The Gamblers
of the Old West

THE GAMBLERS

By the Editors of

TIME-LIFE BOOKS

TIME-LIFE BOOKS / ALEXANDRIA, VIRGINIA

Time-Life Books is a division of Time Life Inc.

TIME LIFE INC.
PRESIDENT and CEO: George Artandi

TIME-LIFE BOOKS
PRESIDENT: John D. Hall
PUBLISHER/MANAGING EDITOR: Neil Kagan
Vice President, Director of Finance: Christopher Hearing
Vice President, Book Production: Marjann Caldwell
Director of Operations: Eileen Bradley
Director of Photography and Research: John Conrad Weiser
Director of Editorial Administration: Barbara Levitt
Chief Librarian: Louise D. Forstall

THE OLD WEST
Editorial Staff for "The Gamblers"
Editor: Jim Hicks
Text Editors: Russell B. Adams, Jr., Bobbie Conlan-Moore, Lee Hassig, David Johnson
Designer: Edward Frank
Staff Writers: Paul Clancy, Susan Feller, Mark M. Steele, Lydia Preston
Chief Researcher: Carol Forsyth Mickey
Researchers: Kris Baker, Michael Blumenthal, Feroline Burrage, Mindy A. Daniels, Barbara Fleming, Pat Good, Richard Kenin, Ann D. Kuhns, Sara Mark, Heather Mason Sandifer
Art Assistant: Van W. Carney
Editorial Assistant: Barbara Brownell

EDITORIAL PRODUCTION
Production Editor: Douglas B. Graham
Operations Manager: Gennaro C. Esposito, Gordon E. Buck (assistant)
Assistant Production Editor: Feliciano Madrid
Quality Control: Robert L. Young (director), James J. Cox (assistant), Michael G. Wight (associate)
Art Coordinator: Anne B. Landry
Copy Staff: Susan B. Galloway (chief), Patricia Graber, Elise Ritter, Celia Beattie
Picture Department: Linda Hensel

CORRESPONDENTS: Elisabeth Kraemer (Bonn); Margot Hapgood, Dorothy Bacon, Lesley Coleman (London); Susan Jonas, Lucy T. Voulgaris (New York); Maria Vincenza Aloisi, Josephine du Brusle (Paris); Ann Natanson (Rome). Valuable assistance was also provided by: Carolyn T. Chubet, Miriam Hsia (New York), Guy Shipler (Reno), Mimi Murphy (Rome), Janet Zich (San Francisco).

The editors are indebted to Valerie Moolman, text editor, for her help with this book.

The editors wish to acknowledge with thanks the help and advice of William R. Williamson of Santa Barbara, California, whose large collection of gambling artifacts has greatly enriched the illustrative content of this volume. Specific references will be found on page 234.

For information on Time-Life Books,
please call 1-800-621-7026 or write:
Reader Information
Time-Life Customer Service
P.O. Box 85568
Richmond, Virginia 23285-5568

Library of Congress Cataloging in Publication Data
Time-Life Books.
    The gamblers.
    (The Old West)
    Bibliography: p.
    Includes index.
        I. Gambling—The West—History.
I. Title. II. Series: The Old West (New York)
HV 6715.T55   1978   364.17'2'0978   78-12281

ISBN: 0-7835-4903-2
Printed in 1996. Fourth printing. Printed in U.S.A.
© MCMLXXVII Time-Life Books. All rights reserved.

CONTENTS

1 | A frontier gone gambling mad

Obliged to share their makeshift gambling den with the barber, patrons of a Southwestern tent-town saloon sit down to a hand of cards.

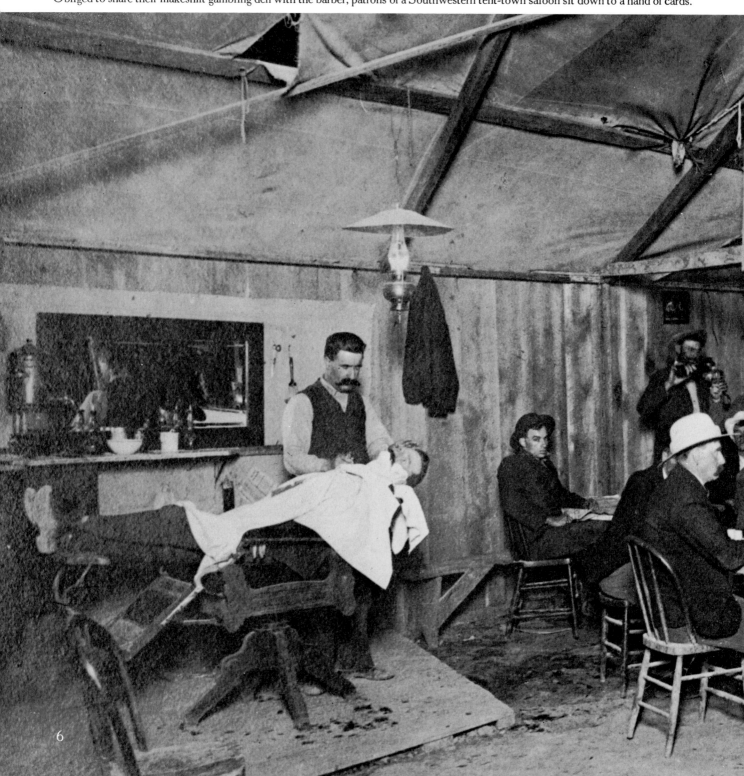

Almost everybody gambled in the Old West. Prospectors and dance-hall girls, cattle barons and cowpokes, clergymen and gunfighters all gathered around gaming tables to wager their newly won fortunes—or their last possessions—on the turn of a card or the spin of a wheel. Even 10- and 12-year-old children, reported one observer, patronized gambling houses, "losing their hundred dollars at a pop with all the nonchalance of an old gambler."

Gambling was a Western mania, the only amusement that could match the heady, speculative atmosphere of frontier life itself. In infant mining and cattle towns, where the games sprang up with the first rude tents and shacks, the action served as a kind of fiscal barometer—the higher the stakes, the more prosperous the community.

In remote areas, far from the rowdy saloons that beckoned every payday, cowboys, loggers and railway workers gambled compulsively among themselves. Or they took on perhaps the eagerest Western gamblers of all—the Indians, who had been losing their ponies, tipis and wives to one another centuries before the white man arrived.

Four Texas cowhands break their day's routine with a game of hearts. Cowboys wagered everything from coyote paws and wolf scalps— redeemable for bounty money—to payday IOUs on impromptu range and bunkhouse games.

A group of lumberjacks play dice in a bunkhouse at a logging camp in northern Minnesota. Western loggers were such chronic gamblers that one California lumber company paid workers in vouchers drawn on local gambling houses.

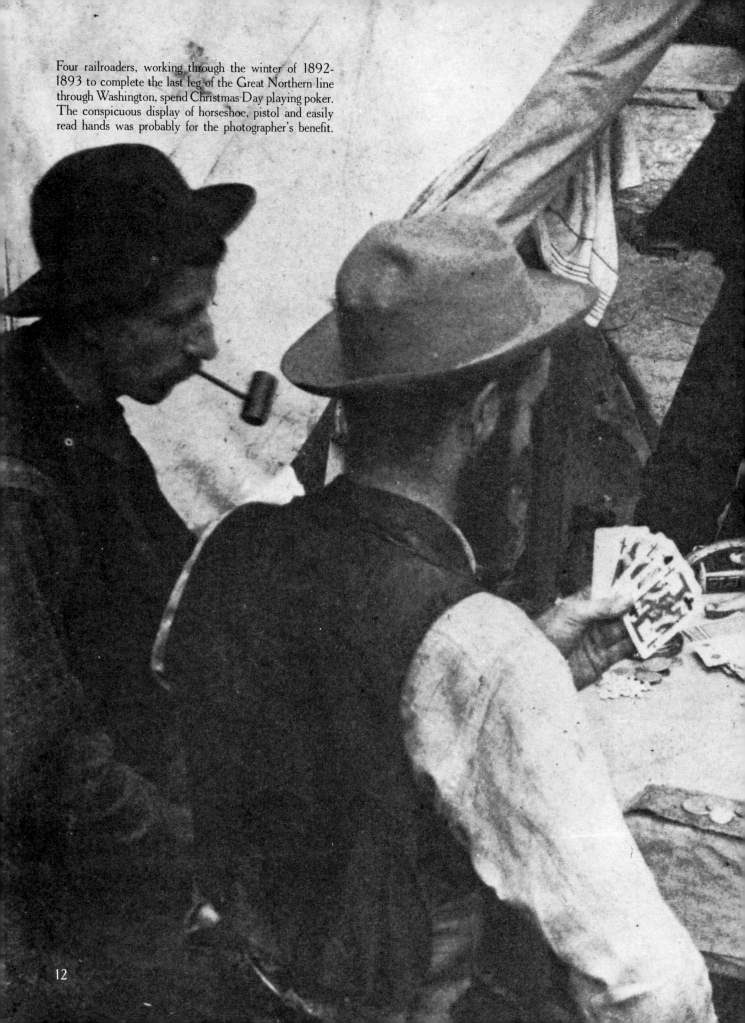

Four railroaders, working through the winter of 1892-1893 to complete the last leg of the Great Northern line through Washington, spend Christmas Day playing poker. The conspicuous display of horseshoe, pistol and easily read hands was probably for the photographer's benefit.

Patrons of the Merchant's Hotel in Columbia, Nevada, place bets on faro *(left foreground)*, craps *(right)* and roulette *(behind the faro table)*. The three fast-action games were popular in the Western boomtown casinos where gamblers were continually impatient for speedy results.

The indigenous wagerers: Indians who would bet all they had

Gambling was as prevalent in the West as dust storms, cowboys and sudden death. Long centuries before white men put in their appearance, the aboriginal Indians were addicted to wagering on games of chance. For them, betting was an element in their sacred ritual and an activity they took with seriousness—sometimes with deadly seriousness.

The emigrants who began to arrive in the West—not only emigrants of European origin, but Mexicans, blacks and Chinese as well—hewed to the tradition; they routinely gambled their spare cash and possessions and sometimes everything they had on a feat of skill, the turn of a card or a mere difference of opinion. *The Annals of San Francisco,* that city's first history, emphatically asserted that gambling in the early 1850s was omnipresent: "*Everybody did so.* Gambling was *the* amusement—*the* grand occupation of many classes. Judges and clergymen, physicians and advocates, merchants and clerks, tradesmen, mechanics, laborers, miners and farmers, all adventurers in their kind—every one elbowed his way to the gamingtable, and unblushingly threw down his golden or silver stake." That description could as well apply to virtually every tent-strewn mining camp, dirt-street cattle town or roughneck railhead in the West.

In Santa Fe, New Mexico Territory, Albert Richardson, roving reporter for the Boston *Journal,* noted in 1859 that the natives of Spanish lineage "are inveterate gamblers. Soon after he learns to walk, the child risks his first penny; and the grey haired man tottering into the grave, stakes his only coat or his last dollar.

Chippewa Indians gamble intently with checkers at Fort Snelling, Minnesota, in the 1840s. The high stakes, including the pipe and weapons next to the players, indicate the seriousness of the contest.

Americans too plunge into games of chance with their national recklessness. Though times were now dull, the city contained fifty American 'sporting men,' as professional gamblers are politely termed. At the Santa Fe hotel I often saw three monte banks in a single room in operation from daylight until mid-night. They were attended by a motley crowd of Indians, Mexicans and whites, darkening the saloon with tobacco smoke. The deep silence was broken only by the jingle of coins and the suppressed breath of players. Enormous piles of silver weighed down the tables, and frequently ten thousand dollars changed hands in ten minutes."

Sante Fe gamblers ranged from the affluent to the indigent, the foolish to the prudent, Richardson observed. "Business men would publicly lose or win a thousand dollars with the greatest nonchalance. One evening I saw a clerk with only five dollars sit down to the game. In a few hours he had won a thousand, but before morning he was penniless. A young surveyor after winning twelve hundred dollars, left the table, saying, 'When you have a good thing, keep it.'"

The stakes did not have to be as high as this for a gambler to become involved in his game. In fact, most of the saloon bets in San Francisco averaged less than five dollars. Some of the most modest wagers ever in the West must surely have been those that were made by three Indians in Austin, Nevada. A local newspaper, the Reese River *Reveille,* printed this report: "In front of the Cosmopolitan Saloon, yesterday afternoon, three stalwart Piutes were engaged in a game of Indian poker, the stakes in which was chewing-gum. Each player would bite off a piece from the wad in his mouth and place it in the 'pot,' and the one holding the high hand would rake down the three pieces and put them in his mouth."

In Dodge City, Kansas, in 1878, a reporter for the *Globe* noted that the cowboys and the cattle were

arriving in bellowing herds from the south, and so were the gamblers: "Just 403,901 (?) gamblers (large and small fry) are already in Dodge, prepared to help themselves to the pickings this summer." The question mark was apparently meant to tell the reader that the reporter had plucked a humorously exaggerated figure out of the air, but his point was clear.

In Truckee, a logging town on the border of Nevada and California, lumberjacks of the 1880s were paid not in cash but in company vouchers. When they hit town after a month in the woods, they promptly visited the local gambling houses and exchanged the vouchers for chips, which they soon lost. The loggers then went back to felling trees, while the citizens of the town gambled among themselves for what the lumbermen had left behind.

Westerners gambled in the mining towns and in the railroad towns, in the mountains and on the plains. And they gambled on the rivers, riotously, intemperately and notoriously. Betsy Taliaferro, a lawyer's young wife journeying along the Mississippi aboard a sternwheeler, complained that the nocturnal rites of gamblers in the men's cabin disturbed the quiet decorum of the ladies' cabin. "They gamble all night— scarcely can draw my breath— and afraid to open the doors," Betsy wrote indignantly. "A dull monotony— nothing but the clink of those incessant gamblers, day and night." The next night she confided yet another distressed comment to her diary: "Those gamblers were quarrelling loudly in the Gents' Cabin. Oh! This odious vice— what does it not lead to!"

Never in United States history had gambling been more widespread or more socially acceptable than it was in frontier days. Westerners wagered enthusiastically at games of poker, brag, euchre, all fours, Boston, seven-up and pitch. They bet at Spanish and three-card monte, roulette, chuck-a-luck, *vingt-et-un, rouge et noir,* faro, cassino, whist and keno. They lost or won at cockfights, prize fights, dogfights, horse races, steamboat races, billiards and thimblerig. They plunged on lotteries, mining stocks and town lots. Wherever the outcome of an event or situation appeared to be in doubt the gamblers convened.

One reason for the prevalence of gambling lay in the rigors, loneliness and boredom of frontier life. A large

painting. A white who watched many such matches said Indians "frequently stake their last piece of property on the issue of the game."

proportion of the men in the West, particularly in the mining camps, were young—and youth, far from home and Mother, is always eager to draw to an inside straight or bet which shell the pea is under. After a spell of brutally hard work on the prairie, in the forest, on the railroad or in a mine, a young bachelor needed relaxation and a little excitement. When he came roaring into town he found both in the saloons, the natural habitat of professional gamblers.

Almost every saloon had its resident sporting man; and somewhere close at hand, perhaps even upstairs, there was likely to be a sporting girl or two as well. Without the recreation provided by the saloonkeeper, the prostitute and the gambler, a good many men might have gone home or gone mad.

Westerners gambled for the thrill of risking a big stake or simply to pass the time. Some saw the gaming tables as a kind of substitute gold mine, an opportunity to strike it rich quick; the professionals gambled as a career and made an erratic living at it, constantly veering between flush and flat broke. They were not, on the whole, a noble lot. Many of them, in fact, were rapacious predators who ran thinly disguised swindles and held it as an article of faith that one never gave the "mark," or sucker, an even break.

The West had its spoilsports, of course—men and women who felt that wide-open wagering degraded their communities, and fought it tooth and nail. These crusaders invoked the bugaboo of the pathological gambler who plunged himself and his family into ruin. As early as 1848 antigambling activists in San Francisco succeeded in passing laws that abolished public gambling, but such legislation, while it eventually closed the doors of the devil's casinos, simply drove devil-worshipping gamblers underground.

The white man's moralizing and legal maneuverings had no discernible effect on the original Western gamblers, the Indians. Since the beginning of their history, Indians had whiled away their spare time betting at games of skill or chance. Part of their affinity for gambling was religious: with the flight of an arrow or a throw of the dice, Indians mimicked the actions of their mythical heroes in the spiritual world.

The creation myths of many tribes involved the divine Twins, gods who were the offspring of the sun.

One lived in the East, the other in the West. One ruled the days and summer; the other prevailed at night and during winter.

As competitive as their contrasting realms, the Twins, according to a Zuñi myth, "divine men's chance, and play games of hazard, wagering the fate of whole nations in mere pastime." They were thought to be the primal gamblers; they were the patrons of betting, and it was their games that mortals learned to play. Sacred objects discovered at Zuñi shrines to the divine Twins are indistinguishable, except in their degree of ornate craftsmanship, from the Indians' everyday gambling paraphernalia.

Among some tribes, the mythical associations of gambling were of overriding importance; the Wichita tribe, for example, played games of chance and skill only in connection with ceremonies. They were the exception; most Indians played whenever they had a little time on their hands and some possessions to wager. Whether an Indian played a game to attract rain or to while away an afternoon, he rarely if ever played without trying to take his opponent for everything he had. To fleece their fellows, Indians gambled at a variety of games, some emphasizing skill or dexterity, others, such as dice games, dependent on pure chance.

The dice that Indians used bore little resemblance to the six-sided ivory cubes that whites were accustomed to. Since prehistoric times, Indian dice had had only two faces. They could be made of a variety of materials, with one or both sides painted, carved or decorated with bits of colored abalone shell. In some of the games the dice were shaken in a bowl or a basket and in others they were tossed up into the air to fall on blankets or hides. A player scored points according to which sides of the dice landed up.

Edwin Denig, a fur trader, was one of the first white men to record details of Indian dicing. In an 1854 report to the governor of Washington Territory, Denig noted that the Assiniboin Indians of North Dakota used a flat-bottomed, polished wooden bowl in which 25 assorted dice were shaken at once. Some of these dice were crows' claws painted red on one side, black on the other; others consisted of plum stones, pieces of blue china, vest buttons and brass tacks. The Assiniboins assigned a different numerical value to each kind of die: five for the claws, as little as one for the tacks. If,

Two sailors watch as Costanoan tribesmen, among the few Indians who wore beards or mustaches, cast dice for a small animal.

Crow Indians bet cartridges on a sleight-of-hand game. To win, a player had to guess which of his opponent's hands hid an object.

for instance, a claw landed with its red side up, the thrower won five points; black side up won nothing. If the claw stuck end up in the ground, the thrower collected 25 points. An exceedingly rare, perfect throw of all 25 dice totaled 100 points. Despite the variety of dice and values, the game was played swiftly; Denig marveled that the Indians, "by much practice," were able to total the number at a glance.

Generally, Indian dice games lasted much longer than those played by whites, since the winner returned half the stake to the loser at certain moments during the betting and the loser thus had many chances of reversing his bad luck. This prolonging of the painful pleasure was an important consideration for the Assiniboins, who seemed to live for gambling. Sometimes they also died because of it. "Most of the leisure time, either by night or by day," wrote Denig, "is devoted to gambling in various ways, and such is their infatuation that it is the cause of much distress and poverty in families. Many quarrels arise among them from this source, and we are well acquainted with an Indian who a few years since killed another because he refused to put up his wife to be played for."

To illustrate how the Assiniboins kept a dice game going for hours and hours, as well as the readiness of the gamblers to risk all their possessions, Denig described a hypothetical game between two men. Each wagers a knife at the outset, and they toss the dice alternately until one of them scores 100 or more points and wins the knives. For the next game of 100, the loser puts up a shirt, equal in value to both knives.

This double-or-nothing play continues until the stakes are quite high—a considerable pile of miscellaneous goods against a valuable gun, for example. If the loser is victorious at this juncture, he gets back everything he has lost. On the other hand, if the winner's lucky streak continues, he retains only the gun and in propitiation refunds all of the other property he has already won. Denig pointed out that the game was "often kept up for two or three days and nights without any intermission, except to eat, until one of the parties is ruined. We have known Indians to lose everything—horse, dogs, cooking utensils, lodge, wife, even to his wearing apparel, and be obliged to get an old skin from some one to cover himself and seek a shelter in the lodge of one of his relations."

Wives, when lost by husbands at gambling, had nothing to say about the matter but simply took up residence with the winner. The loser, said Denig, never committed suicide on such occasions but sought "some other outlet—in war expeditions or some way to acquire property that he may again play and retrieve his losses. There are some who invariably lose and are poor all their lives. A man may with honor stop with the loss of his gun. He also has a second opportunity to retire on losing his horse—but when a regular set-to takes place between two soldiers it generally ends as above described."

The betting scheme of the Assiniboin dice game was uncommonly complex compared to most Indian wagering. Usually, players and spectators alike offered some possession as a stake. Instantly it was matched by someone from the other side with an article of equal value. On occasion, individual bets were tied together so that each Indian could identify his portion of the pot after the game. But more often, the stakes were tossed willy-nilly into a single pile—which was watched over by medicine men so that neither side could bewitch the pot and procure an advantage in the game. In group betting of this kind there would be multiple winners, who split the spoils among themselves.

Dakota Indians played an eerie game of dice with a dead man in which the living risked nothing and the deceased opponent lost all. The game, connected with the Indians' funeral rituals, began after an Indian died. His relatives divided his possessions into small lots and invited tribe members to gamble for them with the man's spirit. "One Indian is selected to represent the ghost," said a report published in 1881, "and he plays against all the others, who are not required to stake anything on the result, but simply invited to take part in the ceremony, which is usually held in the lodge of the dead person. The players play singly against the ghost's representative. If the invited player succeeds in beating the ghost, he takes one of the piles of goods and passes out, when another is invited to play, etc., until all the piles of goods are won."

Contrasting with the pure chance of dice games was the artful deceit practiced in certain Indian guessing games such as the hand game, which resembled button-button-who's-got-the-button. In the 1890s an ethnol-

Two Indians struggle to unhorse each other as they gallop hard after a third during a
polo-like game on which high stakes were
bet. Indians played with short, clubbed
sticks, rather than long-handled mallets.

FREDERIC REMINGTON

ogist named James Mooney watched excited Arapahos in Oklahoma playing this game.

"Frequently there will be a party of twenty to thirty men gaming in one tipi, and singing so that their voices can be heard far out from the camp," wrote Mooney. "The players sit in a circle around the tipi fire, those on one side of the fire playing against those on the other. The only requisites are the button, usually a small bit of wood. Each party has a button, that of one side being painted black, the other being red. The leader of one party takes the button and endeavors to move it from one hand to the other, or to pass it on to a partner, while those on the opposing side keep a sharp lookout, and try to guess in which hand it is. Those having the button try to deceive their opponents as to its where-abouts by putting one hand over the other, by folding their arms, and by putting their hands behind them, so as to pass the button to a partner, all the while keeping time to the rhythm of a gaming chorus sung by the whole party at the top of their voices."

Mooney was intrigued by the gamblers' chanting. "The song is very peculiar and well-nigh indescrib-able," he wrote. "It is usually, but not always, unmean-ing, and jumps, halts and staggers in a most surprising fashion, but always in perfect time with the movements of the hands and arms of the singers. All this time the opposing players are watching the hands of the other or looking straight into their face to observe every tell-tale movement of their features, and when one thinks he has discovered in which hand the button is, he throws out his thumb toward that hand with a loud 'that!' Should he guess aright, his side scores a certain number of tallies, and in turn takes the button and begins another song. Should the guess be wrong, the losing side must give up an equivalent number of tally sticks. So the play goes on until the small hours of the night. It is always a gambling game, and the stakes are sometimes very large."

High stakes spiced another protracted sleight-of-hand sing-gamble near Renton, Washington, where a team of Black River and Cedar River Indians took on some Puyallups in 1894. The game had not been played in that area for more than 30 years and members of the younger generation, who had known nothing but effete Eastern card games, stood around bug-eyed while the oldest Indians took part in the contest. The scorer was an ancient Puyallup named Seatcum, re-ported to be 101 years old. "He certainly looks it,"

Four Crow Indians *(right)* are poised for the start of a cross-country race in 1910. Three of them are barefoot; one has donned light moccasins to protect his feet.

During the Flute Ceremony, Hopi priests *(above)* watch from behind their feather-decked prayer sticks as three runners race across the parched desert clay in 1901.

Navajo runners grimace from the strain of racing under the harsh Southwestern sun. Tribe members bet everything from household tools to livestock on such contests.

Running for riches, rain and a state of grace

Foot races—from short dashes on swept tracks to miles-long relays on foot-scarring prairie stubble—were highly popular Indian betting events.

Sometimes the contestants wagered only a blanket; on other occasions, the stakes were huge. A newspaper reporter wrote of a Zuñi foot race in 1890: "Money, silver belts, bracelets and rings, turquoises, horses—in fact anything and everything of value are offered by a resident of the pueblo in support of his favorites." A Papago Indian related that his people "bet everything. Sometimes when people went home again, they had not a pot or basket in the house. They would dig holes in the ground to serve food."

Besides being great sport, the races had a religious significance for many tribes. The Hopis held races to venerate the great power of nature. The Zuñis raced each year before they planted corn as part of their spring rites to bring rain for the germinating seeds. Thus, while race bets could materially increase individual fortunes, the very act of holding the races might enhance the fortunes of the entire tribe by putting it in good stead with its gods.

remarked a reporter who covered the event for the Seattle *Post-Intelligencer.* "He resembles an Egyptian mummy come to life after being dried for a thousand years." The whole affair, according to the reporter, "proved a howling success, and the somber tone of the tom-tom and blood-curdling chant of the painted, feather-bedecked bucks made night hideous for a radius of two miles."

The wagers included 40 horses, wagons, buggies, saddles, blankets, jewelry, rifles, bed quilts, shawls, clothing and $150 in cash—just about everything that these impoverished tribes possessed. Even the winter's supply of food and clothes were put up. The Puyallup Indians at least had a reservation to walk back to if they lost. However, the Black River and Cedar River Indians, if they turned out to be the losers, were in imminent peril of starving to death, unless the white residents of Renton took pity on their plight and provided them with the necessities of life.

Fortunately, it never came to that. The Indians gambled and chanted without rest for five days and nights. To win the game, one side had to get 66 points ahead of the other. It was a constant seesaw among the three tribes. The Puyallups came closest, with 53 points, but eventually they lost their advantage. The Indians were so intent on their game that they did not so much as pause when an Indian woman named Mrs. Moses "was suddenly taken ill with symptoms of insanity." While the medicine man drove the evil spirit out of Mrs. Moses' body and into a keg of cold water, to the accompaniment of appropriate dances and chanting, the gambling continued.

Eventually sheer exhaustion put an end to the game and a tie was declared. The players were so weary that they "did not quit their seats, but doubled up, and in fifteen minutes the noise of the tom-tom and the chant was replaced by the sound of deep snoring."

There were assorted versions of the hand game. Sometimes a row of players held a blanket in their teeth as a screen and exchanged the button behind it. Occasionally they tied bits of fur and cloth to their wrists and fingers, fluttering them to aid in distracting attention when the button was passed. The "buttons" differed from tribe to tribe—pebbles, beans, polished bones, bullets, sticks and other small objects were used. When tribe played against tribe for stakes that were as high as

guns and horses, medicine men might be called upon to participate in the games. Many of these sorcerers were highly skilled sleight-of-hand artists. The skill was a part of their magical repertoire, and when one of them was brought into a game it was akin to slipping a professional player onto a team of amateurs.

In one celebrated contest a Kiowa-Apache medicine man named Dävéko was hastily summoned to help out his losing fellow tribesmen against their Cheyenne opponents. He must have had the dexterity of a highly gifted vaudevillian. A spectator left this account: "He rolled his sleeves way up, so his arms were bare. They thought he had the bean in his hand, but he shook hands with them and there was nothing there. He shook hands again and the bean was there. The Cheyennes tried to guess Dävéko again, but he did not have it. He reached in the fire and pulled the bean out." Faced with such an opponent, the Cheyennes wisely withdrew from the game.

Even recovery from illness could depend on the outcome of the hand game. The Pomo Indians of California believed that some sicknesses were caused magically, by enemies. Against this kind of illness a skilled medicine man could work wonders. Unfortunately, successful treatment was expensive; no one who had only a small amount of money to offer the doctor ever recovered. To increase the pile of money—and the patient's chance for improvement—members of the invalid's family gambled against the enemies who, for their part, hoped to ensure the effectiveness of their black magic by winning the pot.

A different kind of guessing game, one played by the Zuñi Indians of New Mexico, was called hidden ball. The object of the game was for one team of players to divine which one of four tubes marked a ball that had been buried in a mound of sand by the members of the other team. Frank Cushing, an enthnologist who was intrigued by Indian games and gambling, described how hidden ball was played in the 1880s:

"A crowd began to gather. Larger and noisier it grew, until it became a surging clamorous black mass. Gradually two piles of fabrics—vessels, silver ornaments, necklaces, embroideries, and symbols representing horses, cattle, and sheep—grew to large proportions. Women gathered on the roofs around, wildly stretching forth articles for the betting."

After a team concealed the ball, "one by one three of the four opposing players were summoned to guess under which tube the ball was hidden. At each guess the cries of the opposing parties became deafening, and their mock struggles approached the violence of mortal combat. The last guesser found the ball; and as he victoriously carried the latter and the tubes across to his own mound, his side scored 10."

However, that was only the beginning. To win, one of the sides had to accumulate 100 points. "Noisier and noisier grew the dancers," continued Cushing, "more and more insulting and defiant their songs and epithets until they fairly gnashed their teeth at one another. Day dawned on the still uncertain contest; nor was it until the sun again touched the western horizon, that the hoarse, still defiant voices died away, and the victorious party bore off their mountains of 'gifts from the gods.'"

Indian gambling was not always as sedentary as the dicing and guessing games. Indians also wagered wildly on the outcome of physical contests, some of which were so violent that they might easily have been mistaken for battles. Bloody noses and cracked shins were routine among participants in sky's-the-limit ball games in which stakes were often high.

In the 1830s Choctaw Indians in present-day Oklahoma gathered for a game that they called simply "ball play"; it was, in fact, a kind of wild and woolly version of lacrosse. George Catlin, the famous artist who recorded the villages, games, ceremonies and faces of Western Indians between 1829 and 1838, was a spectator at this game. In order to miss none of the action, he arrived at the playing field on the afternoon before the event and watched the opposing teams build goals consisting of two upright posts, some 25 feet high, six feet apart and surmounted by a vertical pole. Midway between the two goals, which were about 750 feet apart, a stake was driven to mark the spot where the play would begin.

Tribal elders, who had supervised the work on the field, next drew a long line that served the same function as betting booths at a racetrack.

As soon as the line was drawn, wrote Catlin, it was inundated by "a great concourse of women and old men, boys and girls, and dogs and horses. The betting was all done across this line, and seemed to be chiefly left to the women, who seemed to have marshaled out a little of everything that their houses and their fields possessed. Goods and chattels—knives—dresses—blankets—pots and kettles—dogs and horses, and guns; and all were placed in the possession of stakeholders, who sat by them, and watched them on the ground all night." With the stakes running this high, it is little wonder that the ballplayers were all grimly determined to win.

The opposing teams assembled the next morning, and Catlin noted that there were about 700 players, all vigorous young warriors, crowded onto the field. Each man carried two ball-sticks or rackets "bent into an oblong hoop at the end, with a sort of slight web of small thongs tied across, to prevent the ball from passing through. The players hold one of these in each hand, and by leaping into the air, they catch the ball between the two nettings and throw it, without being allowed to strike it or catch it in their hands." The men wore no moccasins or protective clothing of any kind, only breechcloths and manes and tails of colored horsehair.

At the start of the match the ball was tossed among the players gathered around the stake in the middle of the field—and the melee began. "There are times," wrote Catlin, "when the ball gets to the ground, and such a confused mass rushing together around it, and knocking their sticks together, without the possibility of any-one getting or seeing it, for the dust that they raise, that the spectator loses his strength, and everything else but his senses; when the condensed mass of ball-sticks, and shins, and bloody noses, is carried around the different parts of the ground, for a quarter of an hour at a time."

The game ended late in the afternoon, when one team had scored 100 points. The players were badly in need of refreshment, not to mention medical attention. They had brought whiskey with them, but their priorities were clear: first they settled the bets and only then did they turn to the liquor, which "sent them all off merry and in good humor, but not drunk."

Among the Mandan Indians of the upper Missouri River, Catlin observed an archery contest, which was a much less strenuous athletic event. It was not, as might have been expected, a test of accuracy. Hitting a distant target was not of foremost importance to the Man-

dans. They killed buffalo and Indian enemies at close range from galloping horses, a maneuver that required the Mandans to shoot arrows rapidly rather than with long-range accuracy.

Thus the Mandans had "a favourite amusement which they call the 'game of the arrow,'" wrote Catlin, "where the young men who are the most distinguished in this exercise, assemble on the prairie at a little distance from the village, and having paid, each one, his 'entrance-fee' such as a shield, a robe, a pipe, or other article, step forward in turn, shooting their arrows into the air, endeavouring to see who can get the greatest

number flying in the air at one time." As Catlin watched, one of the young men managed to send aloft the remarkable total of eight arrows before the first one hit the ground, and for this performance he collected all the stakes.

Each Plains Indian customarily made his own arrows, yet a quiver taken from a warrior fallen on the field of battle often contained arrows bearing the personal markings of other individuals. This apparent contradiction puzzled whites until they learned that warriors got these alien arrows by gambling. A game of the Pawnee tribe observed in the 1830s by an early stu-

poles through a hoop as it rolled away from the throwers. The hoops of many tribes were netted or spoked and in effect became rolling dart boards; the scoring depended upon which space within the hoop the pole penetrated. "The game was very difficult," said one spectator after watching a match in 1889, "and misses were more frequent than scores."

The Apaches made hoop and pole still more difficult when they reduced the size of the hoop and used a longer pole. In 1868 Colonel John Cremony observed a game played by Mescalero Apaches in New Mexico with 10-foot poles and a hoop that was only six inches in diameter.

Apache women were not allowed to play hoop and pole or even approach the contest, "because they always foment troubles between the players, and create confusion by taking sides and provoking dissension," as an old Apache told Cremony.

Men, whether spectators or participants, were required to attend the game unarmed. "When people gamble," the same authority explained, "they become half crazy, and are very apt to quarrel. This is the most exciting game we have, and those who play it will wager all they possess. The loser is apt to get angry, and fights have ensued which resulted in the loss of many warriors. To prevent this, it was long ago determined that no warrior should be present with arms upon his person or within near reach."

Though Indian women were barred from hoop and pole, they had their own gambling games at which they competed just as fiercely and wagered just as recklessly as the men—within their more limited means. Assiniboin men sometimes prohibited their women from gambling, but to no avail; even the threat of a sound thrashing did not deter the ladies. As soon as their men went hunting, the women began gambling.

The women of the Papago tribe of Arizona were devoted to double ball, a field game in which opposing teams used hooked sticks to launch a pair of balls, joined together with string, toward the opponent's goal. Papago myths tell of women who became so absorbed by the game that they left their children untended and traipsed from village to village in search of a challenge. As recently as the 1890s, Catholic nuns periodically confiscated the sticks and burned them in an effort to focus the women's attention on domestic chores.

dent of Indian ways, John B. Dunbar, explains how gambling for arrows worked among the Pawnees. "One person shot an arrow," wrote Dunbar, "so that it should fall upon the ground at a distance of from forty to sixty paces. The players then in succession endeavored to shoot so that their arrows should fall immediately across this arrow. Whoever succeeded took all the arrows discharged."

Arrow games, however, were not as widespread among Western tribes as a game that was commonly known as hoop and pole. It varied from tribe to tribe, but the basic aim of the contest was to hurl javelin-like

In a game of *ne añg-puḳi,* or kill-the-bone, a Paiute Indian attempts to guess the hand in which his opponent conceals the marked bone. The tally sticks between the players are used to indicate the score.

Tossing plum stones in a basket, Sioux Indians bet which combinations of decorated and plain sides will land face up. The game was a favorite of elderly women but young women, and men, also played.

In winter, when it was too cold to play double ball outdoors, young Papago women gambled indoors at stick dice. They usually bet articles of clothing or things that they had made. An old woman told an anthropologist how she had once won a shawl and a necklace. Her opponent, hoping to recover the lost possessions, challenged her to a foot race, a favorite contest among Indian women as well as Indian men.

Before the start of the race, the challenger "brought out everything she had to bet," recalled the woman, "a sleeping mat, a basket and a big pot. We went to the racetrack and all our relatives came with us. They were all betting. We chose two umpires, one of her male relatives and one of mine. Then they laid hair ropes down at each end of the track and the two men started us. All the people yelled. But pretty soon her relatives stopped yelling; she was not winning. I came in first and the people brought the things she had bet up to my house. I heard her crying that night out in the desert, because she had lost everything."

Although it was the custom for Indian men and women to play their own games and to wager their own possessions, the Teton Dakota Indians made an exception of one game. In this contest, several deer hoofs that had been drilled through with holes were tossed up into the air and impaled on a stick as they fell. Even though men and women played the game separately, they were not especially concerned about whose property they wagered. "The women," reported one observer, "when they play this game, bring their husbands' goods without the knowledge of the owners, and sometimes lose all of them. When the men play, they sometimes stake all of their wives' property, and occasionally they lose all."

White men rarely shared in the rich and varied gambling heritage of Western Indians, but those who did could consider it to be a special privilege. One such man was George Belden, a cavalry trooper who in the 1860s joined some Dakota Indians for a game of

Yakima Indians in Washington interrupt their card game for a visiting photographer around 1900. Yakimas gambled constantly and their professional gamblers enjoyed the same high esteem accorded to outstanding athletes.

shinny, in which a ball was knocked around a field with a club-headed stick.

White Bear and Little Dog Soldier, the Dakota chiefs who organized the contest, each picked several dozen warriors for their teams. Belden, whom the Indians held in such high esteem that they had made him a chief, was chosen early by Little Dog Soldier. After the teams were settled, the betting started. The warriors could bet directly against one another, according to Belden, or they could toss their articles on a pile of objects belonging to their team; "instantly it was matched by the judges against some article of corresponding value from the pile of the other side. Thus I bet a hunting knife, half a pound of powder, a pair of moccasins and a small hand mirror, which articles were appropriately matched."

A pair of goal posts was erected at each end of a bumpy field and the players attempted to drive the ball, a spherical wad of buckskin-covered rags the size

of an orange, through the area between the posts with their sticks. After a long and bloody scrimmage in which the ball was several times lost from view among tufts of grass on the field, Belden noticed that an opposing player was trying to hide it beneath his foot. Belden ran "against him from behind with such force as to throw him on his face" and then drove the ball down the field to a teammate who easily tapped the ball between the posts, ending the game.

"I was declared the winner," said Belden, "and Little Dog Soldier congratulated me on my success. Then we all smoked, and went over to the stakes to receive our shares. As winner I was entitled to a general share of the spoils; but I declined in favor of the young Indian who had helped me drive the ball, saying that, as he had last hit it, and actually forced it between the stakes, he was, in reality, the most deserving. This argument was loudly applauded by the old men, and the young warrior, who had not been friendly for some time with me, was so touched by my generosity that he came and thanked me, saying frankly, 'You, and not I, won the game.' However, I forced the general stakes upon him, a saddle, half a pound of powder, six yards of wampum beads, and a handsomely braided knife-scabbard."

Although few other whites gambled with Indians at their own games, members of the two cultures competed fiercely wherever they shared common interests. Firearms and marksmanship, for example, led to a spirited shooting match between a white man and an Indian in the winter of 1861.

A group of rancher-prospectors, holed up in a camp called American Fork in the mountains of western Montana, organized the shooting match between one of their number and an Indian named Pushigan. The whites' chosen marksman was a young man named Granville Stuart, who had a new breech-loading Maynard carbine rifle, .50 caliber, that fired reloadable brass cartridges. Pushigan, the champion of a mixed band of Bannock, Shoshoni and Turkuarika Indians, was equipped with a decrepit old muzzle-loading rifle that weighed a staggering 30 pounds. "He had taken a piece of hoop-iron and improvised a sight by slightly turning up the end in which he filed a notch," wrote one of the white men. "This contrivance was fastened to the gun-barrel with buckskin thongs, and by means of a

Primitive art in the hands of card-happy Apaches

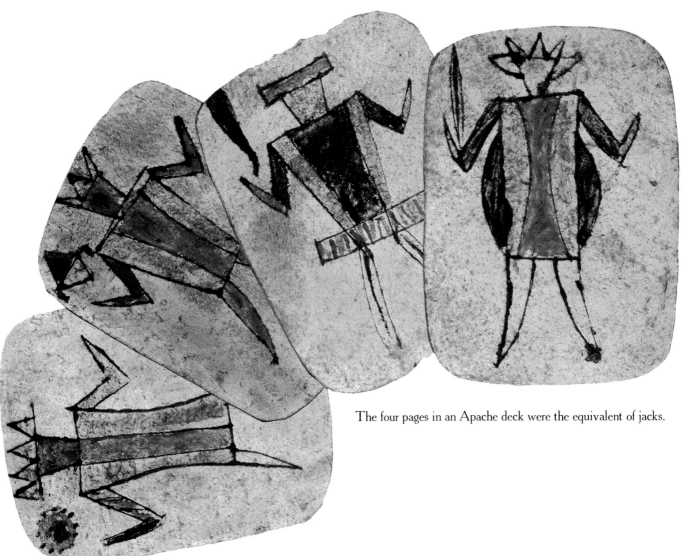

The four pages in an Apache deck were the equivalent of jacks.

As tensions between whites and Indians in the Southwest increased in the mid-19th Century, Apaches found themselves unwelcome at the settlers' trading posts and thus unable to buy the playing cards with which they loved to gamble. Determined to continue playing cards, the tribesmen began fashioning their own decks.

Most Apache cards—such as those from four different decks, shown here—were hand painted on durable hides. Variations in the backs of the cards were unimportant since the Apaches' favorite game was Spanish, or Mexican, monte, a game in which the bets were decided by the card on the bottom of the deck.

The Apache monte deck consisted of 40 cards with 10 cards in each suit: an *as* (ace), *rey* (king), *caballero* (knight), *sota* (page), and numeral cards 2 through 7. The suits were borrowed from Spanish decks—cups, swords, coins and cudgels—though the Apache artists often modified the designs. Swords were sometimes painted as arrowheads. Cups, articles not generally used by the Indians, were represented merely as combinations of triangles bearing only the vaguest resemblance to a covered goblet.

  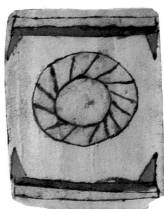 

These cards are in a deck made by a White Mountain Apache. From left: knight of swords, ace of cudgels, ace of coins, king of swords.

  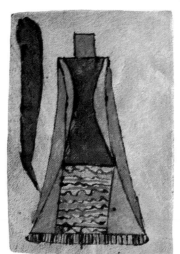 

In this deck robed Spanish kings become almost abstract. From left: king of coins, two of cudgels, king of cudgels, knight of swords.

  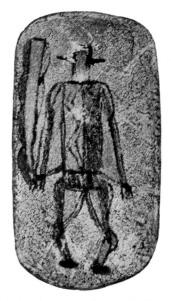 

The maker of this deck preferred cards with round corners. From left: knight of swords, ace of coins, page of cudgels, five of swords.

small wooden wedge he could raise and lower the sight
to suit his fancy."

On the day of the match the entire white population
of American Fork turned up at the shooting range with
beads, robes, blankets, butcher knives, horses and cash
to bet on their favorite. At the same time, a swarm of
Indians arrived to wager on Pushigan. A paper bull's-
eye was fastened to a wagon tail gate and a firing line
was drawn 100 yards away. According to rules established beforehand, the target was to be moved back
100 yards after each round, up to a distance of 1,000
yards. The white men knew that the Indian would be a
good marksman at the shorter distances but were confident that Granville Stuart's superior rifle and considerable skill would tell at the long range. So to begin with,
they made only small bets.

On the first round Pushigan went to the firing line,
raised his massive old muzzle-loader and scored a
bull's-eye. Stuart fired afterward; he not only failed to

hit the target but also missed the entire tail gate. This,
as one of his supporters remembered with quiet irony,
"was not very encouraging, considering the close prox-
imity of the mark."

The match continued. As the distance between
marksmen and target increased, Pushigan consistently
drilled the bull's-eye and Stuart invariably missed it.
Then at 600 yards, Stuart scored. "Up to this point,"
observed the chronicler of the event, "we had been
making very light bets, but now confidence was re-
stored with a whoop and betting ran high." One opti-
mist wagered two horses against one; others put up
nearly everything they had.

But at 700 yards Stuart missed and at 800 yards
and 900 yards he missed again, while the cool and
confident Pushigan scored relentlessly. The target was
never moved to the 1,000-yard mark because by that
time "our crowd was 'flat broke,' with not a pony,
blanket or butcher knife left. We had to foot it back to

the camp, arriving late in the evening, tired and hungry, much sadder and wiser men than when we started out so gayly in the morning." The Indians, to vary the cliché, went home happier, if not wiser, at least richer.

Stuart realized later that he had been the victim of his own carelessness. He had loaded some of his cartridges with too much gunpowder and others with too little. Consequently, his shots flew wildly high or low of the mark and his single score at 600 yards was a fluke. This analysis was of small solace to his friends, one of whom sourly remarked, "Too bad you didn't bet that gun and lost it."

Besides being expert marksmen, Indians valued speedy horses. Among Plains Indians, a single race-winning horse might be traded for several general-purpose mounts. Artist George Catlin noted that horse racing was "one of the most exciting amusements, and one of the most extravagant modes of gambling of the Indians." Catlin also discovered firsthand that an Indian horse race could make unusual demands on a tenderfoot from Pennsylvania.

During a visit to a Minataree village, Catlin decided to race against a warrior who had lost heavily in two earlier outings. Generous to a fault, the painter deliberately chose a slow pony to give the disappointed Indian a chance to recoup his losses. When he arrived at the starting line, Catlin learned two startling rules of the race: he was expected to ride without a saddle and, like the Indian, without his clothes. "Reader! Imagine yourselves as I was," exhorted Catlin in his book about North American Indians, "with my trembling little horse underneath me, and the cool atmosphere that was floating about and ready to embrace me at the next moment when we 'were off.' Though my little Pegasus seemed to dart through the clouds, my red adversary was leaving me too far behind for further competition." So Catlin sheepishly returned to the starting line and his clothes, disappointing a crowd of women and children gathered at the finish line to witness his exposure.

If Catlin's Victorian modesty was troubled by this kind of horse race, his sense of self-preservation would probably have stopped him from participating in certain Indian horse races that must have appeared downright suicidal to white men. In these contests, Indian riders charged headlong at an immovable object, the one who first touched it being the winner. In one such contest described by Colonel Richard Dodge, who was a soldier and a student of Indian customs, the racers rushed "at a heavy pole placed horizontally about six feet from the ground, resting on forks firmly set. If the rider stops his horse a moment too soon he fails of touching the pole; if a moment too late the horse passes under the pole, leaving the rider dangling to it or thrown to the ground."

There were other kinds of Indian horse races that a white might enter without risking life or limb. But if he did so, he risked considerable injury to his self-esteem, since these races required superb horsemanship and, often enough, specially trained ponies. For one such race, two strips of buffalo hide were laid on the ground six to 10 feet apart and about 200 yards from the start. "The game," wrote Colonel Dodge, "is to run at full speed, jump the horse between the strips, turn him in his tracks, and return to the starting point. The horse which fails to get beyond the first strip with all four of his feet, or which gets a single foot beyond the second strip, is beaten, even though he makes the best time."

The Indians assimilated card playing into their gambling repertoire as readily as they took up horse racing. Both horses and playing cards were, in fact, introduced to the Indians of the West by Spanish conquistadors. By 1795, a Spanish missionary among peaceful Apache Indians in present-day Arizona was complaining to his superior that Spaniards and their playing cards had thoroughly corrupted the natives. "In the conference I had with them on the afternoon of my visit," reported Friar Pedro de Arriquibar, "when I played a game of chance with them (to which they are highly addicted, and chiefly the 'boys' and even the women), they told that this and the other card games they play is the first milk they sucked from the Christians; that in their country they knew nothing of this."

Indians soon learned to make their own playing cards out of tree bark, painting them to resemble, more or less, the white man's product. At least one pack of Indian cards is on record that is reported to have been made out of material considerably more exotic than tree bark. The pack had fallen into the possession of Captain E. M. Kingsbury, who was a trader at the San Carlos Indian Reservation in Arizona. Each of the

The hazards of the game when white met Indian

Although whites and Indians were equally passionate gamblers, they had few opportunities to bet against one another. When whites did gamble against Indians, they frequently found themselves rudely surprised by their opponents' skills.

Charles Russell, an artist known for his shrewd sense of humor, painted one such occasion in the pictures at right. A cowboy and an Indian meet on the range to play cooncan—the name is a corruption of the Spanish words *con quien,* "with whom" —a popular 19th Century Mexican game that was the forerunner of rummy. Having stripped the cowboy of his possessions—from his horse to his gun and kerchief—the victorious Indian rides off, leaving only the cards that led to his victim's downfall.

A real-life encounter between veteran gambler George Devol and a group of Indian poker players ended more explosively. Playing "more for the novelty of the thing than to win their money," Devol found himself being cheated by an old chief whose partner stood behind Devol, telling the chief in their Indian language what cards the white man held.

Devol retaliated by palming cards until he had accumulated a winning hand. He then put his good cards into play (keeping them hidden from the spy behind him) and made a sizable bet. The chief matched him with a bag of silver. When Devol showed his hand, the camp erupted. The enraged chief reached for his tomahawk and attacked his hapless informant. In the resulting confusion, Devol disappeared with his winnings—and counted himself a lucky man to have escaped with his scalp.

He later advised others who gambled with Indians to "play a square game and keep their eyes skinned for the big buck that talks to the chief."

Their mounts standing by, a cowboy and an Indian concentrate on a game of cooncan.

The game over, the broadly grinning Indian rides off on the stunned cowboy's horse.

cards had a brightly painted face and spots on it. At first glance one might have guessed that the material was cowhide or horsehide, except that the cards were too thin. The mystery persisted until the captain was informed on the reservation—possibly accurately—that the cards were made from tanned human skin, taken from the hides of white men.

Though Spaniards introduced cards, the card *game* Indians honored was brought west by emigrants from New Orleans in the 1800s. It was poker. In the 1830s, George Catlin reported that Indians enjoyed slapping down their tree-bark playing cards in imitation of white poker players, even though they had no clear idea of how to play the game. In time, Indians filled in this gap in their knowledge. By the 1870s, passengers stepping off the train at any Nevada stop on the newly completed transcontinental railroad were likely to be greeted by the sight of a group of shabby ex-warriors, clutching a greasy deck of cards and so intent on their game of poker or pedro as to be oblivious of everything else around them.

By that time the Indians were constant poker players and some of them were exceedingly proficient at the game. Among the best was a native son of the Pacific Northwest whose Indian name was White-Geese-Sounding-on-Waters. The whites rechristened him Poker Jim. A diligent student and canny philosopher of the game, Poker Jim uttered a principle that poker players everywhere who are tempted to wager a sum of money on a marginal hand of cards ignore only at their peril. What Poker Jim stated, with noble simplicity, was: "Two pair not much good."

Although little is known about the further fortunes of Poker Jim, another inveterate gambler was an Indian whose name has been noted around the world. During his years of captivity at Fort Sill, Oklahoma, the great Apache war chief Geronimo devoted much of his time to card playing and other gambling activities. Geronimo could be as fierce at card games as he had been at the game of war.

Elbridge Burbank, a young artist who visited Fort Sill in 1897 to paint Geronimo's portrait, vividly remembered the old man at a Fourth of July sports meet, playing a game of monte, dealing the cards with the finesse of a riverboat sporting man and shouting at the top of his voice as he scooped up his winnings.

Any account of Indian gambling in the West would be incomplete without a word or two about cheating. Among Indians wagering at their own games, fair play seems to have been the rule. Nevertheless, where there was an opportunity to take unfair advantage of the competition, Indians, like their white counterparts, would certainly do so. In foot and horse races, for example, false starts were common, each contestant vying for that potentially decisive half-step advantage over his opponents.

When intertribal rivalry was involved, the temptation to fudge could be too strong to resist. In the 1870s, the numbers of Paiutes and Shoshonis living near Austin, Nevada, were about equal, and a fierce competitiveness sprang up between them. The tribes frequently gambled against each other, and one day the editor of the Reese River *Reveille* was approached by a Shoshoni who said he wanted instruction in the art of marking cards.

"Why?" asked the *Reveille*'s editor, to which the Shoshoni replied, "Me heap break every Piute sonofabitch in Austin!"

As it turned out, the Paiutes beat the Shoshonis at their own game. The *Reveille* reported the entire affair a couple of weeks afterward: "A short time ago, a couple of Piutes went to a store on Main Street and purchased the entire stock of playing cards. They took them to their camp, and having secretly marked each one, came back to the store, and putting on that look of misery only an Indian knows how to assume, offered to sell them back for one-fourth of what they had paid. The pasteboards were purchased on these terms and were subsequently sold, one pack at a time, to the Shoshones.

"The Piutes knew that the Shoshones made their purchases at this particular place; and the guileless Shoshones, unaware of manipulation, played poker with the wily Piute, without a suspicion that all was not 'on the dead squar.' The result was that there is weeping and wailing and gnashing of teeth in the camp of the Shoshones."

The journey of Indian gamblers from ritual to ruse had been a long one. It was undoubtedly hastened in its later course by the example of slick professionals from the East—like those suave sharks of the riverboats who could devour unwary passengers in a single gulp.

An artist's portfolio of spectator sports

"It is no uncommon occurrence," wrote artist George Catlin, describing a Choctaw game akin to lacrosse, "for six or eight hundred or a thousand young men, to engage in a game of ball, with five or six times that number of men, women, and children surrounding and looking on."

Such immense crowds gathered less frequently in other tribes, who were not so numerous as Choctaws. And not every Indian game could accommodate so many participants. Nevertheless, ball games, races and tests of skill like the ones depicted in the Catlin oil paintings on these pages often attracted sizable numbers of both competitors and onlookers, most of whom made bets on the events.

The number of players could be substantial even in games that might be expected to involve only a few people. Ute Indians in Colorado, for example, gambled at a contest in which a player tried to guess which of his opponent's hands concealed a small object. The game required only two people, but often drew more than 20 men at once, the participants arrayed in two long rows of opponents facing each other.

On occasion, spectators performed a role that could directly affect the result of the contest. Among the Papagos, the crowd at foot races against neighboring Pimas and Yumas formed a human screen to conceal their champion from the opponents' medicine man until the start of the event. If the runner were exposed, the Papagos believed, the medicine man could cast a spell that would cause him to lose the race.

Sioux women vie at double ball for a few pots and pieces of bright calico, while tipsy male onlookers urge them on. In some tribes, miniatures of the sticks and ball used to play the game were suspended from the cradles of baby girls, probably in hopes of instilling future skill at the sport.

A pennant and a crowd of eager Indians mark the finish line
of a race between two Hidatsa horsemen. Two referees,
one representing each rider, stand apart from the spectators
at the finish to render judgment in case of a close race.

44

Mandan Indians wager weapons, hides and a small game animal as they compete to get the greatest number of arrows airborne at once. Warriors of some other tribes shot at a ball tied to a stick or at a sheaf of grass thrown into the air.

2 | Dirty dealing on the wide Mississippi

Riverboats nuzzle up to the waterfront at St. Louis, a headquarters for what one ex-gambler called "predatory excursions" on the river.

"Cast off your stern line!" bawls the captain. "Cast off your spring line!"

"All clear!" returns the mate, and a stately sternwheeler, her ties to the mundane riverbank severed, churns into mid-channel. There she will provide the perfect setting, sovereign and impregnable, for some of the most outrageous sharpsters of the West—the Mississippi riverboat gamblers.

These scoundrels could choose among hundreds of boats out of New Orleans, Vicksburg, St. Louis and other cities. The steamers, some of them waterborne palaces, were full of wealthy planters, land speculators, settlers. And the gamblers were ready to pluck them of crops, cash or anything else. "It was dead easy money, too," said one veteran practitioner.

During the 1840s and 1850s hundreds of riverboat gamblers propelled their profession to new heights of knavery, and most of them did so without a flicker of conscience. Suckers, one gambler is supposed to have said, had no business with money, anyway.

A waterborne paradise for cardsharping knaves

There is no record that a committee of Western professional gamblers ever drew up plans for a paradise on earth. But there can be little doubt about the principal features they would have prescribed. First, a great system of navigable waterways closely resembling the Mississippi and the rivers of the West; second, hundreds of steamboats equipped with spacious saloons dispensing fine food and passable drink; third, an ever-changing list of passengers, most of them carrying large bank rolls and all of them gullible. Finally, the gamblers would surely have wanted the opportunity to deal an occasional card from the bottom of the deck.

With or without the advice of gamblers, such a paradise was created, and there has never been anything else quite like it in the history of gambling, of the West or even of the world. The great work was not accomplished overnight. But once the first step was taken, it went ahead as briskly as a game of three-card monte at a riverboat gambling table.

The first step was the Louisiana Purchase of 1803, which opened the Mississippi for commerce and made New Orleans a part of the United States. Almost from the time of its foundation by the French in 1718, New Orleans had been a lively place, the frequent haunt of pirates, prostitutes, thieves and gamblers, but it had been isolated from the rest of the Continent. Now, with the great river open, New Orleans became the fountainhead from which gambling could spread north along the Mississippi and west along its tributaries—the

Red, the Arkansas and the Missouri Rivers. By 1810 New Orleans had a population of only about 17,000, but that small city may have had more gambling houses than Philadelphia, Baltimore, Boston and New York combined. New Orleans was also sending out scores of cardsharps to establish outposts at Natchez, Vicksburg and St. Louis.

The early gamblers along the Mississippi were uncouth in appearance and murderous in inclination, quite unlike the suave, courtly gentlemen of riverboat legend. Their principal customers were the violent and tough flatboatmen who floated downriver from the hinterland carrying the products of farm and field. Gambling was a popular pastime aboard the cramped flatboats, and when crewmen went ashore they generally looked for more of the same kind of diversion at the nearest river-front dive.

Left only to the brawling flatboatmen and the first wave of card-playing thugs out of New Orleans, gambling on and along the Western waters might have remained a matter of small stakes, loud oaths and ready fists. But in January 1812, Robert Fulton's *New Orleans* chuffed into her namesake city and brought the steamboat age to the West. For gamblers, a whole new era was about to begin.

The first few pioneering steamboats were slow and cumbersome, and were used primarily as freight carriers. But in 1815 the Fulton interests launched a second *New Orleans*—the first had sunk—with respectable passenger accommodations where a man had room to stretch out and shuffle a deck of cards. She was 140 feet long, 28 wide, and could make 10 miles an hour downstream and four up, carrying 200 tons of freight and about 50 passengers, who were segregated by sex. The women's quarters consisted of a 30-foot cabin belowdecks; the men slept in what one early traveler called "an elegant roundhouse" abovedecks. Atop this

Wearing the sharply tailored frock coat that became known as the gambler's uniform, a lone passenger lolls on a deck of the *J. M. White* in the 1880s. In fact, many gamblers preferred to travel incognito, dressed as farmers, merchants or preachers.

Amid the squalor of a steamboat's cheapest accommodations, located on the lower deck, one passenger rifles another's trunk while the unsuspecting victim is absorbed in a card game. Thievery, like gambling, was common on the Mississippi River.

An intent flatboatman arranges his cards in this 1847 study for a painting by George Caleb Bingham. Although the crews of muscle-powered river craft often sought more raucous entertainment ashore, gambling was a favorite pastime when afloat.

they enjoyed "an elegantly decorated walk with iron railings and nettings" where they could "sit comfortably and have a commanding view over the boat, river and land, and enjoy the cool breeze."

This was a promising beginning for the gentlemanly gamblers. They had nothing against women—far from it—but they believed that the proper place for the fair sex was out of the way. Most of the ladies did not approve of games of chance and thus had an inhibiting effect on them.

Many more vessels followed in the wake of the *New Orleans*. By 1820 there were an estimated 69

steamboats plying the Western rivers. By 1845 there were 557 and by 1860 the number had jumped to 735. And the ranks of gamblers, adept at such games as poker, whist, brag and three-card monte, easily kept pace with the growing fleet of steamers.

With the possible exception of the steely eyed frontier gunfighter, few figures in the history of the American West were so embellished by popular folklore as riverboat gamblers, though few gamblers themselves had any illusions about their trade. In 1896 Cole Martin, who had spent much of his life on the rivers, looked back on his career and remarked: "It's very

A gambler's tale of a captain and a grand river lady

On May 6, 1871, the steamboat *Great Republic* was auctioned off in St. Louis. She was a beauty—the biggest riverboat, and one of the most lavish, of the era. Built at a cost of $235,000, she deserved her reputation as "the finest steamer afloat." Her columns were fluted, her walls frescoed, her main saloon graced by floral carpets and crystal chandeliers.

But she was a white elephant, burning $5,000 worth of fuel on each round trip between New Orleans and St. Louis. Her first owner went broke, and at a St. Louis auction the great four-decker was knocked down at a mere $48,000 to a riverboat captain and ex-gambler named William Thorwegan.

Thorwegan had lost a previous vessel in a fire and presumably was without the funds to buy the *Great Republic*. How he got them constitutes a romantic tale in which fact and fiction are hard to sift. According to one Henry Hill, who told his story 65 years after the event, the steamer was a gift from him to Thorwegan for kindnesses shown him in his youth.

Hill, from a Southern aristocratic family, had turned gambler and fallen on evil days. "Many steamboat captains refused to permit gambling and often set us ashore," he reminisced. Booted off his last boat, deserted by all his friends except the loyal Thorwegan, Hill decided to quit the profession and go west, where he made a killing in land speculation.

Returning to St. Louis, Hill read two separate items of news: Thorwegan had lost his boat and the *Great Republic* was for sale. "Next day I met some planters from the lower Mississippi," said Hill. "They wanted a game of poker and I agreed to sit in. We played from 3 Saturday night until 4 Monday morning and when I cashed in, I had won $350,000."

Hill claimed that he bought the boat with part of that windfall and gave her to a tearful Thorwegan.

Maybe. But Thorwegan's boat had burned in 1867 and he acquired the *Great Republic* in 1871. And the newspapers of the time clearly state that Thorwegan did his own bidding at the auction. Perhaps Hill provided him with the cash. Or perhaps the story was merely an old gambler's flight of wishful thinking.

At any rate, Thorwegan owned the boat for six years, rechristened her the *Grand Republic* and made her bigger and even more splendid. When she too went up in flames, in a fire of suspicious origin, she lighted up the St. Louis sky, awing onlookers with her "molten magnificence."

pretty to read about, but the real thing was not so nice. The black-eyed, black-mustached hero gambler that you read about was anything but a hero. There was no chivalry in his nature, and he was ready for any dark deed that would profit him. Of course I am speaking of the professional gambler, for everyone gambled; if they had not done so the professional's occupation would have been gone. The chivalrous ones were the young Southern planters, reckless, but not mean, who would play the full limit and get fleeced."

The appearance of the professional riverboat gambler was sometimes as crude as his morals. Fat and red-nosed, his waistcoat blotched with food stains, the gambler often affected the nondescript dress of an itinerant preacher or a hinterland farmer. Others came closer to the romantic image of gamblers as gaudy dandies. In this version, the gambler was resplendent in his knee-length, black, broadcloth coat and a ruffled white shirt whose bosom sparkled with a huge stud—sometimes a diamond, sometimes a fake—called a "headlight." His vest was black, decorated with hand-painted hunting scenes or flowers. On his nimble fingers he wore gold or diamond rings; his high-heeled boots were made of the finest leather and his underwear came from Paris.

Many riverboat gamblers, at least when their luck was running high, carried massive gold watches. Their particular favorites were the European-made Jürgensens, costing as much as $1,000, with one-carat diamonds set in their stems. The watches were sometimes attached to heavy gold chains that were remarkably long—Jimmy Fitzgerald, who was perhaps the greatest dandy on the Mississippi, boasted a chain that was almost 20 feet in length and looped several times around his neck. Another consummate dude, James Ashby, carried a gold-headed cane in each hand and, when he wished to be particularly impressive, sported a diamond-studded gold pencil, which he clenched in his teeth like a cigar.

Whatever their wardrobes or their jeweled accessories, the gamblers who worked the Western riverboats were at least the spiritual descendants of the crude, shore-bound gamesters of New Orleans. For a time, these

The *Grand Republic* steamed down the Mississippi River loaded with a glittering list of passengers and a cargo hold full of cotton.

cardsharps and con men led amphibious lives. While still maintaining their seamy resorts in the river towns, they also worked on the steamboats, where they came to be regarded quite early in the game as a breed apart from the ordinary traveler. Indeed, in 1817, when a boiler exploded on board the *Constitution* and scalded 11 passengers to death, one of the survivors noted of the fatalities: "Among them was a gambler, who was buried separately."

The opportunities for such permanent displays of disapproval were rare. However, public resentment of the early professional gamblers was common enough—not because they played games of chance, but because they almost always won by cheating. And even more disruptive to public order, a gambler frequently responded to a challenge by means of a bullet, a blow or a knife.

An aroused citizenry passed numerous laws to ban or restrict gambling on and along the Western rivers, but such regulations were spottily enforced. Gambling was so much a part of American life that only a minority of moral zealots wanted to do away with it com-

pletely. George Washington, after all, had often gambled at cards; Thomas Jefferson, at the same time he was composing the Declaration of Independence, maintained meticulous records of his winnings and losings at backgammon and lotto. And Andrew Jackson was quite a horseplayer.

It was difficult enough on land for the law to proceed against crooked gamblers while leaving the games of honest gentlemen alone. The problem was intensified on the steamboats, where travelers with ready cash found themselves on long and monotonous journeys, far from the watchful eyes of their home communities. For the most part, the steamboats were beyond the practical jurisdiction of state and local authority as well, and it was customarily up to the captain to maintain proper order as he saw fit. Wise captains knew that card playing—along with drinking—was the most popular amusement among male passengers and they were loath to interfere with the diversions of paying customers. They knew, too, that professional gamblers represented a steady clientele for the steamboat lines, and they did not want to discourage such a sure source of revenue. Small wonder that the Western rivers became a gamblers' paradise.

Most of the captains permitted gambling on board their vessels, even if some of them did post discreet signs warning the unwary that they wagered at their own risk. However, few if any of the steamboat captains condoned flagrant cheating at cards or at any other game of chance, and offenders were frequently dealt with harshly.

In the 1850s, two cardsharps aboard the *Robert J. Ward* were busily bilking a young traveler out of a considerable sum when the captain happened to pass their table. When he saw that a crooked poker game was in progress, the captain slapped one of the gamblers across the face, scooped up the pot, and forced the two cheats to return their winnings. At the next woodyard, he had the pair put off his boat.

Occasionally, if a number of gamblers were observed with additional aces dribbling from their sleeves, the riverboat captains would signal for assistance from ashore, hoisting a police flag that summoned a force of constables to the dockside at the next port. There, the gamblers would be duly arrested, but whether because of bribery or the lack of evidence, they usually did not spend very much time behind bars.

At least one captain was hardy and determined enough to go ashore and take direct action against gamblers who had wronged an innocent passenger. The incident occurred in the 1830s, when Captain John Russell's Mississippi steamer was docked at the small community of Natchez-under-the-Hill, which was one of the most notorious hangouts for riverboat gamblers between voyages. One of Captain Russell's passengers, a wide-eyed clergyman, wandered off the vessel, possibly in search of firsthand information about the ways of sinners. Whatever his intentions, the clergyman wound up in a gambling house and got taken for every cent he had.

When the minister returned to the steamboat, he told Russell of his misfortune. Angered that a gang of gamblers would stoop to bilking a naïve man of the cloth, the captain armed his crewmen and led them ashore. There he visited every gambling establishment he could find, and demanded the return of the minister's money. To a man, the gamblers laughed at him and slammed their doors in his face.

Russell was not one to give up easily. He sent some of his men back to the boat for a heavy spar and ordered them to batter down every door that seemed to lead to a gambling den. Still, he recovered no money. And when he threatened to start dragging the district's buildings into the river, the gamblers laughed at him even more than they had before.

Now Russell was furious, and proceeded to show that he meant business. Unmooring his boat, he told some of his men to fasten a thick rope to one of the gambling houses. Then he tightened the rope on the capstan of his vessel and called for full speed astern. The house had lurched away from its foundation before one of the gamblers managed to dash out and slice through the rope.

The captain next ordered his armed men to replace the severed rope with a chain. As the house started to inch toward the river once again, the gamblers realized that they had been beaten. The minister got his money back. And he may have picked up some material for a sermon or two.

Sometimes a good Samaritan from among the passengers took on crooked gamblers alone. One night in 1832, four men sat at a poker game aboard a Mississippi River steamer. One of them, a young man from Natchez who was coming back from a honeymoon trip to New York, was a heavy loser. Worse still, he was not playing with his own money. While he had been in New York, he had collected some $50,000 from Eastern merchants on behalf of the Southern planters, and now all but about $5,000 of that sum was gone. As even that remnant started to dribble away, a knot of spectators gathered around to watch the game. Among them, wearing a broad-brimmed hat and a plain black suit, was James Bowie, who was the inventor of the bowie knife and later a hero of the Alamo. He saw immediately that the game was rigged.

When the young man's last dollar was gone, he leaped to his feet and dashed out to the deck, where he attempted to climb over the rail and hurl himself into the river. Bowie, looking for all the world like a kindly preacher, helped to restrain the desperate loser and led him back to his cabin. Bowie returned to the bar and got into a game with the three gamblers. They played for high stakes, and it was not long before the table was piled high with bills of large denomination. Then

A sportsman's handy games and ready assets

A gambler in the 19th Century West could carry the essential tools of his trade with him, often in the form of some pocket gaming device or accessory, so that he would be able to gamble anywhere at any time.

Particularly well suited to a sporting man's itinerant life and flamboyant style were items such as mother-of-pearl dice in a hinged gold case that was worn as a watch fob, and solid gold dice in a matching canister only one inch tall. Less ostentatious, but equally convenient, was a miniature roulette wheel, operated much like a stop watch, that might be used as a come-on to entice a passing sucker into a more serious game.

Decorative nongaming equipment also served a gambler's purposes. Silver matchsafes embossed with a gambling motif, or a timepiece with playing cards to mark the hours, served—if produced at the proper moment—as convenient forms of advertising. And when the chips were down and money was scarce, baubles such as these were transformed into reserve assets for gamblers who pushed them into the pot to take the place of hard cash.

SILVER MATCHSAFES

POCKET ROULETTE

GOLD DICE AND CUP

WATCH-FOB DICE

PLAYING-CARD WATCH

On the Mississippi and Ohio River steamers in the 1850s, the handsome game box below—and the natty appearance of Alexander Bonnett who carried it—announced the presence of a professional gambler.

Bonnett's game box was fitted for three sizes of mother-of-pearl markers and an implement vital to a gambler of the era: a pistol. For travel, Bonnett's pocket-size .44 caliber nestled against a deck of cards and a pair of ivory dice.

While Bonnett's box equipped him for a variety of games such as poker, euchre and brag, the two boxes at right, which were used on the riverboat *Natchez* in the 1880s, were designed for more specific diversions. A box used for the game of crown and anchor has compartments edged in velvet to accommodate paper squares that, when set on a table, form the "layout"

on which bets are placed. Two dice and two paper squares, missing from this timeworn set, were marked with the crown and anchor that give the game its name. The other case, simpler in style, contains a backgammon game.

The Steamboat cards are an inexpensive grade popular with gamblers during the late 1800s. They were rarely carried: on the riverboats, cards could be purchased from bartenders.

RIVERBOAT GAMBLER ALEXANDER BONNETT *(ABOVE RIGHT)* AND HIS GAME BOX

BACKGAMMON SET

CROWN AND ANCHOR SET

STEAMBOAT PLAYING CARDS

Bowie noticed that one of the gamblers was flicking a card from his sleeve.

Almost in a single motion, Bowie pulled an enormous knife from his shirt bosom with one hand and gripped the gambler's wrist with the other. "Show your hand!" he cried. "If it contains more than five cards I shall kill you!" The gambler made an effort to wriggle free but Bowie held him like a vise. He twisted the man's wrist and six cards fell to the table: four aces, a queen and a jack.

"I shall take the pot," announced Bowie, "with a legitimate poker hand, four kings and a ten." The pot, which contained some $70,000, was eminently worth the taking.

"Who the devil are you, anyway?" questioned the gambler.

"I am James Bowie."

"The voice was like velvet," according to an old account of the incident. "But it cut like steel into the hearts of the chief gambler's confederates and deterred them from any purpose or impulse they might have had to interfere. They, with the crowd, shrank back from the table, smitten with terror by the name. Bowie softly swept the banknotes into his hat and lightly clapped it on his head." At that point Bowie gave most of the money to the young honeymooner, making good the $50,000 loss, and kept the remaining $20,000 for himself.

Few of the victims of fast-shuffling riverboat gamblers were fortunate enough to find a champion as formidable as Jim Bowie. And those who sought to stand up for themselves frequently discovered that they were no match for the violent breed of men who preyed on unwary travelers. In 1838, an Illinois publication reported that numerous men who had gone to the West had "taken passage on board of a boat, and never been heard of again." Although friends and families sought in vain to obtain information about the missing travelers the publication had little doubt about their whereabouts. "Could the deep and turbid waters of our rivers reveal their secrets," it said, "they would tell but too often the long silence of those absent friends. The midnight gambling, the fierce quarrel, the dirk, the sullen plunge of the ghastly corpse, with heavy weights attached, all follow in quick succession, and with the unerring certainty that effect follows cause."

Despite their shadowy reputations, riverboat gamblers were often considered to be good company, at least until they were caught cheating. "They were fine fellows, educated men who could talk to anyone about anything, and as polite as anything you ever saw." To be sure, the author of that statement was a gambler himself, an old Mississippi professional named Tom Ellison, but many riverboat passengers would have agreed with him.

The passengers themselves were a mixed lot. An observer in 1855 ticked off a fair sampling that included "immigrants from every nationality in Europe, the aristocratic English lord, the conservative bishop, the wealthy planter, the farmer from the arctic regions of Lake Superior, the frank, open-handed men of the West, politicians of every stripe, and religionists of all creeds," not omitting "the graceless gambler." In this case "graceless" may not have referred to the gambler's lack of social polish, but to his slim chance of salvation.

The principal quarries of the gamblers were of course the passengers who had money, and these were numerous. At the height of the South's prosperity in the 25 years preceding the Civil War a good many large fortunes were made in cotton, rice, sugar and tobacco. The steamboats commonly carried rich merchants, planters, cotton factors and land speculators who were heavily laden with gold and banknotes. Businessmen, carrying money to make important purchases or returning with the cash proceeds of a sale, were frequent passengers.

In the steamer's cabin—often called the social hall or main saloon—there were always tables where a man might play a friendly game of poker. Women, although not excluded by any law or regulation, customarily left the tables to the males, who frequently did not break off their games until waiters appeared. There was invariably a well-stocked bar and drinks were strong: brandy smashes, milk punches, mint juleps, eggnogs and straight bourbon, gin, rum and brandy. If the supply of authentic French brandy ran out, bartenders would substitute Kentucky whiskey fresh from the still, flavoring it with burnt peach stones, a dash of nitric acid and a bit of cod-liver oil.

The bartenders also sold another product that was even more lethal: playing cards. When a gambler started a game he often bought a deck from the bartender and ostentatiously broke the seal and tore off the wrapping. His victims could hardly doubt that the fresh cards were pure and unmarked, or suspect that the bartender had been bribed to replace his stock with a few dozen decks of cards that were known in the profession as "readers."

All riverboat gamblers were expert at cheating, and perhaps 99 per cent of them, either occasionally or all the time, did cheat. One authority on the subject, who estimated that there were at least 2,000 gamblers on the Western waters in the mid-19th Century, could think of only four who were honest. One of these, a man named John Powell, was not only honest but afflicted with a conscience.

In 1858, on his 50th birthday, Powell added up his accounts and concluded that he was worth half a million dollars. But in that year he chanced to get into a poker game with a young English traveler on one of the boats and took the lad for all his money ($8,000) and all of his luggage. The Englishman turned up in the dining saloon the next morning, shook hands with his fellow passengers and then shot himself. Powell was so upset that he sent the $8,000 and the luggage to the young man's family and quit gambling for a year. When he returned to his profession he was still unnerved and soon lost his entire fortune. He was never able to recoup it and died broke, an example to his colleagues of the dangers of compassion.

A good cardsharp was so skilled at his chosen craft that the gambler Tom Ellison was moved in his later years to confess that what went on at riverboat gaming tables was not really gambling at all—it was more like robbery. "But that's what went as gambling in those times," he explained. "The fellows had to be pretty slick, I can tell you.... I've seen fellows pick every card in a pack, and call it without missing once. I've seen them shuffle them one for one all through from top to bottom, so that they were in the same position after a dozen shuffles that they were in at first. They'd just flutter them up like a flock of quail and get the aces, kings, queens, jacks and tens all together as easy as pie. A sucker had no more chance against those fellows than a snowball in a red-hot oven. They were good fellows, free with their money as water, after scheming to bust their heads to get it. A hundred didn't bother them any more than a chew of tobacco would you."

Ellison once saw a planter "lose his whole tobacco crop in one night and get up and never mind it particularly. Many a time I've seen a game player just skin off his watch and ring and studs and play them in. Men often lost their goods playing in their way bills. I've seen them betting a bale of cotton at a crack, and it wasn't at all uncommon to hear an old planter betting off his Negroes on a good hand. Every man who ever ran on the river knows that these old planters used to play in their lady servants, valuing them all the way from $300 to $1,500. I saw a little colored boy stand up at $300 to back his master's faith in a little flush that wasn't any good on earth."

Riverboat gamblers rarely operated alone. They preferred to stalk their prey in pairs or in teams of three or a half a dozen. Often they boarded the boats at different times or at different towns and pretended not to know each other. When one of them got into a poker game his partners would deal him winning hands or, standing near the table as interested spectators, signal what cards his opponents held. This process, called "iteming," often involved puffs of cigar smoke like Indian signals, or the casual scratching of ears, nose or eyebrows. One gambler favored a walking stick, which he held at various angles; another, who pretended to be an affable half-wit, wandered through the saloon sawing out coded snatches of music on the violin.

Poker was commonly played on the riverboats, but the real killer was three-card monte. This was not truly a game, but a brief and brutal exercise in sleight of hand. Its ancestor was the ancient shell game, played with three walnut shells and a pea. The operator of the game put the pea on a tabletop, covered it with one of the shells, and placed the empties alongside. He then manipulated the three shells in a halting, clumsy manner and invited an onlooker to locate the pea. No matter how sharp his eyes, the victim almost invariably overlooked the lightning move of the operator when he extracted the pea and caught it between his fingers. Vast sums have been lost at this game since antiquity.

Three-card monte was played with a couple of insignificant cards, perhaps a pair of fives or sixes, and a face card or an ace, which was called the "baby." The professional gambler slapped the three cards facedown on a table, manipulated them, and bet that the spectator could not locate the baby.

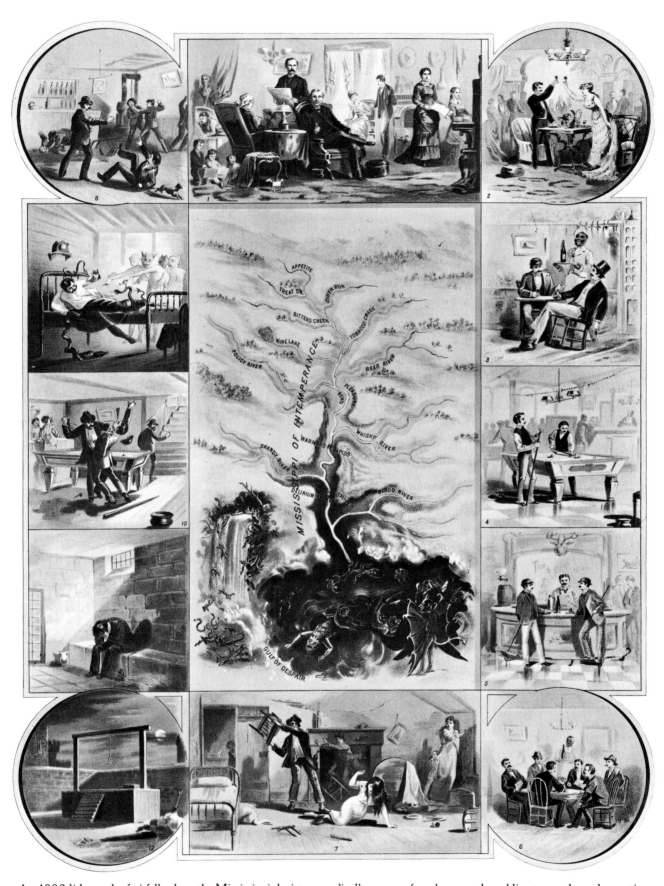

An 1882 lithograph of pitfalls along the Mississippi depicts a prodigal's progress from booze and gambling to murder and execution.

This ultimatum led to a shoot-out with gamblers and the hanging of five of them. When the gamblers fled Vicksburg, they met hostile receptions in other river towns as a storm of antigambling sentiment swept the Mississippi valley in the mid-1830s.

Notice.

AT a meeting of the citizens of Vicksburg on Saturday the 4th day of July, it was

Resolved, That a notice be given to all *professional* GAMBLERS, that the citizens of Vicksburg are resolved to exclude them from this place and its vicinity, and that *twenty-four hours* notice be given them to leave the place.

Resolved, That all persons permitting Faro dealing in their houses, be also notified, that they will be prosecuted therefor.

Resolved, That one hundred copies of the foregoing resolutions be printed and stuck up at the corners of the streets, and the publication be deemed notice.

Vicksburg, July 5, 1835.

The three-card monte dealer was commonly called a "thrower," or, because cards were often known as "broads," a "broad pitcher." He began his game with a first-rate spiel that appealed to both the skepticism and the greed of the onlookers. "Here you are, gentlemen; this ace of hearts is the winning card. Watch it closely. Follow it with your eye as I shuffle. Here it is, and now here, now here, and now—where? It is my regular trade, gentlemen, to move my hands quicker than your eyes. I always have two chances to your one. The ace of hearts. If your sight is quick enough, you beat me and I pay; if not, I beat you and take your money. Who will go me twenty? It is very plain and simple, but you can't always tell. Who will go me twenty dollars?"

The gambler admits that sleight of hand, or at any rate some fast shuffling, is involved. But he appears so mediocre, even inept, as he shuffles the cards that the spectators suspect he is an apprentice, a fool or a drunk—or perhaps all three. Why not risk $20? At this point the gambler's assistant, often called a "capper," steps up to place a bet. Everybody follows the ace with no trouble, and the capper wins with ease. Appearing to be angry, the gambler offers to bet $50. The capper agrees to this and wins again. By this time the onlookers are digging for their wallets and hoping that the gambler will be foolish enough to bet $500 or even $1,000.

Now the capper moves in for the kill. While the gambler seems to allow his attention to wander, per-

haps even casting his eyes heavenward in despair at his miserable luck, the capper quickly marks or turns up the corner of the baby card. Everyone except the gambler notices this. The gambler bets $100 and once again he loses. The rank smell of avarice is heavy in the riverboat saloon. The baby card is plainly marked. How could a man lose?

The seemingly discomfitted gambler complains that he is having the worst streak of luck ever known on the Mississippi, and has only $1,500 left. He will have to bet it all just to get even, he says. Will anyone go him $1,500? Up steps a rich and eager planter who is willing to lay down $1,500. The planter feels sorry for the poor gambler—but not so sorry that he will not bet on a sure thing.

The gambler moves the cards, deftly palming the marked ace and substituting a losing card that has an identical mark, or turned-up corner. The planter, who has been following the action with what he is convinced is a very careful eye, triumphantly jabs his finger at a particular card. The gambler then turns the card over, smiles sympathetically—it is a loser—and scoops up his $1,500.

The planter can hardly complain. He had meant to cheat the gambler—and now, having been cheated himself, he must quietly pay up. Had he been true blue he might have warned the gambler that the baby was marked, but now he can only ponder the wisdom of the old saying, "You can't cheat an honest man." ◉

A red-hot race for pride and money

In the summer of 1870 a bitter rivalry between two headstrong riverboat captains turned the muddy Mississippi into a gigantic raceway, the setting for one of the biggest gambling events of the 19th Century.

The two captains were known for the verbal abuse they hurled at each other. John W. Cannon of the *Robert E. Lee* referred to Thomas P. Leathers of the *Natchez* as an "old scoundrel" and Leathers branded Cannon

A CARD.

Reports having been circulated that steamer R. E. LEE, leaving for Louisville on the 30th June, is going out for a race, such reports are not true, and the traveling community are assured that every attention will be given to the safety and comfort of passengers.

The running and management of the Lee will in no manner be affected by the departure o other boats.

Je19—otf2dp   JOHN W. CANNON, Master

Cannon announced a false destination for the *Robert E. Lee* to deter passengers, and stripped his boat of nearly everything but fuel.

a "mealy-mouthed, egg-sucking this-and-that." Both knew the fastest boat would attract the most cotton shipping business. So when they published notice cards (below) piously denying any intent to compete in a 1,200-mile race from New Orleans to St. Louis, few believed them.

Newspapers in Europe as well as the United States proclaimed it the race of the century. Millions of dollars were bet as crowds descended on river towns along the route and flooded commercial exchanges and telegraph offices throughout the world.

Public excitement was as hot as the fires in the steamboats' boilers as they slipped their moorings at about 5 p.m. on June 30 and, trailing plumes of sparks and charcoal-black smoke, plowed upriver. In riverside towns like Natchez, Vicksburg, Memphis and Cairo, odds changed frequently and new wagers were struck by the light of bonfires as the days wore into nights.

Fiercely determined to win, Cannon staged a running refueling from another boat he had waiting in mid-river and plunged dangerously forward through the fog (any sane man would have laid up, Leathers snarled). After three days, 18 hours and 14 minutes—more than six hours in front of the *Natchez*—the *Robert E. Lee* panted into St. Louis to a tumultuous greeting. Her time was never equaled.

A CARD TO THE PUBLIC.

Being satisfied that the steamer NATCHEZ has a reputation of being fast, I take this method of informing the public that the reports of the Natchez leaving here next Thursday, the 30th inst., intending racing, are not true. All passengers and shippers can rest assured that the Natchez will not race with any boat that may leave here on the same day with her. All business entrusted to my care, either in freight or passengers, will have the best attention.
T. P. LEATHERS,
Master Steamer Natchez.
Je25—5t2dp

Practical even when racing, Leathers put extra passengers and cargo aboard the *Natchez*. "I am not afraid of Cannon's trickery," he said.

Moonlight reveals an awesome scene: a pair of exquisitely graceful riverboats in a close and fiery struggle for mastery of the Mississippi. In truth, the two vessels were never as near each other as this painting suggests; the *Robert E. Lee* started four minutes before the *Natchez* in the timed race and never surrendered the lead.

One of the greatest three-card monte throwers in all of riverboat history was George Devol, who left behind a curious and lively autobiography called *Forty Years a Gambler on the Mississippi.* Devol could hardly be considered an upstanding citizen. One of his contemporaries who bought a copy of his autobiography noted on the flyleaf that George "was always, and is yet, a 'bad egg.' " In his own way, Devol may well have agreed with this assessment. In the book, he observed wryly that "some men are born rascals, some men have rascality thrust upon them, others achieve it." A born rascal, Devol led his life in a manner that seemed almost dedicated to the magnification of this hereditary trait.

Devol told his stories of gambling with a wicked relish, but he had some slight streak of Christian charity. "I caught a preacher once for all his money, his gold spectacles, and his sermons," he said. "Then I had some of those queer feelings come over me, so I gave him his sermons and specks back."

Born in Ohio in 1829, Devol ran away from home when he was only 10 years old and hired on as a riverboat cabin boy at four dollars a month. In some ways he was an antecedent of Mark Twain's Huckleberry Finn, but he was actually closer to another fictional character called Simon Suggs. Created by a largely forgotten writer named Johnson Jones Hooper, Simon was widely known to readers throughout the American frontier, principally from *Some Adventures of Captain Simon Suggs,* which predated *Huckleberry Finn* by more than 30 years.

In Hooper's fiction Simon Suggs's father is a preacher and Simon is a guileful lad who is bent on gambling. Says the preacher: "Simon! Simon! you poor unlettered fool. Don't you know that all card-players, and chicken-fighters, and horse-racers go to hell? And don't you know that them that plays cards always loses their money, and—"

To this Simon gives a memorable reply. "Who wins it all then, daddy?"

George Devol did not win it all. But he was a winner in the sense that he survived to the age of 73 and enjoyed a career of his own choosing. In his prime he was about six feet tall and powerfully built and weighed 195 pounds. Like many another in his profession, he was a combative man. Gamblers on the Western waters customarily carried derringers—short-snouted, over-and-under double-barreled pistols of about .45 caliber. Such firearms were deadly at poker-table range, but they were not much good beyond that. Devol did carry an efficient revolver, which he referred to as Betsy Jane, but his main weapons in a fight were his fists and his head. Even allowing for a certain amount of exaggeration, Devol's hands must have been enormous. "My old paw is large enough to hold out a compressed bale of cotton or a whole deck of cards, and it comes in very handy to do the work. I could hold one deck in the palm of my hand and shuffle up another."

Devol's head, as he said, "must be pretty thick, or it would have been cracked many years ago, for I have been struck some terrible blows on my head with iron dray-pins, pokers, clubs, stone-coal, and bowlders. Doctors have often told me that my skull was nearly an inch in thickness over my forehead. I never have my hair clipped short, for I would be ashamed to take my hat off, as the lines on my old scalp look about like the railroad map of the State in which I was born."

The tactic that Devol utilized in fights was keeping his head low and hoping that opponents would break their fists on it. When the opportunity occurred he would deliver a bone-crushing butt. Noted one witness: "George was a great butter. He could use his head with terrible effect and kill any man living, white or black, by butting him."

In spite of his general toughness Devol had an agile mind. As a lad, he learned his profession quickly. At the outbreak of the Mexican War in 1846 he traveled on a steamboat to the Rio Grande, hoping to fight Mexicans. On the way there, he was taken in hand by a gambler who taught him how to cheat at cards. Instead of fighting, young Devol wound up gambling with United States Army troops. In a short time he was able to return to New Orleans with the handsome sum of $2,700 in his pockets.

Before he retired from gambling for good in the 1880s Devol managed to win perhaps two million dollars more but, like most of the men in his profession, he could not hold onto it. "It is said of me that I have won more money than any sporting man in this country," Devol wrote in 1886. "I will say that I hadn't sense enough to keep it; but if I had never seen a Faro bank, I would be a wealthy man today."

Gamblers fleece unwary river travelers in two illustrations from the autobiography of cardsharp George Devol (left). Aboard the *Sultana (top)*, Devol purposely loses to a shill—causing an onlooker who backed Devol to drop $4,000. On the *Mayflower (bottom)*, Devol's partner Canada Bill uses a marked queen to win $2,000 at monte.

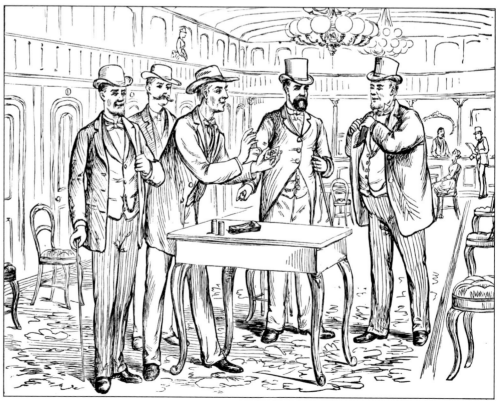

Faro was Devol's fatal weakness. He was a master of such games of chance as three-card monte, poker and cassino, and was also intimately familiar with all of the arts of cheating at cards. However, he was a prime sucker at faro. After a successful voyage on the river, his pockets bulging with his winnings, he would rush ashore to the nearest faro game, where he would be trimmed as easily as any wide-eyed yokel. Devol never offered an explanation for this failing. Perhaps he thought that none was necessary—the history of gambling, after all, is full of stories of people who were wizards at one game and dolts at another. However, some philosophical illumination may be cast by Devol's longtime friend and gambling confederate, "Canada Bill" Jones.

Canada Bill, according to Devol's description of him, "was a character one might travel the length and breadth of the land and never find his match, or run across his equal. Imagine a medium-sized, chicken-headed, tow-haired sort of a man with mild blue eyes, and a mouth nearly from ear to ear, who walked with a shuffling, half-apologetic sort of a gait, and who, when his countenance was in repose, resembled an idiot. His clothes were always several sizes too large, and his face was as smooth as a woman's and never had a particle of hair on it.

"Canada was a slick one. He had a squeaking, boyish voice, and awkward, gawky manners, and a way of asking fool questions and putting on a good natured sort of a grin, that led everybody to believe that he was the rankest kind of a sucker—the greenest sort of a country jake. Woe to the man who picked him up, though. Canada was, under all his hypocritical appearance, a regular card shark, and could turn monte with the best of them. He was my partner for a number of years, and many are the suckers we roped in, and many the huge roll of bills we corralled."

Three-card monte was Canada Bill's specialty, but he was constitutionally incapable of limiting himself to that. He would take an eager hand in a large variety of other games and almost invariably lose. "He loved gambling for its own sake," explained Devol, "just as the moralists love virtue for its own sake. No man that I ever came in contact with ever struck me as being so fond of gambling. I never knew Bill to play at a short card game that he did not quit loser, and I have known

him to play as long as seventy hours at a sitting."

Canada Bill's immortality does not rest, however, on his curious appearance or manner or on his penchant for getting out of his element and losing his shirt. It rests upon a single line that he once uttered, a phrase that has been repeated by countless thousands of other gamblers. Canada Bill was playing faro one evening in a one-horse town located on the Mississippi riverbank, and losing, when a friend of his tugged at his sleeve and asked, "Bill, Bill, don't you know this game is crooked?"

"Yes," answered Canada Bill, "but it's the only game in town."

Like Canada Bill, George Devol loved gambling for its own sake. He admired men who lost their money without complaint, and sometimes he quietly returned part of it. He would not gamble with youngsters. "Young men and boys have often stood around the table and bothered me to bet. I would tell them to go away, that I did not gamble with boys. That would make some of the smart Alecks mad, and they would make a great deal of noise. So, when I was about to close up, I would take in the young chap. He would walk away with a good lesson. But when I had to win money from a boy to keep him quiet, I would always go to him and return the money, after giving him a good talking to."

Devol despised sore losers. Once, while he was playing three-card monte on board the famous steamboat *Robert E. Lee,* one of the passengers stepped up to the table and slapped down $800. "I knew it was all the money he had," Devol acknowledged, "for he tried to make it $1,000 by putting up his watch; but in those days I would not turn for a watch unless it was a Jürgensen or very fine make. When he had lost his money and spent a few moments studying, he whipped out a Colt's navy and said, 'See here, friend, that is all the money I have got, and I am going to die right here but I will have it back.' I cooly said, 'Did you think I was going to keep the money?' He replied, 'I knew very well you would not keep it. If you had, I would have filled you full of lead.'

"Pulling out a roll of money, I said, 'I want to whisper to you.' He put his head down, and I said that I didn't want to give up the money before all these people; that then they would want their money back.

70

'But you offer to bet me again, and I will bet the $800 against your pistol.'

"That pleased him. 'All right,' he said, and the $800 and the pistol went up in my partner's hands. Over went the wrong card. I grabbed the pistol, and told my partner to give me the stake money. Pulling the gun on him, 'Now,' I said, 'you have acted the wet dog about this, and I will not give you a cent of your money; and if you cut any more capers, I'll break your nose.'"

For all his occasional shows of meanness, Devol did not have, in the flatboatman's phrase, "a clear meat-axe disposition all the way through." He was soft-hearted about animals. Once, he was traveling on the *Princess* when the boat stopped at the mouth of the Red River to take on passengers. "I saw the negroes carrying some long boxes built like chicken-coops," Devol recalled. "I asked Captain Holmes what was in the boxes. He said, 'Alligators.'

"So I went down stairs and found the man that owned them. I took him up to the bar and had a drink; then I asked him what he was going to do with the alligators.

"He said he had a side-show, and he was going to play the fairs all over the entire Northern country, and he wanted them to draw custom. I told him I thought it an excellent idea, and said, 'I have a ten-legged wolf in a cage that I will get on board at Vicksburg, and I will sell him cheap.' This pleased him, and we took another drink.

"After supper we got to playing whisky poker, as I told him I never gambled much, only once in a while, as planters would play a quarter antee. He insisted on changing it into a little draw; and as I had some very good cards in the bar, I was not hard to coax. We commenced at a quarter antee, and after we had been playing about an hour he insisted on raising it to $1. He flattered me more than I ever was flattered before, in telling me I was the luckiest man to draw he ever saw. The result was, before we reached Natchez I had won all his money and his alligators."

Tables of diners stretch into the distance in the typically elongated saloon of the *Dubuque*. At such sumptuous meals, gamblers could mingle with wealthy planters and merchants, singling out suckers for the game to follow.

Devol could not bring himself to keep the alligators. When he observed that his opponent "took it so much to heart about losing his pets, I sold them back to him and took his note." Devol was not certain that the note would ever be made good. Therefore, as an additional gesture of kindness, he decided that upon his death he would leave it "with my dear old mother-in-law for collection."

Devol's exuberant autobiography contains many such anecdotes, and a number of them were set down with considerable embellishment. The everyday reality of his existence, and that of hundreds of his gambling contemporaries, was somewhat quieter. They worked the riverboats year after year, voyage after voyage, trimming the suckers by superior card play or by cheating, but they rarely ran into a fight or an extraordinary experience. For them it was a business, and very few of them bothered to record its details any more than a commercial canner would bother to write about the distinguishing features of every can that he packed. But Devol seemed to run into more eyebrow-raisers than most. There was, for instance, the time he tried to turn a catfish into a pike.

As Devol related the story, he and a partner—who must have been more proficient at the game than Devol was—had been playing in an all-night faro game in New Orleans, and wound up several hundred dollars ahead. Before they went to bed, they decided to take a stroll to the French market in order to have a cup of coffee. When they got to the market, Devol recalled, "we saw a catfish that would weigh about 125 pounds; its mouth was so large that I could put my head into it."

Devol stared at the fish while his partner, a man named Bush, stepped a little way into the market. An old man came up to Devol and said, "That is the largest catfish I ever saw."

Deciding to have some fun and perhaps a bet with the man, Devol signaled to his partner and replied, "You are the worst judge of a fish I ever saw; that is not a cat, it is a pike, and the largest one ever brought to this market."

The old man looked at Devol and then at the fish and said, "Look here, my boy, where in the devil were you raised?"

"I was born and raised in Indiana," said Devol.

The old man allowed that he could have guessed that Devol hailed from a state where the people knew little about fish—or anything else, for that matter. "I appeared to be mad," said Devol, "and offered to bet him $100 that the fish was a pike. Says he, 'Do you mean it?' I pulled out a roll, threw down $100 and told him to cover it. He lammed her up, and I said, 'Who will we leave it to?'

"We looked around and saw Bush, with a memorandum book in his hand and a pen behind his ear, talking to a woman who sold vegetables, and he was acting as if he was collector of the market. I said, 'Maybe that man with the book in his hand might know.' The old fellow called Bush, and said to him, 'Do you belong about here?' 'Oh, yes; I have belonged about here for a good many years,' says Bush. 'Well, sir, you are just the man we want to decide our bet,' says the old gent. 'We want you to tell us what kind of a fish this is.'

"Bush braced himself up, and said, 'I have been market-master here for twenty years, and that is the largest pike I ever saw in this market.' 'Well! Well! Well!' says the old man, 'I have lived on the Tombigbee River for forty-five years, and I never saw two bigger fools than you two.' "

Devol was a diehard. When he finished working the riverboats in about 1885, the pickings had grown so slim that most of his colleagues had long since abandoned the waterways in favor of fresher fields on the booming frontier. Spurred on by stories of gold in California, many of the riverboat gamblers had departed decades before, bound for the Pacific coast and its hordes of newly rich miners who were eager to chance small fortunes on the turn of a card. Other gamblers journeyed on to the brawling cattle towns and the gold and silver camps of the rugged interior territories, where they set up their gambling tables in settings that were far less luxurious than the opulent saloons of the river steamers.

Behind them these roving gamblers left a betting man's paradise that had been changed forever by the Civil War. The rich planters, men who were willing to play against a three-card monte thrower at $1,500 a turn, had vanished—their fortunes had been destroyed by the collapse of the Old South. More and more, travelers shunned the tedium of river travel in favor of

the much swifter railroads, where the displaced riverboaters attempted on occasion to start up a game or two in the smoking car. Trips on trains were too rapid for anybody to settle in for some really serious gambling, however, and the railroad crews turned out to be far less tolerant of gamblers than the steamer captains had ever been.

Steamboats continued to plow through the waters of the West, but all of the old glitter had vanished. The world of the riverboat gambler was preserved merely in memories, many of which were heavy with violence and despair. Perhaps the most poignant of all was the story about the captain, enticed into a crooked poker game in the 1840s, who at last, holding four kings, was driven to put up his two-thirds interest in his steamboat. With a sly smile, the professional gambler spread his cards on the table. They showed four aces.

Half an hour later, in his stateroom, the captain shot himself through the heart. In the letter he left behind, he observed that "a man who would bet his last dollar on four kings doesn't deserve standing room on earth."

Down amid the cargo, the roll of the bones

In a blur of action, a group of roustabouts shoots a fast game of craps in the midst of barrels of cargo on a riverboat's main deck in 1889.

Once while ambling along the boiler deck of the Mississippi steamboat *City of Chester,* a professional gambler heard "a Negro cry in a stentorian voice, 'come 7 or 11,' then another man calling out 'chill'en cryin' fo' bread." Then came the dry clatter of something rolling across deck planks. Going below to the main deck, he witnessed his first game of craps. Joining in the fun, he immediately lost $15.

Throughout the riverboat era, off-duty deck hands could be found crouched on the main deck among the freight and furnaces. Here these roustabouts rolled "the bones" in this fast-paced game that blacks had developed from a European dice game, hazard.

One passenger who gambled down below—and found his life changed as a consequence—was Pinckney Pinchback, the black servant of renowned riverboat gambler George Devol. "Pinch," as he was known, knew his boss's tricks and he applied them on the main deck. He won so much at monte, seven-up and poker that he quit working for Devol, entered politics—and wound up serving as governor of Louisiana during the carpetbag era.

Enthusiasm for a crap game aboard the riverboat *Natchez* about 1910 gives a deck hand an opportunity to pick a crew mate's back pocket. Such pilfering was commonplace; a deck officer in charge of roustabouts on a river steamer allowed that the deck was downright "dangerous for people with money in their pockets."

3 | Betting fever in gold-rush country

Portsmouth Square, with casinos like the Bella Union and El Dorado, was San Francisco's gambling center until 1855.

California during the height of the gold rush had everything a gambler could want: wealth and opportunity galore. From 1848 through the early 1850s, $350 million worth of dust and nuggets was scratched from the soil of California by a devil-may-care throng who were notorious for being the most reckless gamblers in the country.

They "are mad, stark mad," wrote a New York reporter in 1849. Prospectors dusty from the diggings swarmed into San Francisco and Sacramento and laid their glittering heaps on gaming tables that had tiny scales to weigh the bets. When faro, monte or roulette palled, miners squandered their gold on roisterous Spanish blood sports

and exotic amusements from China.

Such exuberance, such abandon infected the entire populace. From destitute miners who panned for gold in saloon sweepings to big-wheel casino operators, Californians rashly wagered everything they owned, confident that a fortune lurked under the next card or, if not, outdoors under the next rock.

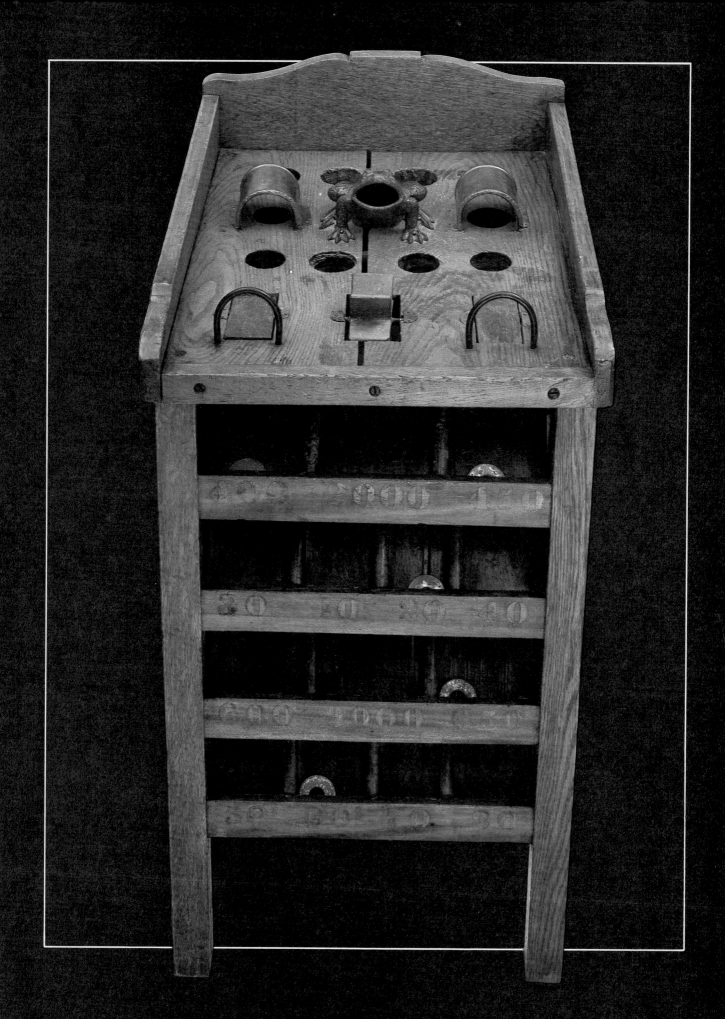

Relieving Californians of their golden burdens

Gamblers knew how brutally heavy gold is—a fist-sized leather bag full of nuggets and dust weighs about 10 pounds. A lad who carried such a lump in his side pocket could develop a dangerous list. Muscular strain, sciatica, lumbago and even hernia could result, particularly in ignorant fellows who had never borne such a concentrated burden before. Gamblers felt bound in charity to lighten the load of their fellow men.

So when gold was discovered in California in 1848, gamblers throughout the country saw immediately the once-in-a-lifetime chance to perform good works, and hundreds swarmed to the West Coast.

There, in virtually every settlement of half-a-dozen tents or more, the gamblers set up facilities—a variety of health clinics, one might say—to ease miners of their glittering and weighty affliction.

Consider the selfless dedication of one William B. Thorington, a dexterous surgeon skilled at separating gold from men. "Lucky Bill" Thorington was a thimble-rigger, a vulgar name perhaps but an accurate one for a practitioner of the shell game. In the spring of 1851, Lucky Bill stationed himself at the west end of the porch at Lee's Exchange, which was the largest gambling house in Sacramento, and sought to attract bullion-burdened miners to his humble surgery. This is what he said:

"Here, gentlemen, is a nice, quiet little game conducted on the square, and especially recommended by the clergy for its honesty and wholesome moral tendencies. I win only from blind men; all that have two good eyes can win a fortune. You see, gentlemen, here are three little wooden cups, and here is a little ball, which, for the sake of starting the game, I shall place under this one, as you can plainly see—thus—and thus—and thus: and now I will bet two, four or six ounces that no gentleman can, the first time trying, raise the cup that the ball is under; if he can, he can win all the money that Bill, by patient toil and industry, has scraped together."

In a mere 60 days, Lucky Bill managed to relieve miners of nearly 100 golden pounds. It was only incidental—and a crass point to bring up—that the gold was worth $24,000.

Thorington's low-life establishment on a Sacramento porch was short on elegance compared to the big gambling saloons in San Francisco. And no wonder. That city was the mecca for most professional gamblers. There, within a few years of the discovery of gold, perhaps as many as 1,000 "resorts" featuring games of chance were going full blast. It was the greatest carnival of gambling in the nation's history.

The casinos were sumptuous by the standards of the time. They were "the most splendid in the world," wrote one witness, who may have been a trifle carried away, "fitted up with superb furniture and appointments. On the gilded walls, often painted in fresco, are grouped copies of the most beautiful gems of modern and ancient art. The couches, lounges, divans, etc., scattered along the sides of these temples of chance, heaped with cushions of crimson, green and gold, purple and azure, are of every graceful and lovely shape. Upon the marble tables are scattered flower-shaped vases of alabaster or Bohemian glass of every hue, and quaint jars of costly porcelain. The lamps are veiled, until their light softly floats in the air, and mysteriously reveals the surrounding objects."

When the British diarist J. D. Borthwick stepped into one of the first-class gambling rooms, he found "a

El Sapo, the toad, squats atop a game of skill bearing his name. Californians adopted this amusement from the Spanish and bet on who could score highest by tossing disks at the toad's mouth and nearby holes.

selected. If the customer had picked or "caught" five of the characters he was paid two dollars. If he had six he got $20, seven $200, and so on up to 10, for which the payoff was $3,000. Those were poor odds but the game was a favorite of the California Chinese, in part because the tickets could be bought for as little as 10 cents. There were hundreds of small shops, laundries and restaurants in San Francisco where the tickets were available and the game was by no means restricted to the Chinese. Whites are estimated to have invested more than three million dollars a year in it.

Gamblers in general have always been a superstitious group, however Oriental gamblers far outdistanced their Occidental counterparts in putting stock in signs and portents. The owners of Chinese gambling houses, who naturally preferred to have the good luck on their side rather than the customers', were careful to avoid the use of all colors except for white in their gaming rooms. In the Chinese culture, white is the color of mourning and of the robes of the dead, and gamblers associated it with the idea of losing. A customer obliged to play fan-tan in an all-white room expected to have trouble.

Careful proprietors went so far as to display inscriptions to the tutelary spirit on white paper and to burn white candles in front of their shrines, instead of the red ones that were ordinarily used in religious ceremonies. On the other hand, some proprietors frequently placed bits of orange peel among the coins and porcelain buttons in the fan-tan boxes. This, they piously averred, was for purification purposes, but everyone knew that it was actually done to bring good fortune to the house: for Chinese who came from Canton Province, orange was an auspicious color and babies were washed in orange juice at their birth.

The patron of Chinese gambling parlors had his own superstitious recourses to counter the disadvantage of betting in an all-white house with orange peels in the fan-tan boxes. Most of these were warning signs that told him when to stay away from the tables. If on his way he was jostled by someone in the street or encountered even a minor obstruction such as a parked wagon, his luck was off; he turned back and postponed gambling until another day. When seated at supper in a gaming house—most of those in San Francisco had a resident cook and served excellent meals—he took

care to eat in silence, or at least to avoid all gambling talk; he also avoided sitting at a table where several persons had already commenced eating. To violate these taboos was to court misfortune. It was also unlucky to touch another gambler's hand when laying one's stake on a number; if that happened, however, the player could cancel the bad omen by choosing a different number.

Inauspicious words were avoided, and one of the worst of them was the word for "book" (shü), which in provincial Chinese patois sounds dangerously similar to a verb that means "to lose." Since gamblers frequently checked out their lucky and unlucky days in the almanac, t'ung shü, they took care to refer to this book as "lucky stars," kat sing. In this way they flattered the gods of fortune and avoided the fatal shü in one neat phrase.

Enthusiasts of the gaming table had more positive ways of helping their luck along. They could, for instance, visit a temple and burn a stick of incense at the altar. If the smoke drifted toward their favorite joss (idol) it was a sign of good luck; if it drifted away, the gambler temporarily gave up his betting plans. At shrines sacred to Kwan Tí, God of War, a box holding 80 bamboo divining sticks and marked with the 80 characters of the lottery tickets was kept for the convenience of pak kop piu players. After the customary rites, the pious gambler would select as many sticks as the numbers he wanted to play and throw them into the box, like so many dice. The characters on which the sticks landed were the ones that Kwan Tí was recommending for the day, and the gambler would dot his lottery ticket accordingly.

Players resorted to all sorts of methods in trying to divine the winning numbers in pak kop piu. Less inventive bettors merely shut their eyes and dotted their tickets at random. Others made a lucky symbol with their dots, or asked strangers or children to do the dotting for them, or marked a group of characters that, when read in succession, formed a sentence conveying a fortuitous promise.

The Chinese, of course, did not restrict themselves to their own games or to playing with other Chinese. On most occasions, mixed gambling sessions ended uneventfully with some winners, some losers and no hard feelings. But in 1891, there occurred a poker game that precipitated a rare and bizarre case of murder and mayhem.

One April evening that year Ah Tia, a successful merchant of Bridgeport, California, got into a poker game with a group of Indians, including an expert player named Poker Tom, who quit the game when he was ahead $200. Ah Tia, nettled by this, persuaded Poker Tom and the others to resume the contest on the following night. However, when Poker Tom's Indian friends turned up at Ah Tia's store they discovered that the doors were locked and the curtains were drawn. One of them, peering through a gap in the drapery, observed Ah Tia and Poker Tom inside grimly concentrating on cards. Assuming that the game had turned into a private head-to-head affair, they returned to their homes.

There were no witnesses to the next development but apparently Poker Tom won still more of Ah Tia's money or otherwise hurt his feelings, for the Chinese fell upon the Indian and slew him. Ah Tia then dismembered his victim's body, putting the arms and legs in a vat of brine and carefully chopping the heart, liver and other plumbing into stew-sized pieces, which he tossed into a large cauldron along with some sliced carrots and onions. As a good cook should, he added soy sauce. Ah Tia then took what remained of Poker Tom—principally his torso and a few odd fragments—and stuffed them into a trunk, which he threw into the nearby West Walker River.

During the next few days Ah Tia removed the Indian's limbs from the vat of brine, cut them into chops and sold them in his store as goat meat, six cents a pound. He also invited the other Indians of the original game to a grand stew dinner, which they ate with expressions of gratitude.

Soon the trunk was discovered in the river and nearby were found a saddle, blanket and coat that had belonged to Poker Tom. The Indians, recalling the dinner Ah Tia had served them, were quite put out. There was an inquest and Ah Tia was charged with murder. But the county prosecutor failed to produce evidence conclusively linking the Chinese merchant with the crime, and Ah Tia's well-paid defense attorneys moved successfully for dismissal of the case. The judge told the defendant that he was free to leave the courtroom but Ah Tia, glancing outside, was reluctant to depart: the street was jammed with Indians, and all of them seemed out of sorts.

Ah Tia asked for bodyguards, promising five dollars a day to anyone who would protect him, but before arrangements could be made the Indians swarmed into the courtroom and dragged him outside. His defense attorneys and the officers of the court were unable to help him further. The Indians threw Ah Tia to the ground, roped his ankles and dragged him behind a horse to a field at the edge of town, where they dispatched him in bloody fashion.

It was a celebrated case. In August 1891, the U.S. District Court sent an army colonel to Bridgeport to investigate. The colonel reported that Ah Tia should have been given better protection by the townsfolk. He did not come straight out with it but he seemed to feel that Ah Tia had been treated too severely for a flawed poker player, and he condemned the Indians as "a barbarous tribe."

Although frequently unkind to Chinese, Indians and other minority groups, Californians liked women, even if they gambled. Indeed when the first lady gamblers in all of the West appeared in San Francisco they were greeted with cries of joy. When one saloon hired a female dealer in 1850, other saloons were obliged to hire women to meet the competition and within a few weeks most of the major gambling houses in town had at least one lady dealer. Later, when mining and cattle towns sprang up all across the inland West, women worked behind gambling tables as a matter of course. If they made mistakes in favor of the house or were caught cheating, the customers merely chuckled indulgently at the little darlings and went ahead with the game. It was considered a pleasure to lose to a lady, and offenses that might have cost a male dealer his life were readily overlooked in a pretty woman with a low décolletage.

Madame Simone Jules could lay claim to being the first lady cardsharp to appear on the California scene. An attractive, dark-haired young woman in her twenties, she was employed at a roulette wheel by San Francisco's Bella Union. Her appearance and personality were so charming that her table immediately began to draw an immense trade. But, mysteriously, she disappeared from the San Francisco scene in 1854.

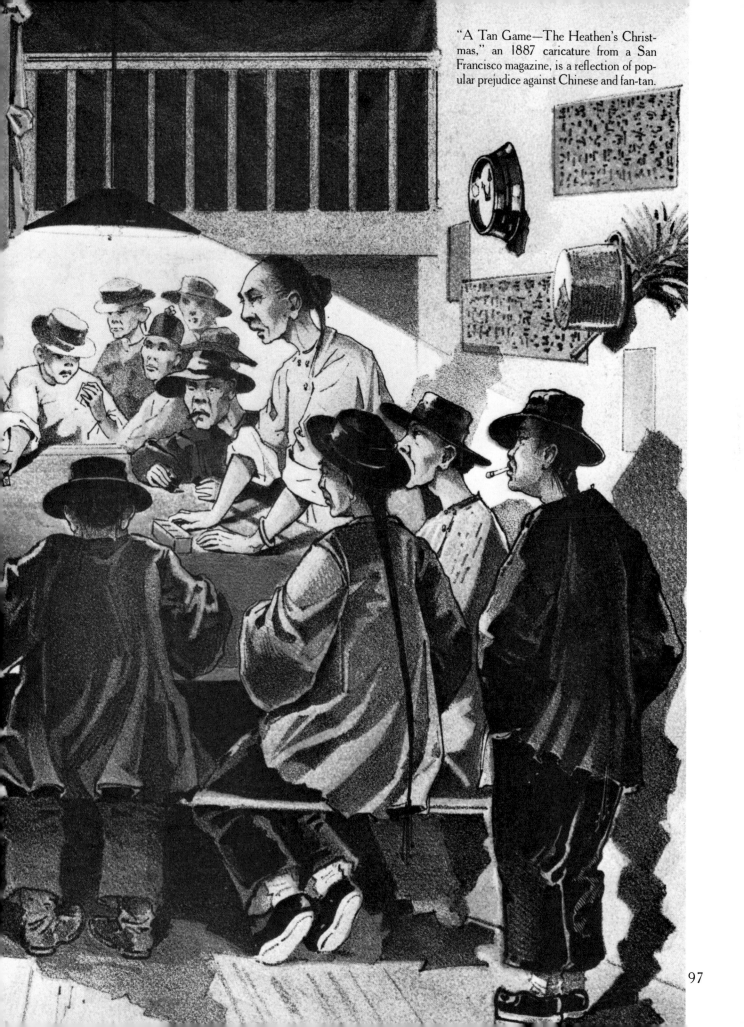

"A Tan Game—The Heathen's Christmas," an 1887 caricature from a San Francisco magazine, is a reflection of popular prejudice against Chinese and fan-tan.

The gaily painted wheel of fortune above, made in the late 1860s, once spun in the Barbary Coast district, the heart of San Francisco's underworld. Similar wheels, mounted on a wall or post, were popular attractions in rude casinos throughout the West. In the latter part of the century, though antigambling legislation drove many games underground, the gaudy wheels continued to operate openly—in carnivals, stores and at charity events like the one advertised in the broadside at left.

THE WHEEL OF FORTUNE
TRY YOUR LUCK!
$50,000
GOLD COIN.
Pajaro Valley Benevol'nt Ass'n
GRAND GIFT CONCERT,
Watsonville, Santa Cruz County, Cal.
TICKETS, $2.00 GOLD COIN
FOR SALE HERE.

In that same year a stagecoach northbound from San Francisco arrived in Nevada City, California, carrying an attractive cargo. When the stagecoach lurched to a stop in the dusty street, the local male onlookers, lusty as goats, were delighted to see that a trim, handsome woman was emerging from it. She was well dressed—perhaps a trifle flamboyant in her jewels and the low cut of her gown, but obviously not a prostitute. Nor was she, it was soon learned with relief, a schoolteacher, temperance worker or the fiancée of any of the men in the vicinity. Indeed, she had the same dark good looks, flashing eyes, ready smile, piquant French accent and downy upper lip of the missing Madame Jules. Even though she called herself Eleanore Dumont, the odds are great that she was the pioneer lady gambler herself.

Miss Dumont took a room in a hotel, emerging occasionally to dine alone. She smoked cigarettes, which she rolled deftly in her fingers. From time to time she sipped a glass of wine, but avoided the hard stuff. And she seemed resolutely chaste. When men approached her, she turned them aside with polite dignity or, when the need arose, with a level gaze that could pin a lecher to the wall.

After a week or so the purpose of Miss Dumont's visit to Nevada City became clear. She rented a room in a store on Broad Street and opened a game of *vingt-et-un.* Gold miners flocked there, at first in curiosity and then in flat-out admiration. She insisted that they wear jackets, take off their hats, swear in moderation and refrain from brawling. With smiles, personal greetings and her air of virginity, she maintained better order than a professional bouncer might have done with a bung starter. Her gambling house prospered.

Soon she was obliged to take larger quarters, hire assistants and find a secure place to store her money. But in 1856, when the fortunes of Nevada City began to decline, she found it necessary to move on. For the next 23 years she was an itinerant gambler, surfacing intermittently in Nevada, Idaho, South Dakota, Oregon and Montana, but she never again found a town where she was treated with the unquestioning respect she had enjoyed in Nevada City. Her beauty faded fast. Before she was 30 she had become plump and the few dark, downy hairs above her upper lip had grown embarrassingly profuse. By the early 1860s, Eleanore Dumont was drinking whiskey, not wine, and raw jokes had begun to displace her refined pleasantries. She no longer made her money exclusively by gambling but, for a good fee, would sleep with favored customers. At about this time, as men studied her lips at close range in the lamplight, she acquired a cruel but accurate nickname, Madame Moustache.

In the 1870s, when she was past 40, Madame Moustache reportedly ran a saloon and brothel in Fort Benton, Montana, on the upper reaches of the Missouri River. A literate steamboatman named Louis Rosché, an occasional drinker, carouser and gambler who had a tendency to exaggerate, visited her establishment to have a look at the notorious woman.

"The click of dice," wrote Rosché, "the rattle of the roulette ball, and the slap of cards greeted my ears as, with my heart beating fast with excitement, I entered the door of the weather-beaten two-story frame building and stepped into the gambling hall." He sat down at a table in the corner. "A rickety set of stairs led up to a second-floor balcony where I saw doors leading to about a dozen smaller rooms. The place was foggy with smoke and smelled of sweating, unwashed bodies and cheap whiskey. The floor was filthy. The male customers, nearly all of whom were chewing, were remarkably bad marksmen, the spittoons, placed at strategic locations, all going unscathed.

"The none-too-clean-looking bar ran along one wall. Faintly from one of the upstairs rooms I could hear the gibberish of a drunken man and the high, shrill laughter of a woman who was quite sober.

"I noticed a square platform in the middle of the room with a single table on it. The table was empty, although roughly dressed men were gathered about a number of other tables." Rosché supposed, correctly, that the table on the platform was reserved for the proprietress.

A whore, "rouged like a clown," approached and sat down beside him. He gave her a silver dollar and asserted with bravado—at least as he remembered the events—"I'm here for a fling at the cards tonight with your lady boss. Now you take this and buy yourself a drink. Come around after I clean out the Madame, and maybe we can do a little celebrating." The whore lifted her skirt, put the coin in a purse in her stocking and said, "Better not hold your breath."

Soon there was a hush in the room and Eleanore Dumont came in. "If I had not seen the unbelievable black brush on the woman's upper lip," marveled Rosché, "I would not have known that this was the famous Madame Moustache. She was fat, showing unmistakably the signs of age. Rouge and powder, apparently applied only half-heartedly, failed to hide the sagging lines of her face, the pouches under her eyes, the general marks of dissipation. Her one badge of respectability was a black silk dress."

Rosché watched as the woman sat down at the table on the platform and began shuffling cards, her rings flashing as she did so. "Two large, rawboned men, six-shooter holsters swinging from their hips, strolled up and leaned on a post directly behind her. I knew that they were bouncers."

Mustering up his courage, Rosché walked over to the table and took out his wallet. "Ma'am," he began, "there's more than two hundred dollars there. Let's get going now, and I don't want to quit until you've got all my money or until I've got a considerable amount of yours."

The woman was quietly amused and asked him what game he wanted to play. Rosché had no preference. "Very well, then," she replied. "It shall be *vingt-et-un.*"

The game was brisk. The sheep was soon shorn. "It would be painful to exhume the memories of the hour that followed," said Rosché. Having lost all his money, he stood up to leave.

"No, no, no," protested Madame Moustache. "The steamboatman must not go before he has had his drink on the house. Jake!" she called, turning toward the bar. "Bring over the special drink."

"I'm not thirsty," Rosché said. But then he noticed that the two men lounging against the post had suddenly straightened up.

"The Madame wants to set 'em up," one of them advised, "and I believe it'd be right healthy for you to let her do it."

Soon the bartender put a glass on the table and Rosché saw to his astonishment that it was filled with milk. "Your special drink, Mr. Steamboatman," announced Madame Moustache.

Rosché drank. "I later found out," he said, "that it was her custom after trimming a sucker to set him up to

a glass of milk. I never heard it said whether she did this because she felt any man silly enough to lose his last cent to a woman deserved a milk diet or whether it was her idea that the milk would keep him going until his next meal." Rosché went back to his boat.

The final scene of Madame Moustache's life took place in California, where her career had begun. She was running a small gambling house in the gold-mining town of Bodie in 1879, when professional gamblers broke her bank. Leaving no apology, no request for sympathy, no message at all, she walked out of town and killed herself. She was about 50 years old. The Sacramento *Union* of September 9, 1879, carried only this item from Bodie: "A woman named Eleanore Dumont was found dead today, a suicide, about a mile out of town. She was well known throughout the mining camps."

Other California gamblers, unlike the taciturn Madame Jules-Dumont-Moustache, did leave notes and occasionally a poem when they cashed in their own chips. Pat Hogan, who began his career in gold-rush days and successfully operated faro games in San Francisco and Virginia City for many years, finally hit a fearful streak of bad luck and shot himself. In his pocket he had placed an ace of hearts on which he had written:

Life is only a game of poker, played well or ill;
Some hold four aces; some draw and fill;
Some make a bluff and oft get there,
While others ante and never hold a pair.

In spite of that lugubrious rhyme, gambling in California was frequently a light-hearted matter and was an almost universal practice. At cigar stands and in bars men commonly shook dice with the proprietors to determine whether a smoke or a drink was free or double the price. "The Italian fruit peddlers who go around among the stores and offices," according to one gambler, "are always supplied with a dice box and the clerks, and even the solid business men, call the cubes into requisition to settle the price of a bunch of grapes or a dozen of bananas."

The phrase "you bet," signifying strong affirmation or approval, was more widely heard in California than anywhere in the country. In the 1860s a New York newspaper reporter, who had journeyed west to study the customs and manners of the natives, wrote:

Women who dealt themselves into wealth and legend

If a man in a saloon out West listened carefully, he might have heard, behind the clink of coins and the rattle of dice, the soft rustle of crinolines and a sultry voice inquiring, "Anyone for twenty-one, gentlemen?"

Women gamblers were sprinkled sparsely throughout the West. And although sensationally popular in female-starved towns, most of them achieved little more than brief local notoriety. Nonetheless, a few remarkable women like Belle Siddons and "Poker Alice" Ivers rose above a one-town reputation and became part of Western legend.

Belle Siddons, a well-educated Missouri girl, served as a Confederate spy during the Civil War. After the War, she married a United States Army surgeon who took her to a post in Texas. When her husband died in 1869, Belle began to support herself by gambling. For the next dozen years she wandered across the West, operating her own casinos in Wichita, Denver, Deadwood and other towns. She changed her name at least twice, first to Madame Vestal and then to Lurline Monte Verde, and apparently made a handsome living at cards.

In Deadwood, she fell in love with Archie McLaughlin, a stagecoach robber. When Archie was caught and lynched in 1878, she took to drugs. In 1881 she was found unconscious in a San Francisco opium house and died soon after.

Though many lady gamblers came to equally sad ends, one who beat the odds was Alice Ivers, generally called Poker Alice. The daughter of an English schoolteacher, she married a Colorado mining engineer who, for her amusement, took her to assorted gambling establishments. Alice learned fast.

After her husband died she fell to full-time gambling and during the next 40 years operated in New Mexico, Arizona, Oklahoma, Kansas, South Dakota and Texas. Her English heritage soon dropped away: she learned to smoke cigars, married twice again, packed a revolver, shot two men—one fatally—and was found guilty of running a combination gambling den and whorehouse. She was, however, smart enough to retire with a few dollars and outlived many of her contemporaries, dying in 1930, an amiable old lady of 79.

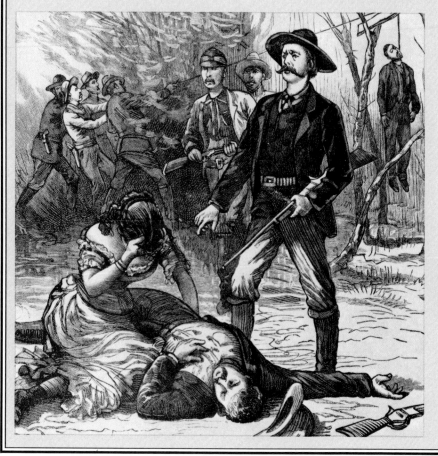

Poker-faced Poker Alice dressed fashionably and extravagantly in her heyday. Once she spent $6,000 during a New York shopping spree; in later, leaner years she wore army-surplus clothes.

Belle Siddons, dressed for an evening at the casino, weeps over the body of her highwayman lover. In the background of this romanticized contemporary drawing, vigilantes string up his partner.

"That 'you bet' is the most popular and the most used ejaculation heard in San Francisco goes without saying it. Everybody uses it.

"Only a few evenings ago at a party I asked a fashionable young lady who had been exquisitely entertaining those present with some finely executed selections from Verdi, if she had the music and would she play a selection from the opera 'Martha' and she replied, 'You bet.'

"I entered one of the first class French restaurants on Dupont street and meeting the affable and bowing proprietor I asked him: 'Do you speak English?' He replied: 'Oui. Oui, Monsieur. I speek ze Anglais. You bet.'

"Entering a streetcar at the foot of Market street and not knowing the location of the street at which I desired to get off I asked the conductor to tell me when to do so. He nonchalantly replied, after taking the fare: 'You bet.'

"On the sidewalk of a business street I met two gamins, one of whom carried, slung from his shoulder, a box boot shining outfit. I accepted their offer to shine 'em up for a bit. After placing a foot upon the box I asked the urchin wielding the shining brush what his partner, apparently standing idly by, did. 'He spits on the blacking,' was the reply, 'An' he's some spitter, too. You bet.'

"Thus, with the elite down to the lowly, this idiom is used to give stress to any assertion made."

As the reporter noted, a willingness to bet was as prevalent at the top of the social and financial ladder as at the bottom.

In the private rooms at the Palace Hotel, the Baldwin and the Pacific Club in San Francisco, for example, California's most solid citizens engaged in some of the richest card games ever dealt in the U.S. Poker had finally caught on in California by the late 1860s and it was poker that these high rollers preferred. Among the players were men who had made fortunes in the Comstock Lode in Nevada, including James C. Flood, a mining-stock manipulator of vast and shady skill. William Ralston, president of the Bank of California sat in on the games along with no fewer than four Nevada senators: John P. Jones, James G. Fair, William Stewart and William Sharon. When these gentlemen tackled each other in the 1870s it was not unusual for pots

How The Law Against Gambling

A stolid constable sits ready to warn gamblers of raids in this 1876 lampoon of a lenient San Francisco police chief. California passed an antigambling law in 1872, but underground games flourished.

is being Enforced in San Francisco, under Chief Ellis' administration

103

to contain as much as $100,000 and on occasion the figure was considerably higher. The largest single hand of which there is any record was reported by a connoisseur as follows:

"Five of the big fish were in the game and they were playing jack pots. Sharon opened and Ralston and two others stayed. There was some light chipping of $100 and $200 several times around, when Ralston strengthened his play and began raising by thousands. Sharon and Ralston soon had the play to themselves, and it was not long before there was $150,000 in the pot. Then Sharon met a raise with a $50,000 counter. Ralston studied only a moment and then came back with a raise of $150,000."

With upward of $350,000 on the table "Sharon did not take long to decide his play. 'I quit, Bill,' he said, and shuffled his cards into the deck.

"Ralston was so delighted over having made his bold partner lay down that he spread his hand, disclosing a pair of tens. Sharon never told what he held in his hand until after Ralston's death. It was a pair of jacks."

It must have been discouraging to be bluffed out of a $350,000 pot but Sharon never complained about his loss. Why should he? During 15 years of play at one club alone, the Pacific, he won more than one million dollars.

Californians would have been a dull lot indeed had they limited their betting to recognized games of chance. In fact, they made all kinds of assertions and were ready to back them up with hard cash. Many of these argumentative bets took place in saloons, the natural leisure-time habitat of the predominantly male population of any settlement's earlier years. The bartender was usually the stakeholder and referee, and any of the onlookers had the option of swelling the kitty by putting their money on whichever side of a contention seemed more likely to win.

The subjects of the bets—at least those known to history—rarely reflected higher modes of thought, and some were downright trivial. After an earthquake, two Sacramento men wagered on whether a cracked saloon wall would collapse and fall inside or outside the building. A miner, flush with liquor and success after making a gold strike at Indian Diggings in El Dorado County, boasted about the deadly accuracy of his throwing arm.

His companion contemptuously bet that he could not hit the bar mirror at 20 feet with a beer glass; the miner accepted the challenge, won the $1.50 bet and cheerfully paid the barkeeper $175 for a new mirror. A cavern-mouthed Digger Indian from Folsom, remembered only as Billy, won drinks for the house by devouring seven pumpkin pies in 23 bites. Contentious Californians laid down their money to prove that they could shear more sheep, cut more wood, or cash a larger check than anybody else.

In the town of Marysville, two rival ice dealers named Mayoux and Tomb "hurled the defi" at each other—to use the then-current slang expression for a challenge—over whose 150-pound block of ice would melt slower underneath the full rays of the July sun. The rigid awning of a saloon on the corner of E Street was chosen to be the judgment place. News of the wager had spread rapidly throughout the town and businessmen closed down their shops so that all of Marysville could gather to watch the ice drip. By sundown it was evident that Mayoux would be the winner—not because his product was superior but because he had had the foresight to lay his cake of ice on its broad side so that it melted evenly, while Tomb had placed his block on end and by noon miniature rivulets were rapidly eroding its flanks.

Tomb conceded defeat and paid Mayoux $100, but by now the citizens of Marsyville had found an even more fascinating eventuality to bet on: namely, the hour and minute when the last drop of water would drip from the awning. It was clear that the ice would continue to drip through the night and the bets clustered around 10 a.m. At 9 a.m., the county judge, having agreed to act as referee, mounted a stepladder before an expectant crowd and stood over the awning with a stop watch, observing the last remnants of the ice melt away. One hour and 28 minutes later he announced solemnly that the last drop had dripped. History does not record who the happy winner was.

A bet placed on a frog in Sacramento's Arcade Hotel is probably unique. Thomas Guinean, proprietor of the Arcade, had a pet bullfrog of large dimensions, which perched on a brick set in the center of a glass bowl filled with water. The bowl was placed on the bar, and there the frog sat all day, occasionally darting out its tongue to catch a passing fly.

GREAT ATTRACTION
AT THE IOWA HILL
Amphitheatre
Panther!
AND
BEAR FIGHT

THE PROPRIETORS HAVE PROCURED

A LARGE AND FEROCIOUS PANTHER,

Caught near the summit of the Sierra Nevada Mountains, and purchased

THE CELEBRATED GRIZZLY BEAR, LOLA MONTES,

WHICH THEY WILL FIGHT

ON SUNDAY, NOVEMBER 5.

Rich and Rare Sport may be expected, as both animals are in fine condition. The Panther is one of the largest of the species, and the Bear unequalled for his weight. They have also procured

A NUMBER OF FINE GAME CHICKENS!

Which they will fight. Any persons having Game Chickens, and wishing to test them, can have an opportunity either for sport or wager

The whole to conclude with a Match Fight between the
FAVORITE DOGS, UNION AND STAR!

FISH & BROWN.

Mr STEVENS will enter the celebrated Dog, Major, with **$500** attached to his neck, challenging any Dog of his weight for a Rough and Tumble Fight.

Fighting dogs in a clinch *(below)* and a
bear tussling with a bull *(bottom)* provided
action-packed spectacles for California
gamblers. Dogs were eager to fight, but
bears and bulls sometimes needed goading.

A citizen of the town, observing Guinean's frog, told the proprietor that he also had a frog, a small green one that he had raised from a tadpole and had taught to perform a remarkable feat. His frog, he averred, could climb the rungs of a tiny ladder and, when it gained the top, hang there by one leg. Guinean, considering himself an expert in the ways of frogs, denied that they could be taught ladder-climbing or anything else. Like his big bull on the bar, frogs could only sit, hop, croak and eat flies.

Inevitably the defi was hurled and caught. The wager was a bottle of champagne that cost five dollars. Within a day or two the citizen returned with a pasteboard box that contained his little frog and a miniature ladder. The glass bowl on the bar seemed to be a sensible place for the demonstration, so the brick was removed, the bullfrog disappeared into the water, the little green frog was dropped in, and the ladder was propped up inside the bowl. The citizen then started whistling softly and the little frog emerged from the water and began to ascend the ladder, guided by an occasional tickle from a straw that his trainer had plucked from a broom.

All was going well when suddenly, like a shot from a cannon, Guinean's bullfrog leapt up from the watery depths and swallowed the little climber whole. Or almost whole. Actually, one leg dangled for a while from his mouth. The horrified trainer grabbed for it, but too late; like the rest of his performer, it disappeared down the bullfrog's gullet.

According to the strict rules of wagering, Guinean had won. The little green frog had not reached the summit nor had it hung there by one leg. But Guinean handsomely conceded defeat and handed the dejected winner his bottle of champagne.

Not all saloon critter-bets were on the up-and-up. Just as sharpers hovered thickly around the gaming tables, confidence men could be encountered almost anywhere in California's swarming towns—especially in a saloon with their elbows propped on the bar. Two crooked sporting men toured saloon back rooms in the 1850s with a sure-fire routine involving an ant and a louse. They would enter a drinking emporium separately, pretending to be strangers. Mixing with the crowd, they would turn the conversation toward races of various kinds—horse races, dog races, foot races.

Suddenly, as though the thought had just occurred to him, one of the swindlers would wonder aloud, "Which could hightail it off a hot plate faster—an ant or a louse?" The other would then state categorically that in a race of that sort the ant would be the inevitable winner; everyone knew that an ant was a whirlwind compared with a stick-in-the-flesh louse. His secret cohort would disagree and a bet would quickly be arranged to settle the argument. Meanwhile the on-lookers, being Californians, would be drawn into the betting, most of them putting their money on the ant, whose advocate hardly needed to assure them (though he privately did) that they were betting on a sure thing.

The louse man would then retire briefly in order to procure a contender from some portion of his anatomy and the ant man would go outside to the nearest anthill and return with a captive specimen. After a dish or plate had been heated thoroughly over a lighted candle or the barroom grill, it would be placed in the center of a table. The bettors gathered eagerly around, and the ant and louse were dropped simultaneously onto the center of the hot plate. The ant scurried straight to the edge and circled there, vainly seeking an exit, while the less frantic and more practical louse merely lumbered to the edge and tumbled off. The louse man collected all the stakes and departed, to be joined later by his partner to divvy the profits.

Naturally this swindle could be perpetrated only once in any town, but the historian who recorded the details said the two "gathered in a good many ounces of gold dust before all the diggings were worked."

Californians were particularly fond of betting on foot races, a gambling sport widespread in the West. Every sizeable town in the state had a champion and there was heavy wagering when one runner challenged another. The races were sprints, usually of 100 yards or so, and they were always held on the main street. The backers of the racers ranged themselves on opposite sides of the thoroughfare and generally bet all their available cash on their favorites. The popularity of foot racing was so great that professionals, some of them college-trained sprinters from the East, used to wander from town to town hurling the defi at the local boys.

Most town champions were too proud not to accept the challenge and most townsfolk too confident not to bet. The locals were almost invariably trimmed. The professionals kept themselves in fine physical condition and often further improved their chances by having their aides and backers offer the local runners a few belts of whiskey before the starting gun. That was not difficult to do because racing headquarters were in saloons. Observing this melancholy state of affairs and noting that horses and other mute beasts were not susceptible to strong drink, one local sage came up with an aphorism that seems as sound today as it was a century ago: "Never bet on anything that can talk."

But that rule was no protection against animals—camels in one case—that were too dumb to bet on. Bizarre though it may seem, the War Department in the 1850s purchased a large number of camels to try as pack animals in the southwestern desert. But the Army lost interest in the experiment during the Civil War and sold off the camels as military surplus. In the 1860s a herd of them turned up in Sacramento and were purchased by a man who intended to take them to Nevada, where he thought they might be useful in transporting salt from Owens Lake to the Comstock Lode. Meanwhile he tried to make a modest sum from his animals by staging what he advertised as a "Dromedary Race."

Californians were enchanted. What could be more fascinating than a dromedary race in Sacramento? The herd was taken to a fenced oval race track where, after heavy betting by the spectators, the beasts were prodded into running. There were no jockeys. Each camel merely carried a placard on its side bearing a number. The race started out well, amid oaths and shouts from the prodders. However, when the camels came to the first turn, they all sank to their knees and began chewing their cuds.

Horsemen with bullwhips immediately rode out to stop the chewing and restart the running. The camels responded slowly but reluctantly resumed racing. When they reached the second curve on the oval they all sank to their knees once more, resumed chewing and never did finish the race. There were arguments over settling the bets and for years thereafter, at least in the neighborhood of Sacramento, when a man said "I have been to a dromedary race" he meant that he knew how problematical life could be.

Roosters cannot talk, either, and Californians were inclined to wager large sums on them. In June 1862, a series of contests took place that one historian called

"the biggest cocking main that probably was ever pitted in this state." The rival gamesters were from Sacramento and San Francisco and they staged numerous encounters on which they bet $1,000 to $5,000, not to mention the wagers made by spectators. In the main event a rooster named Butcher Stag killed an adversary called Honest John by leaping on top of him and driving a steel spur through his eye and into his brain, while the assembled multitude vigorously applauded the accomplishment.

Cockfighting, one of the oldest of blood sports, did not become a fight to the death until the 18th Century when deadly spurs were first clamped to cocks' heels. Some of these weapons resembled curved upholsterers'

needles; others, invented by the Mexicans, consisted of 3-inch-long, double-edged razors. Thus equipped a bird could, and usually did, kill his rival, and the winner himself rarely escaped without severe lacerations. Sometimes in his awkward thrashing about, the victor cut his own throat.

These feathered battlers, bred from champion stock, were not pitted against an adversary until they were between one and two years old. By then a cock weighed close to five pounds and his instinct for sexual rivalry had been cultivated to make him an aggressive gladiator in the arena. Or so it was hoped. There were always the so-called "runners" who refused to fight or who gave in when they realized they were beaten.

Cockfighting had been introduced to the Western frontier largely by Southerners, the Irish and the Mexicans, and its popularity spread like wildfire. Captain Anthony Greene, whose family crossed the continent and settled in Sacramento in 1850, acquired his first gamecock at the age of seven; from then on the sport became a ruling passion of Greene's life. As he remembered more than a half century afterward, "In the late fifties and during the early sixties California was a hot bed of cockers."

One such Californian, Mike Duffy of Vallejo, learned to pay close attention to what his fighters were fed for dinner. In the 1860s, Duffy came up with a fierce red bird that he called Garibaldi, after the popular red-haired Italian patriot. Duffy placed his gamecock in contention against what one historian called "a coterie of cock pit devotees in San Francisco" and there was heavy betting. Garibaldi was the favored fowl but when brought out to the pit he appeared to be listless. "Instead of giving his usual crow of defiance, emitted from a curved neck and with a restless scratching of the sawdust, he stood lifeless. His antagonist boldly strutted and scratched, he defiantly crowed, but 'Garibaldi' paid no attention to him at all. Mike, remarking that his gaffer must have been taken suddenly ill, forfeited the stake and departed for his home a discomfitted and disconsolate man."

What had happened to Garibaldi soon became evident. Mike, "on entering the kitchen of his house, was surprised to hear something drop with a dull thud upon the floor. Looking down he saw that it was a bullet. Astonished to see such a missile there he stooped to pick it up. In doing so he gave 'Garibaldi,' held under his arm, a squeeze that caused him to lay two more bullets." Garibaldi subsequently discharged six more of the bullets. He had been, as the historian observed, "slugged" by some of Mike Duffy's stealthy and unscrupulous rivals.

A similar fate was suffered by Mark Twain's celebrated jumping frog of Calaveras County, California. Twain was in San Francisco around the time of Garibaldi's misfortune and kept an eye on the newspapers. Perhaps the great author turned Garibaldi into a frog for a story that was, as Twain said, the basis of his reputation. Had it not been for Duffy and his rooster, American literature might well be the poorer today.

Cockfight aficionados jam the pit rail in a Mexican border town as two feathered combatants warily stalk each other. Mexicans in California were no less enthusiastic about the sport and often staked considerable sums on the birds.

4 | Cheating and its perils

Cheating was the gambler's shady colleague, on call at an instant's notice to help him bankrupt some sucker or to rescue him from the hands of any adversary who got too lucky.

No game was immune from cheating and some games—the way they were played—even amounted to outright larceny. The entire West, it appeared, was permeated with itinerant faro cheats, sleight-of-hand shell game artists and poker demons who were masters of the stacked deck and the crooked deal. In order to be successful in their work, cheaters employed, besides a cultivated sensitivity in their fingertips, loaded dice, marked cards and ingenious devices for concealing an extra card to complete a winning hand.

Caught using such novelties or dealing from the bottom of the deck, gamblers faced violent reprisal, and at times the aura of peril surrounding a cheater could become palpable. "I knew," as one ex-cardsharp nicely put it, "that if he detected any cheating my life would be exacted as a forfeit."

When cheating was discovered, or even suspected, the relaxed atmosphere of a friendly game could become charged with tension in the seconds that it took to hurl an accusation. Another instant, and the crack of a pistol might transform a saloon into a murder scene, as on the two occasions depicted by Frederic Remington on these and the following pages.

Fellow players accuse a man of cheating at a card game at Ft. Laramie, Wyoming. Such incidents might pass uneasily, without violence—or erupt into bloodshed.

In Remington's *Misdeal*, human wreckage litters a room filled with gun smoke. Some gamblers, the artist wrote, played craving blood: "There would be little excitement about the game without drawing of cards and revolvers."

AND HE WENT FOR THAT HEATHEN CHINEE

A player's ace in the hole: a card up his sleeve

In 1843 a professional cardplayer along the Mississippi began bombarding the American public with a fusillade of books, whose titles were all variations on one theme: *Gambling Exposed,* "A full Exposition of all the various Arts, Mysteries and Miseries of Gambling, by the 'Reformed Gambler' Jonathan H. Green." Green swore he had seen the error of his ways and was now dedicated to stamping out what he called "that odious and destructive vice."

An opportunist of rare magnitude, Green then took to the lecture circuit, stunning large audiences with accounts of the many evils he had witnessed. He cautioned parents not to allow a child to play checkers, backgammon or chess because these seemingly innocent pastimes led an unwary youth, step by step, "from one degree of degradation to another, until he gets to the despicable game of thimbles," and at last is practicing "artifices so base, so vile, that every honest mind shudders to contemplate them."

The new convert to probity devoted much time to the mechanics of cheating at various games and, as he warmed up to his work on the lecture platform, he would declare that all of the decks of playing cards were manufactured with secret marks for the benefit of professional gamblers; amateurs and honest folk could not see them. To prove his point he would call for a volunteer from the audience, give him money, and send him out to purchase a deck at the nearest store. When the volunteer came back, Green would shuffle the cards, place them face down on the lectern and then, staring at the back of each card as he picked it up, announce its suit and value. The performance never failed to draw

gasps of righteous indignation from the crowd, followed by an ovation for Green. Villainy and rascality are everywhere, he would declare. No one was safe from the cheaters.

The catch was that Green was not reading any secret marks on the backs of the cards. Concealed in the lectern was a tiny mirror, a "shiner," in which he could see the face of each card as he pretended to study its back. Although Green never publicly admitted his deception, his long career on the Mississippi, it would appear, had rendered him constitutionally incapable of a wholly honest performance.

If a famous lecturer on cheating would cheat his audience, the question immediately arises: just how widespread was cheating among gamblers in the Old West? All professionals knew how to cheat. They were obliged to know the tricks in order to protect themselves against crafty amateurs and against other professionals, with whom they often played.

Although no one has assembled any reliable statistics on the matter, it appears that most of the roving gamblers of the West were crooked. The cardsharp who hastened from one boomtown to another, from Dodge City to Dawson, was not concerned with protecting his reputation or building a steady clientele. He was out to make a fast cleanup and cared very little how he did it. Among professionals who specialized in working steamboats or railroad trains, where gamblers and victims were unlikely to meet again, the proportion of cheats was close to 100 per cent. But a good many other professionals cheated only when sorely provoked, and a few never.

Writing in 1888, California historian Hubert H. Bancroft drew distinctions among three classes of gamblers: "There is the legitimate gambler, one who keeps a table and pays his dues to society in shape of license,

---

A shower of cards falls from the sleeve of
Ah Sin, Bret Harte's "Heathen Chinee,"
whose big mistake, as told in the poem,
was to think he could outcheat cheaters.

Decks that "eliminated chance"

One cardsharp stares intently at the backs of his opponent's hands; another imperceptively caresses the cards as he deals; yet another idly thumbs the edges of the deck while shuffling.

These apparently innocent mannerisms were actually the mechanics of cheating with marked cards. The first gambler looked for secret marks on the backs of cards that revealed the sucker's hand. The second felt for punctured surfaces that gave away the high cards. The third found the aces, subtly trimmed to a wedge shape, and placed them on the bottom of the deck.

Nearly every cardsharp worthy of the name was a master of such trickery and utilized it, accepting the danger of exposure for the overwhelming advantage that the marked cards offered. "When successfully used," a reformed sharper observed, "every element of chance is eliminated from the game, and the play is practically reduced to a cutthroat contest, in which the professional alone carries the knife."

Blue-tinted spectacles enabled the wearer to detect marks made on the backs of cards with phosphorescent ink, which was invisible to the unaided eyes of his opponent.

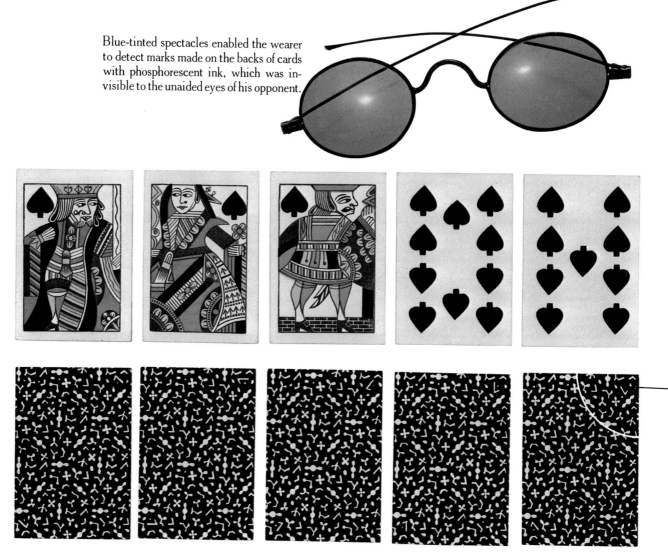

This deluxe card trimmer, brass and steel with an ivory handle, could be used legitimately to renew frayed edges of a whole deck, or illegitimately for shaving certain cards to make them easy to find in a cut.

This corner rounder, ivory-handled companion to the card trimmer, could be employed to cut new corners on an entire deck after trimming or to mark particular cards by slightly altering their corners.

Special markings on the backs of these cards reveal their values to the dealer. The key is a dotted "7" (enlargement) printed in the upper right and lower left corners. The symbol revolves clockwise through eight distinct positions as cards increase in value from 7 through ace. Different marks divulged lesser cards. Suits, less important than card values in many games, were ignored by this marking system.

Depressing the plunger of this brass card pricker drives a needle into the face of the card and raises a Braille-like mark on the back. A crooked dealer could tell from the positions of these bumps what cards were passing through his fingers.

province of penny-ante swindlers. Another professional sharp believed just the opposite, ranking those who used marked decks ahead of "the class of 'second dealers,' 'bottom dealers,' and men who habitually do work with the pack to win."

Although Jonathan Green cheated his audience by using a shiner, he *was* telling the truth about marked cards. Some decks of cards did come from the manufacturer with secret marks already printed on their backs. Called "readers," these cards were first made in the United States around 1830 and for many years were shipped by mail and express to gamblers throughout the West. One of the best-known manufacturers was E. N. Grandine of New York, whose catalogue unblushingly advertised marked cards at $1.25 per pack, $10 a dozen. "These cards are an exact imitation of the fair playing cards in use, and are adapted for Bluff or Poker, Seven-Up, Forty-Five, Euchre, Cribbage, *Vingt-et-Un* or Twenty-One, and all other games of cards, where knowing just what your opponent holds in his hand would enable you to win."

The largest single order for marked cards—though not from E. N. Grandine—was made by American gamblers during the Mexican War. When General Winfield Scott marched into Mexico City in 1847, American cardsharps were only one step behind the troops. The Mexicans were playing a game called Spanish monte, similar to faro, which soon became popular with American soldiers. Much to the astonishment of the American gamblers, the Mexicans were using fair decks—a situation that simply cried out for a little Yankee ingenuity and enterprise.

A syndicate of gamblers headed by an old pro named Bill Clemmens brought in some cheap New York-made readers, but soon found that neither the soldiers nor the Mexicans would use them. The 40-card Spanish decks they normally used were high-quality cards that were manufactured in Mexico by a firm that enjoyed a national monopoly, and the New York cards were simply too inferior. Furthermore, the Mexican manufacturer had never printed marked cards and had no plates for doing so.

Finally, however, a deal was struck between the gamblers and the manufacturer: the cardsharps furnished him the right plates and the manufacturer, for a modest fee of $5,000, proceeded to run off their order

of 100 gross, or 14,400 decks, of cards. But before the job was finished, peace was most inconveniently declared and the American soldiers took off for home, leaving Clemmens and his men holding a colossal bag of queer packs. These could not be utilized in the United States, where Spanish monte was not very well known, and the manufacturer would not allow them to be sold in Mexico.

While the gamblers were considering this rather sizable setback, a kind Providence intervened: gold was discovered in California. Spanish monte was already popular among the Mexicans there and soon proved equally popular with the thousands of miners and adventurers who flocked to San Francisco. The gamblers hurried thither with their marked decks and made such a killing that several of Clemmens' men were able to retire with comfortable fortunes. Others of the company, thinking to play their winning streak a little longer, ordered another 200 gross from the Mexican manufacturer. But by now the California monte dealers and players knew the score and refused to use the syndicate's cards. The greedy sharps were stuck again, this time with more than 28,000 packs of bogus cards, and there was no new El Dorado for them to exploit.

As Clemmens had learned in Mexico City, one of the basic problems with readers was that they usually were of such inferior quality that they were easy to spot. Since the object in printing them was to make a quick buck, the materials used were often shoddy and, if they were intended to imitate the design of genuine cards, the art work was often so sloppy that even a cursory comparison with a legitimate deck would show it up. Thus many gamblers preferred to mark their own cards.

There were probably as many systems for marking cards as there were sharps to invent them. Occasionally the entire deck was marked, but most often only selected cards were altered, giving the gambler an advantage but reducing the risk of detection.

"Strippers" were cards whose ends and sides were trimmed with blades that were razor sharp. Although only about one thirty-secondth of an inch was sliced off, that was enough to allow the practiced gambler to cut to those cards in a deck. The trimming was not always done in straight lines but generally in the faintest of curves, so that the sides of the cards were slightly concave or convex and the ends felt correspondingly wide or narrow to the delicate touch. A gambler who used such cards was said to be "playing both ends against the middle."

Another method was to remove the glaze from a small portion of the back of a card, sometimes with a sharp knife, often with a drop of water that was sponged off after a moment. When the card was held at a certain angle, the spot reflected light differently from the rest of the card's surface. This method was most often used on "club-cards" whose plain white backs did not lend themselves to other kinds of marking. A similar trick, employed on cards with printed backs, involved the use of special dyes to tint a spot on the back of the card—or to tint the entire back with the exception of one spot.

"Line and scroll work" consisted of shading part of the card's design—a particular cluster of leaves, for example—by adding fine lines similar to those used in the original design. A gambler shaded various portions of the leaves according to his own system to denote the suit and value of the card. In the same way, some sharps would use special templates and pins to prick the face of the card, thereby raising Braille-like bumps on its back. If a gambler had not been able to prepare a deck beforehand, he could accomplish his ends during play by scratching or nicking the important cards with his fingernail or a handy "poker-ring" to which a small needle point was attached for that purpose. Another on-the-scene trick was to bend a corner or rimple the card so that it bowed up in the middle.

Marked cards were obviously an advantage, but it took skillful manipulation to make them lucrative. As one old pro told an aspiring disciple, "You have to have the hands, boy. If you ain't got 'em it would do you no good to learn the trick." Therein lay the chief asset of all professional gamblers: hands that were as dexterous as those of a skilled surgeon. The knack was inborn, but complete mastery was bred. Anyone who desired to make a dishonest living at cards or dice had to spend countless hours tediously practicing the moves over and over again.

A cardsharp had to be adept at the false shuffle, in which he appeared to mix the cards thoroughly; at the false cut, in which the halves of the deck were neatly returned to their original position; at dealing seconds, in which he kept the top card in position until he needed it and meanwhile dealt out the cards underneath. Above all, gamblers had to keep their hands uncalloused— "softer than a woman's," said the wife of one gambler—to be able to detect the smallest variation in the surface or shape of the cards. Poker Alice Ivers, a famous woman gambler of the era, remembered dealers whose fingers were "sandpapered until the blood all but oozed through the skin," the better to read the cards that they had marked.

Still, it did a cardsharp no good to be able to do these tricks in the privacy of his room, with only a mirror to watch. "Almost any person, with a little practice, can deal from the bottom," noted one roving gambler in 1873, "but to perform the feat while several pairs of keen eyes are concentrating their gaze on your fingers, without being detected, requires an amount of coolness and nerve which is possessed by not one man in a million." Poker Alice recalled a would-be sharper in the Black Hills district of South Dakota who could perform miracles of manipulation anytime except when it counted. "When he got into a game, with the sharp eyes of professional gamblers upon him," she said, "the courage necessary to that crooked skill wilted and he became only an honest, frightened, exceedingly bad player who lost his stacks of chips almost as soon as they were set before him."

Sometimes even when his courage was adequate a gambler's plan could misfire for lack of attention to a crucial detail, as one pair of Seattle sharpers found when they tried to "ring in a cooler." In preparing a cold deck, or "cooler," the gambler used a pack of cards identical to those to be used in the game. Before play began, he stacked the deck so he could deal excellent hands to his opponents and an even better hand to himself. This assured heavy betting and a murderous outcome. The cooler was concealed until the proper moment and then whisked into the game, often under cover of a handkerchief.

The Seattle cardsharps were in a five-man game, according to one old-time gambler, and were out to skin two of their opponents but not the fifth man, "who was kind of a friend of theirs, although he did not know there was anything wrong about the game." One of the

123

Holdouts for high profits—and high risks

It was hard, in Western saloons, to win consistently at poker; there were just too many good players. So gamblers cheated. Often the edge was gained by holding out a few cards to play when the time was right and the pot was ripe.

Cheating in this manner was a dangerous game. Let a stray card flutter inopportunely from inside a sleeve and the culprit was likely to feel the barrel of a Colt .44 or the cold edge of a bowie knife against his neck before the pasteboard hit the sawdust.

In order to avoid such embarrassment, a sharp often used a holdout, which gripped spare cards and stopped them from appearing until needed. With a holdout under the table or strapped to his body, a cheat could hide up to a whole deck of cards.

A holdout could be a simple device with no moving parts or, like the Kepplinger model overleaf, so complex that even the professionals were amazed.

These bizarre-looking contraptions could be purchased by anybody from manufacturers who brazenly touted their merchandise in catalogues. An advertisement for a particular holdout bragged that "anyone can operate it with very little practice."

Despite such claims, however, there was always the risk of mechanical failure and the ultimate drawback: getting caught. While an extra card on the floor might signify no more than a clumsy misdeal, the pulleys, hinges and springs of a holdout were, if detected, indisputable evidence of a cheat.

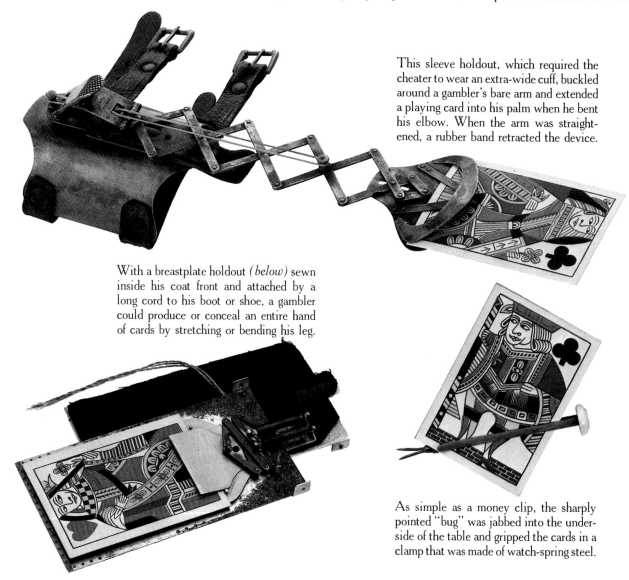

This sleeve holdout, which required the cheater to wear an extra-wide cuff, buckled around a gambler's bare arm and extended a playing card into his palm when he bent his elbow. When the arm was straightened, a rubber band retracted the device.

With a breastplate holdout *(below)* sewn inside his coat front and attached by a long cord to his boot or shoe, a gambler could produce or conceal an entire hand of cards by stretching or bending his leg.

As simple as a money clip, the sharply pointed "bug" was jabbed into the underside of the table and gripped the cards in a clamp that was made of watch-spring steel.

A black cotton bag hides a spring-loaded frame for holding an entire deck of cards in reserve. Strapped around the cheater's waist under his vest, this device, like its cousin the breastplate holdout *(opposite)*, was manipulated by the cardsharp's leg.

This holdout vest had a single strip of elastic sewn into it for a card or two and included an additional loop for a miniature pencil that was used to mark cards.

THE KEPPLINGER HOLDOUT

A harness of pulleys, cords and telescoping silver-plated tubes, the Kepplinger holdout, named for its inventor, reached from a man's forearm to his shoulders and down to his knees. Worn inside the clothing, this contraption adjusted to any girth and height.

To activate the holdout, the cheat had only to spread his knees slightly and a clawlike "sneak," secreted between the two layers of a special double shirt sleeve, moved toward his hand. A professional magician of Kepplinger's day called the invention "the most ingenious holdout ever devised."

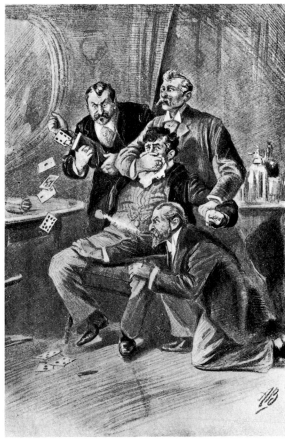

Two astonished gamblers hold and gag P. J. Kepplinger as a third forces his knees apart, activating and exposing the holdout that accounted for its inventor's baffling good luck—and his assailants' losses. The illustration appeared in an 1894 book about methods of cheating, six years after Kepplinger's cronies had uncovered the device and made the cheater promise to duplicate it for each of them.

sharps ringed in a cold deck, dealing great hands to the two intended victims and the winning hand to his partner. "He was careful to give no pair to the man he wanted to befriend.

"Well, to the surprise of the men who had put up the cold deck, the fifth fellow with no pair stayed right in and saw every raise. They didn't dare kick him out or wink at him, so he piled his money in with the rest. In the draw he took a card, and then he was raising more than anyone else around the table. There was $3,600 in that pot at the show-down, and the fellow that had no pair won it all." In his enthusiasm, the man who had fixed the deck apparently had neglected to pay attention to the suits. He had dealt the fifth man four clubs in numerical sequence, and the one card that player drew completed a straight flush—five cards of the same suit in sequence—one of the most powerful poker hands possible.

Poker Alice swore that in all her years of gambling "I handled a cold deck only once, and that for a joke." It seems there was a man in the Black Hills district who always screamed foul when he lost, but believed the game to be fair when he won. "It got on my nerves," was Alice's wry recollection, and the next time she played him she decided to teach him a lesson. The game was poker and the man seemed to be riding a winning streak. "I never saw such luck," Poker Alice said. "By actual count, he had 27 sets of threes without me ever winning a hand. If I held three kings, then he would have three aces; and if I drew the three highest cards in the deck, he would have a small straight to beat it."

When the man exulted "I've got into a square game at last," Poker Alice chomped on her cigar and proceeded to prepare his doom. On her next deal she employed the cold deck and dealt the loudmouth a pat flush—five cards of one suit, a hand that allowed him to stand pat. For herself Poker Alice took a full house—one pair and three of a kind, a better hand than her adversary's. "The betting began," she said, "with my victim pushing forth the chips by the stack." When the carnage was over, Poker Alice had made a profit of some $900.

Being the soul of honesty—at least, that was how she remembered it several decades later—Alice had intended only to demonstrate to the man that he could

THESE DICE
GUARANTEED
TO BE SQUARE.

Beneath bare bulbs, a kerosene lamp and a sign that proclaims fair dice, gamblers crowd around the craps table in a turn-of-the-century saloon. Even in honestly run gambling establishments, players out West rarely bested the house, which usually offered short odds or charged a betting fee.

not tell a square game from a crooked one. However, nothing she said could convince him. After all, had he not won every hand—except the last? "I guess you've got a right to win a hand once in a while," the man told her. In the face of such obstinacy, Poker Alice decided to keep the sucker's dough.

The butt of Poker Alice's joke with the cold deck was just plain stupid. But a good many smarter men were superstitious believers in ideas no more logical than his principle that a good player always wins in a fair game. Whether gamblers out West were high rollers or low, whether they played on the Mississippi or sported so close to the Pacific that they could toss their cigar butts into it, Westerners had a particularly colorful set of cockamamie notions. Many of them can be traced to a gambler's dread of cheats. It lurked behind the belief, for example, that ill fortune came with a kibitzer looking over one's shoulder—as well it might have, particularly if the kibitzer was given to winking or signaling with his finger.

The same fear cautioned that it was disastrous to play poker with a man who had lost an eye. "There's a one-eyed man in the game" meant "Watch out for cheating." According to an early historian of poker the notion arose as follows:

"A little game of draw was in progress in Omaha, and among its participants was a one-eyed man. He was playing in rather remarkable luck, but no one could very well find fault with that. Presently, however, there came a jackpot, and it was the one-eyed man's deal. He opened the pot, and while he was giving himself cards a certain bellicose gentleman named Jones thought he detected the one-eyed man in the act of palming a card. Quick as a flash, Jones whipped out a revolver and placed it on the table in front of him.

" 'Gentlemen,' he said decisively, 'we will have a fresh deal; this one doesn't go.'

"The players were surprised, but as none of them had bettered his hand save the opener, who made no sign of disapproval, they willingly consented.

" 'And now that we start a new deal,' pursued Mr. Jones, carelessly toying with the revolver, 'let me announce that we are going to have nothing but square deals. I am not making any insinuations or bringing any charges, and I will say only this, that if I catch any sonofabitch cheating I will shoot his other eye out.' "

Professionals, not content with marked and manipulated cards, also employed a number of manufactured devices called "advantage tools," such as the little mirror that Jonathan Green hid in the lectern. Small reflectors the size of a dime were sometimes embedded in dummy poker chips or in the bowl of a pipe so that, when the shiners were placed on the table, a gambler could see the underside of the cards as he dealt. Some of the professionals could read the cards in the highly polished backs of their gold watches, cuff links or in specially doctored coins.

Following the Civil War several mail-order houses in addition to Grandine's in New York were able to supply the Western gambler with advantage tools. Chicago and New Orleans had such establishments, and by the 1880s the Will and Finck Company—advertised as "The Only Sporting Emporium on the Pacific Coast"—was doing a lively business in San Francisco. Before U.S. postal laws got tougher, these manufacturers advertised their wares openly in newspapers and flyers sent through the mail, and professional gamblers leafing through the various catalogues could find whatever suited their favorite game.

"Holdouts" were devices for secreting a card or cards—sometimes even entire decks—until the right moment. Will and Finck advertised a table holdout that could "be put under and removed from any table in less than half a minute. Works easily from either knee. It will bring three or more cards up into your hand, and take back the discards as you hold your cards and hands in a natural position on top of the table." In addition, there were sleeve holdouts, cuff holdouts, ring holdouts and something that E. N. Grandine touted in his catalogue as "the latest improved Vest Holdout, which for simplicity, finish and durability is Par Excellence."

Swearing that he occasionally used the vest holdout himself, "as opportunity offers," Grandine waxed eloquent about its virtues: "It will not break or get out of order, anybody can use it, it works smooth and noiseless, and is as perfect as it can be made after many years of careful study. I know it is practical and with an ordinary amount of caution it can be used in 8 out of 10 of all the Gambler's Games in the country. It is a fine Invention and anyone that plays cards for a living needs it more than they do snide Jewelry or Flashy

Clever devices for making dice more friendly

There were several kinds of delicately rigged dice that a Western cheater could use to boost his advantage at the craps table or in a casual game at the bar. Two popular styles were loaded dice, which were slightly unbalanced, and shaved dice, which were subtly misshaped. With both kinds, certain numbers would come up with more than the usual frequency. The rigging was done with odd-looking machines like the two below.

The edge shaver (*below left*) was used primarily to pare material off the edges of a die. If the gambler wanted to improve his chances of rolling, say, a 1, he could shave the edges off the 1 surface at an angle that increased the chances of the die landing with the 6 side (which is opposite the 1) down and the 1 up. To shave a die, the cheater laid it in the trough of the machine and passed it over a blade located beneath the slit in the trough.

A similar advantage could be gained with a dice loader (*below right*). To make the 1 come up, the cheater drilled out two or more spots on the 6 side of the die, filled up the cavities with a heavy metal such as lead or gold, then repainted the spots. Faithful to the laws of gravity, the heavy 6 side usually landed down leaving the lighter 1 side up.

The more the dice were shaved or weighted, the more reliable they were—and the greater the risk of detection. Prudent cheats used moderately rigged dice, which improved their chances by only 5 or 6 per cent, enough to be profitable for a few hours without inviting trouble.

Dice await rigging in a shaver (*left*) and a loader, also shown with its drill secured in its ivory handle (*foreground*) for storage.

Clothes with holes in their pockets instead of Dollars." Then Grandine drove home his point: "There is but *one* way to gamble successfully, and that is to *get Tools to work with and have the best of every Game you get into.*"

One cardsharp who firmly adhered to that principle was a San Francisco gambler named P. J. Kepplinger, who was the inventor of "the very finest holdout the world has ever seen." That pronouncement was given by John Nevil Maskelyne, a 19th Century conjurer who wrote a book called *Sharps and Flats,* "A Complete Revelation of the Secrets of Cheating at Games of Chance and Skill." Writing in 1894, Maskelyne said about the Kepplinger holdout—which was also known as the San Francisco holdout—"this machine in its latest forms is certainly a masterpiece. Yet so little appreciation has the world for true genius, that the inventor of this marvellous piece of apparatus is practi-

cally unknown to the vast majority of his fellow-men." Of course, if Kepplinger had been a bit more subtle and a bit less greedy, his name might never have been known at all.

For several months in 1888, this professional cardsharp had regularly played a merciless game of poker with some of his equally professional colleagues. To use holdouts in a game where "the players were all too well acquainted with the signs and tokens accompanying such devices" would seem worse than useless, Maskelyne wrote, and in fact, "Kepplinger gave no sign of the employment of anything of the kind. He sat like a statue at the table, he kept his cards right away from him, he did not move a muscle as far as could be seen; his opponents could look up his sleeve almost to the elbow, and yet *he won.*"

Kepplinger's poker pals stood it as long as they could. Finally, during one of their games, they am-

SURE BETS WITH A SHAKE OR A SPIN

No frontier saloon was complete without at least one cage, cup or tub designed for the rolling of dice or a spinning top for bartop gambling. Cheaters deftly employed such devices to fleece suckers in fast-paced games like poker dice, hazard and chuck-a-luck. If the cheater kept the stakes low, he could keep winning for hours without the victim ever suspecting a fraud.

"Bird cages," like the one shown at the left, frequently contained metal-loaded dice that the house controlled with hidden electromagnets. Patrons themselves could cheat by throwing rigged dice into the open-topped tub below or the dice chute below at left. Cheaters sometimes used a cup (*above*) with a secret chamber that could swallow up the fair dice and then release the rigged ones into the game—handling even a set of five eight-sided poker dice.

Cheaters' gambling tops resembled those above and below, except that they were so fixed—by being slightly misshapen, or with stems off-center, or by housing a tiny weight that the gambler manipulated by twisting the top's stem—that a prearranged number would land face up when the top ceased spinning. Tops were marked with spots, numerals or symbols appropriate to particular games. Variations included a large wooden top *(above)* for a version of roulette.

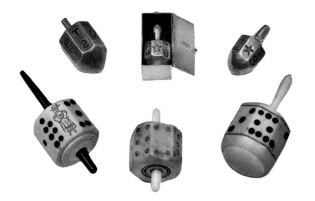

bore such names as sand-tell, coffee-mill, end squeeze, needle squeeze and horse box. Will and Finck marketed 19 different kinds of dealing boxes, of which three were honest—an indication of both the popularity of the game and the likelihood of discovering a square game of faro in the Old West.

Faro dealers were the highest caste among professional gamblers and Western gambling houses paid as much as $100 per week for their services. Considering that the job consisted—at least in theory—of doing no more than pulling cards out of the dealing box, it could be assumed that there was more going on than met the eye. Still, the dealers took a certain pride in being considered honest. Of course, being "honest" meant cheating in the acceptable ways, by manipulating crooked decks and rigged dealing boxes, rather than by tinhorn methods such as shortchanging on bets or attempting to confuse players as to the cards that already had been played. The Will and Finck Company no doubt did a booming business in faro equipment simply catering to "honest" dealers.

There was no game at which the professional gambler could not cheat, and the sporting emporiums were not likely to leave any stones—or bones—unturned. "We wish to call your attention to our Dice Department we manufacture and sell more dice than all others combined, the reason for this is obvious," was the breathless—and underpunctuated—introduction to one company's advertising brochure. "We wish particularly to call your attention to our transparent work. This work is so cleverly executed that they defy detection. If you have never used this work you should not be without it for a single day."

For the sum of five dollars a gambler could order Set No. 100: "This is the fastest winning set known where only two dice are used, and for winning the money fast there is nothing will equal it. No switches required. Put them in the game and leave them stay. They will do the rest."

The self-styled reformed gambler and prolific author Jonathan Green, believing that craps was "fully equal to Faro in its vile deception and ruinous effects," prophesied that "by the time this game is as old as Faro, as many persons will probably be ruined by it, unless some great and mighty check is given to its

Arising from a drunken stupor gun in hand, Ben Graham, a Colorado miner, exposes a cheater and horrifies his friends. Thinking that Graham was dead, the gamblers had been keeping a bizarre vigil by playing cards on the stomach of the "corpse."

prevalence." Indeed, by the early 1900s craps had taken over faro's position as the No. 1 casino banking game in the country.

Craps is played with two dice, the sides of which are numbered from one to six. The two numbers that face up after a throw are added together for the deciding number. If the player shooting the dice throws a 7 or 11, it is a "natural" and wins. A roll of 2, 3 or 12 is a "crap" and loses. If the player shoots a 4, 5, 6, 8, 9 or 10, that becomes his point. To win his bet, he then must throw his point again; if he throws a 7 before he throws his point, he loses.

A professional sharper could—as with cards—rely on his skillful fingers to manipulate fair dice, but it was far better to have the dice on his side. According to E. N. Grandine, "The best way to fix dice for craps is to have one dice with two aces, 2 fives and 2 sixes on, and one with 2 threes, 2 fours and 2 fives on." With dice rigged in conformity with this formula, it was impossible to roll a 7; however, there was a slightly greater chance to throw an 11 than with fair dice. Furthermore, it was impossible to "crap out." Thus, the gambler who used these dice—even though he had little chance of rolling a winning natural on his first throw—was assured of winning his bet since he could count on rolling his point again.

The mis-spotted dice were called "dispatchers"—because they sent the sucker to the cleaners with such dispatch—and their deception was based on the fact that one can see only three sides of a cube at once. The duplicate 5s, for example, were placed on opposite sides of the cube, so at no time would both faces be visible. The only drawback to this hoax was that the sharp had to be a master sleight-of-hand artist to switch the dice in and out of the game—obviously, the sucker could not be allowed to use them—without being caught in the act. For gamblers who preferred a bit less risk, the next best item was "loaded" dice.

Loaded dice were those in which some of the spots were drilled out and filled in with mercury or lead. Will and Finck advertised "selected ivory loaded with quicksilver. Sold in sets of 9 dice, 3 high, 3 low, and 3 fair. Price, per set complete, $5." Unfortunately for the crooked gambler, an alert player could discover which dice were loaded by trying to spin them on one corner, since loaded dice will not spin. Ever-inventive sharps therefore came up with a thoroughly modern contrivance: electric dice.

A core was drilled out of the center of the die between the ace and the 6. A thin disk of iron was placed at the ace end, and a pellet of lead of equal weight was placed at the 6 end. To compensate for this extra weight, the center was filled with cork. Then, as Maskelyne recounted in *Sharps and Flats,* the die was mended with liquid celluloid cement "and the joint is so well and neatly made it is invisible, even though examined with a powerful lens." Used in conjunction with a battery-operated electromagnet hidden in the table, the dice could be made to come up 6s at the flick of a switch.

"The operator has only to trouble himself with regard to two points," Maskelyne observed. "He must press the spring at the right moment, and release it before trying to pick up the dice afterwards. Should he neglect this latter point, he will have the satisfaction of finding the dice stick to the table. In all other respects, he has only to press the button, and electricity will do the rest." Will and Finck marketed the electric die at $2.50 apiece and "Dice Tables, electric, complete, our invention" for $150.

Maskelyne hoped that his exposé would "once and for all render the use of electric dice unsafe under any conditions. The moment the outer world has any idea of their existence, the game is too risky to be pleasant to any sharp." He recommended that players carry "a little mariner's compass, dangling at the end of a watch chain" in order to detect the presence of a magnetized table.

The determination of a crusader like John Maskelyne to reveal the secrets of professional gamblers was one facet of the antigambling sentiment that periodically swept through the country. Convinced that all gamblers cheated and that the habit led to certain moral and financial ruin, upright citizens in Western boomtowns waged a constant battle against the evils of cards and dice. In 1846 the alcalde, or mayor, of Monterey, California, a rather strait-laced ex-United States Navy chaplain named Walter Colton, issued "an ordinance against gambling—a vice which shows itself here more on the sabbath than any other day of the week." Much to the chagrin of the Reverend Colton, however, "the effect of it has been to drive the gamblers from the town into the bushes. I have been informed this evening," he wrote in his journal, "that in a ravine, at a short distance, some 30 individuals have been engaged through the day in this desperate play. They selected a spot deeply embowered in shade, and escaped the eye of my constables."

In San Francisco a few years later, the town council passed strict regulations against gambling, which had taken on such proportions with the advent of the gold rush that it "seriously interfered with business." But, said Californian historian Hubert Bancroft, "a great reform was considered out of place in a small town, and therefore at the next meeting of the council the law was repealed." San Francisco tolerated gambling, Bancroft said, "for the revenue that was derived from it, long after public opinion was against it."

A similar situation existed in Reno, Nevada, some 50 years later. In an article headlined "America's Most Wicked City," the *Kansas City Journal* noted that the town's population of 15,000 supported "in fair prosperity" more than 1,200 saloons, "all of which are gambling resorts."

An outraged bishop, the Right Reverend Henry D. Robinson, referred to gambling as "the greatest evil with which Nevada has to contend at present." In an address reported by the *Journal,* Robinson said: "It is scarcely believable, yet I am assured it is a fact, that some of our businessmen favor the continuance of gambling on the ground that it brings them trade. The income derived by the community from licensing the gambler is so large that many fear lest Nevada's municipalities could not maintain public improvements were this income lost. Nevada's improvements are weighed against Nevada's morals. The tacit assumption seems to be this: Nevada with good streets and bad morals is more desirable than Nevada with bad streets and good morals."

At one point the Reno officials did attempt to curb the pernicious vice. However, the referendum to decide whether or not to drive the gamblers out of town was defeated by 750 votes out of a total of nearly 3,000 votes cast. "The issue was fought by the gamblers in a characteristic method," the *Journal* reported. "A few days before the vote was taken they closed their saloons, left their electric lights unlit, silenced their bands, of which there are scores playing all night long, and shrouded their bars. It was as if the end of the world had come in Reno. Business practically stopped. Silence fell over the city and men talked in whispers, oppressed with the peace that spelled desolation. With their victory at the polls began a saturnalia which was only an exaggerated condition of life in Reno, but which was regarded as necessary and appropriate to celebrate so great a triumph."

Professional sharps who fleeced suckers at cards and dice could, like Poker Alice, take home $1,000 or so for an evening's game against one person. Sometimes, when several woolly lambs were available for shearing, a cardsharp might run his winnings into several thousand dollars. But gamblers who liked to think big gravitated to that old American stand-by, the lottery—where, in one fell swoop, a smart operator could make off with millions.

For many years, even as playing cards and dice were being denounced from the nation's pulpits, lotteries flourished with the blessing of practically everyone. Throughout most of the 18th Century lotteries were taken for granted as a means of financing public projects. Thanks to this wholesale gambling, colleges were founded, churches constructed, roads laid and bridges erected.

But during the next century, by the mid-1800s, most of the lotteries in the country had been taken over by swindlers and sharps. Promoters or agents would decamp with the money, no prize winners would be paid—if, in fact, drawings were even held—and certainly the charitable beneficiary would see little or nothing of the funds that were raised in its name. A more subtle type of swindle was to sell fake tickets in a legitimate lottery or tickets in a purely imaginary lottery, while perhaps the commonest fraud was to rig the drawing for the benefit of a cohort.

Despite growing public indignation and the enactment of laws in many states banning lotteries, this form of gambling continued to draw a loyal, large and ever-hopeful following. In describing the gambling atmosphere that pervaded in California in the latter half of the 19th Century, historian Bancroft noted that around 1870 "a lottery, legalized by the legislature for the benefit of the Mercantile library of San Francisco, caused for a short time an almost entire suspension of business for a hundred miles around."

Such was the state of the art when the legislature in Washington Territory enacted a bill in 1875 authorizing the "Grand Lottery of Washington Territory." Its ostensible purpose was to raise funds to build a wagon road through Snoqualmie Pass, to link the Puget Sound area with the interior of the territory. Seattle citizens had long believed such a road to be the key to their city's growth, and the Grand Lottery was to be effective only in King and Yakima counties, the areas most interested in the road. So popular was the idea that even newspapers that normally frowned on all forms of gambling ventured to endorse the lottery. "To those who must risk their money at hazard," wrote the *Puget Sound Dispatch,* "we can honestly commend the scheme as the best that offers."

One newspaper, however, took a more jaundiced view, claiming that the lottery bill was "simply devised as a boon to an old and respected citizen." The citizen in question was one Henry Yesler, a well-known businessman who had for 40 years been a pillar of the community. Yesler had been the prime mover behind passage of the lottery bill and was exceedingly quick off the mark in getting his lottery set up. Two facts enter into the consideration of whether Yesler's eagerness to act was motivated by pure civic-mindedness. One is that the legislation stipulated that only 10 per cent of the proceeds of the lottery had to be turned over to county authorities for the building of the road; the remaining 90 per cent, though not specifically mentioned, presumably went to the proprietor of the lottery. The second fact is that Henry Yesler was deeply in debt; he owed one creditor alone some $76,000.

Yesler proposed to raffle off as prizes several pieces of property he owned in downtown Seattle (properties he had been trying to sell and whose value he greatly inflated in advertising the lottery), and he hoped to sell

1876 1876

ALKI.

GRAND DISTRIBUTION!

❖ A CHANCE TO WIN $100,000 ❖

FOR THE SMALL OUTLAY OF $5.

WASHINGTON TERRITORY LOTTERY,

Legalized by authority of an Act of the Legislature, in aid of a great road from the City of Seattle, through the Cascade Mountains via Snoqualmie Pass to Walla Walla; Approved by his Excellency, Governor Ferry, Nov. 12, 1875.

$300,000 WORTH OF REAL ESTATE

In the City of Seattle, and in cash, to be distributed.

DRAWS JULY 4, 1876.

60,000 TICKETS & 5,575 PRIZES.

TICKETS $5 COIN EACH, OR ELEVEN FOR $50,

| GRAND | PRIZE, | YESLER'S | STEAM | SAW | MILL |

and Mill property in the city of Seattle, valued at

$100,000 00!

The rents from the Mill and Mill Property equal $700 00 ¡COIN per Month.

Some of the most eligible and best business lots in the city of Seattle will be distributed, including "Hovey & Barker's corner" on Mill and Commercial streets, and the Pacific Brewery property.

The prizes to be drawn and distributed, will be as follows :

1st Prize---The Steam Saw Mill, valued at	....	$100,000
2d " Hovey & Barker Corner " "	....	15,000
3d " Pacific Brewery Property "	....	5,000

Together with 1011 Lots in various parts of the City of Seattle and Additions thereto, valued at from $50 to $1,500 each.

Also 61 prizes in Farming Lands, in King county; and $25,000 in gold coin, divided into 4,000 prizes of $5 each, and 500 prizes of $10 each.

The County Commissioners of King county, Washington Territory, by virtue of said enactment, appointed M. S. Booth, auditor of King county; Capt. Geo. D. Hill, (U. S. A.), treasurer of King county, and John Collins, Esq, President Talbot Coal Company, trustees to whom the whole of the said property has been deeded in trust for the ticket holders drawing the prizes. No scheme of this kind ever offered to the public, presented such great inducements to try for a fortune. The general public can invest with the greatest confidence. The distribution being authorized by law, is guarded in every particular; nothing of the kind can be fairer for all concerned.

MANNER OF DISTRIBUTION.

The drawing will take place at the Pavilion, in the City of Seattle, Washington Territory, and will be made by blindfolded children, from two glass wheels, the contents of which can be seen by all present: one wheel will contain 5,575 gifts on printed slips enclosed in tubes or envelopes; the other wheel will contain tags with numbers corresponding to those on the 60,000 tickets. The contents of both wheels are thoroughly mixed by revolving. The child at the first wheel will draw a number therefrom, then the child at the second wheel will draw a gift therefrom, and the gift thus drawn will belong to the number drawn immediately before it, thus the process will continue until 5,575 gifts and numbers are drawn; an official registry of the prizes drawn will be kept and ticket holders drawing prizes will be satisfied immediately.

OPINIONS OF THE PRESS:

THE GRAND LOTTERY.—Mr. Yesler has been busily engaged during the last week getting his property ready to put in the hands of the Trustees to be appointed by the Board of County Commissioners, as by law directed. The distribution of about $300,000 worth of real property is legalized by authority of an Act of the Legislature, and the greatest confidence is every where felt that it will be conducted fairly and squarely. Mr. Yesler is one of the pioneers of this city, a large property owner, and is known as a gentleman of sterling integrity. The property to be disposed of is situated in the business part of the city, and is of great value. The tickets will be ready for sale on and after January 1st, next, when all who desire to try their luck will have an opportunity to do so with perfect safety. We will in our next issue announce the names of the trustees, and give further particulars of the property to be distributed, together with the Act authorizing the distribution.—Seattle Intelligencer.

"We commend the scheme as the best that offers, not only because it is a home institution, authorized by law and endorsed by public sentiment, but because we know the property put up to the hazard of chance is of real value, and that the drawing will be fairly and faithfully made, without any trickery."—Puget Sound Dispatch.

GREAT LOTTERY SCHEME.—The great, much talked of Yesler lottery scheme has at last reach a stage calling for the appearance in print of its first advertisement, which will be found occupying a column in the present issue of the Tribune. Our space this evening will not admit of more than a brief mention of some of the leading details. The grand prize will be the piece of ground on which the saw mill stands, and in which is included what is known as the Mill Block, a strip extending five hundred feet in length up the left hand side of Mill street to the corner of Front street, and two hundred feet back—valued at $100,000. The second prize is the Hovey & Baker corner, valued at $14,000. The third prize is the North Pacific Brewery property. Altogether, there are to be 5,575 prizes, part of which will be cash and part property. The drawing will come off on the Fourth of July, 1876, or sooner, if the chances are all purchased. Agents will be appointed in various parts of the country to dispose of them, in which undertaking the managers do not anticipate much trouble. Ten per cent of the proceeds of the lottery will be given as an endowment to the improvement of the Snoqualmie Pass road. We will give further particulars from time to time hereafter.—Seattle Tribune.

"The last sensation in Seattle is the advertisement of Mr. H. L. Yesler, in the city papers announcing that his grand lottery in the interest of the Snoqualmie road across the mountains to Eastern Washington, is assuming definite shape, the requirements of which (touching its legality) special legislation was enacted by our last Legislature, I think it pardonable to give a somewhat lengthy notice to it.

$100,000—This first grand prize is to be the mill property, situated in the business part of the city, and valued at one hundred thousand dollars coin. The mill is running steadily, cutting fifty or sixty thousand feet of lumber daily. The water front is excellent, and affords fine facilities for loading vessels with lumber. A good wharf is also included with the mill. This, the first prize, is a fortune, and rents for eight or nine thousand dollars per annum.

The second prize on the list, is a lot on the corner of Commercial and Mill streets, covered by a good substantial wooden building, which rents for a very handsome sum. This location is one of the best for business purposes in the city, and judging by ruling prices, is worth twelve to fifteen thousand dollars.

The third prize is a brewery, situated in a valuable locality, and is rented at a high figure. It will make a very desirable prize. Besides these three first prizes, there will be offered over one thousand lots in various parts of the city, valued at from $50 to $1,500, and several tracts of land outside the city. Also, there will be a great many prizes in coin, so that there will be at least one prize in every ten tickets. Each ticket will be valued at five dollars, and there will be 60,000 tickets, making a capital of three hundred thousand dollars. A large outlay of money will be made in order to properly place this enterprise before the public—more than three tons of paper being required for printing circulars, posters, etc. After the first of January, tickets may be had by applying to Mr. Yesler, in Seattle."—Portland Oregonian.

Agents should get up Clubs at Once and Remit.

☞ Money must accompany the order for Tickets. Money can be sent by mail in registered letter, or postoffice order, or certified draft on any bank, or by express. Write legibly your address.

Agents should apply without delay to

H. L. YESLER, Seattle, W. T.

C. B. BAGLEY, Printer, Olympia, W. T.

Lumberman Henry Yesler offered his saw mill as prize in Seattle's first licensed lottery. A court order canceled the raffle but not before other lotteries had made Seattle "the resort of professional gamblers."

60,000 tickets at five dollars apiece. Unfortunately, there were only 3,000 to 4,000 people in King County and the whole territory itself was sparsely settled. In June 1876, two weeks before the scheduled July 4th drawing, Yesler confessed to a friend that "the sale of tickets is very dull. I am at a loss to know how I am to get out of this trouble."

The whole thing ended quite ignominiously. First Yesler tried to postpone the drawing to the following January. As soon as he made that announcement, however, antigambling sentiment that had been brewing for some time came to a head. Even though the Grand Lottery of Washington Territory—and others that had sprung up in its wake—had been authorized by an act of the legislature, irate citizens took the matter to court. There, a district judge ruled the act void because it gave King and Yakima County residents privileges denied the rest of the territory. Thereupon Yesler and other lottery operators were found guilty of violating the territory's criminal code. Because of his previous good standing in the community, however, Yesler was let off with a small fine—even though about $30,000 from the sale of tickets was never accounted for.

Somehow Yesler managed to appease his creditors and when Seattle boomed in the 1880s and 1890s the real estate that he had not been able to unload in 1876 skyrocketed in value. Yesler thus ended his days in a lavish mansion; he was worth more than a million dollars.

A man who far surpassed Henry Yesler at selling lottery tickets was James Monroe Pattee. A restless writing teacher who was born in New Hampshire, Pattee joined the westward migration at the age of 30 and by 1868 had made a small fortune in land speculation and mining operations in California. In 1870 and 1871, Pattee helped organize something billed as the "Cosmopolitan Benevolent Association of California Grand Fair," a lottery scheme to pay off the debts of the school district in Nevada City. With this experience under his belt, Pattee moved to Omaha and embarked on the career that would earn him the regal sobriquet of Lottery King.

From 1871 to 1873 he held a series of "Great Legal Drawings" which, though they no doubt lined his pocket, too, were for the most part legitimate enterprises, raising money in the time-honored way for libraries and hospitals. But in 1873 Nebraska outlawed lotteries, and Pattee—who had already run into some difficulty over accusations that he had issued duplicate and triplicate tickets in one of his lotteries—found it convenient to locate elsewhere.

In nearby Wyoming, anyone could run a lottery legally by paying $100 to the county sheriff and receiving a license good for three months. The spring of 1875 found Pattee in Laramie, ordering 40,000 circulars from a small newspaper publisher—whose weekly payroll until then had totaled $27—and hiring some 20 clerks. Soon the Lottery King was collecting his mail in a clothesbasket and depositing $4,000 or $5,000 a day in the bank. For a mere $400 a year and three consecutive county licenses, Pattee proceeded to rake in about seven million dollars in ticket sales for the Wyoming Lottery in the first year alone.

Of course, he was not making these gigantic sales to the sparse territorial population. Preferring to keep his suckers at a comfortable distane, Pattee ran frequent advertisements for his lotteries in the *New York Herald* while he remained safely ensconced in Wyoming and attempted to stay in the good graces of the locals by contributing to churches and other charities.

In most lotteries, the number of tickets seldom exceeded about 75,000. Tickets in each of the Wyoming Lottery's monthly drawings numbered a colossal 551,300, at one dollar each, six for five dollars or 20 for $16. Each month 70,755 prizes were offered, totaling $200,000 to $275,000; the grand prize was $50,000. On the face of it, the ratio of the number of prizes to tickets was passable. Unfortunately, only 35 of these prizes were worth more than $100. For the purchase of a one dollar ticket, 70,000 of the winners had a chance to collect the munificent sum of 50 cents.

As a further gimmick, Pattee would notify winners of these paltry prizes that it would cost more to send them their winnings than the value of the prize itself. Pattee would then generously offer to send instead a share of stock worth $10 in a dubious enterprise that he called the "Bullion Gold and Silver Mining Company" and would encourage them to be his agents, receiving a free share for every five that they sold at two dollars apiece.

Despite various editorial campaigns against him, Pattee managed to carry on several such schemes at

James Monroe Pattee sold off millions of these virtually worthless lottery tickets to gullible Americans in the 1870s. The minuscule—and occasionally nonexistent—pay-offs in his raffles earned Pattee a widespread reputation as an arch swindler.

once by judicious use of pseudonymns and front men, not to mention a timely move from Laramie to Cheyenne—where soon sprang up the Cheyenne State Lottery, ostensibly managed by one Marshall S. Pike, president of the "State Bank of Cheyenne."

In February 1877, Orange Judd, who was the editor of the *American Agriculturalist,* lit into the Cheyenne enterprise. "If anyone supposes that the Wyoming lottery is dead while Pattee still lives, he has small knowledge of the nature of things. It still waves its banners, but they are now inscribed 'The Cheyenne State Lottery.'" And Editor Judd lamented, "Poor Wyoming, were not the grasshoppers enough?"

When reformers from out of state got on his trail, Pattee unobtrusively slipped out of Wyoming and set up his operation once more, but this time in Canada. He was apparently none the worse for wear when he left Wyoming, and ticket buyers were generally unaware that they had been taken for a ride. The man appeared to possess an uncanny instinct for getting out while he was ahead. An editor from Kansas who interviewed Pattee recalled, "He seems to delight in boasting of his own villainy in swindling weak human nature. He said his conscience did not trouble him, that people wanted to be humbugged, and it was his business to do it." Spoken like a true professional sharper.

The secret arsenal of the dangerous game

When a gambler's cheating—actual or imagined—was at issue, the weapons that sprang to hand were as macabre as they were deadly. From vests, sleeves, boots and wherever else ingenuity hid them came knuckle-duster knives, dirks and push daggers. And secreted palm guns, derringers and sawed-off belly pistols gave deadly meaning to "the luck of the draw."

The vogue for inconspicuous arms came west with gamblers who were migrating from notorious New Orleans. The push dagger—its crosswise handle making it compact and easy to use—was particularly popular among the Southern gamblers.

But the well-armed sporting man wanted more than a blade, and in the early days of frontier gambling the only available pistols were either too bulky to conceal or relatively weak in stopping power. In the late 1840s gamblers began carrying revolvers with the barrels sawed off, and in the 1850s Henry Deringer's pocket pistol—powerful and accurate enough to cover a poker table, light and compact enough to hide—found a ready market and inspired many imitators.

A sterling-silver knuckle-duster *(below)*, a petite seven-inch push dagger with sheath *(right)* and a double-ring dagger with scrimshawed walrus-ivory handle are typical of the twists of invention and luxury of materials applied to satisfy the gamblers' peculiar requirements. In just two swift strokes the user of the short-bladed knuckle-duster could not only smash an antagonist's jaw but also stab him.

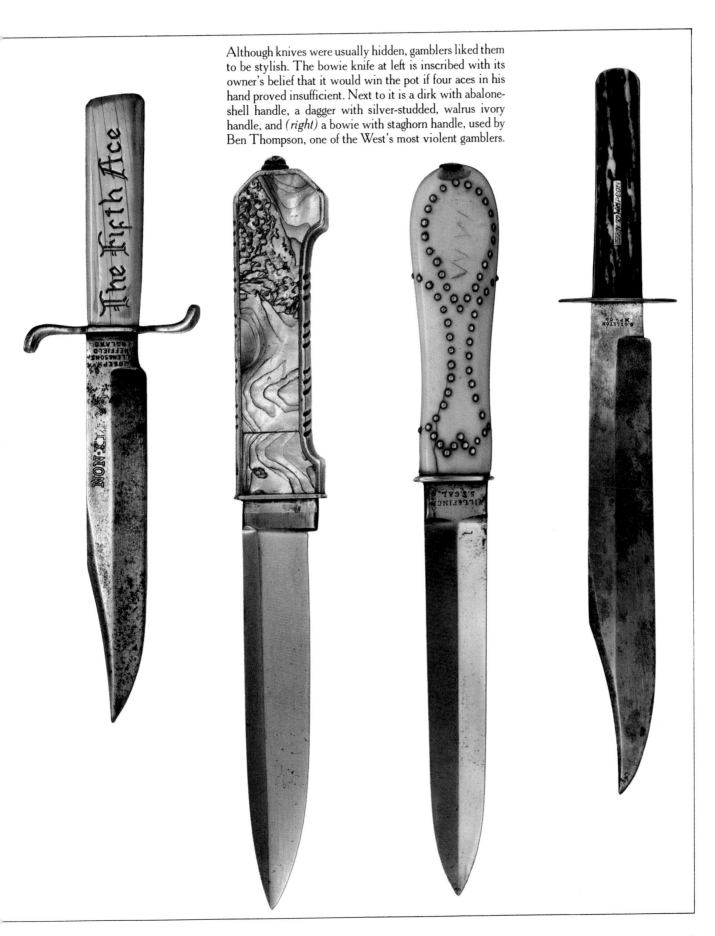

Although knives were usually hidden, gamblers liked them to be stylish. The bowie knife at left is inscribed with its owner's belief that it would win the pot if four aces in his hand proved insufficient. Next to it is a dirk with abalone-shell handle, a dagger with silver-studded, walrus ivory handle, and *(right)* a bowie with staghorn handle, used by Ben Thompson, one of the West's most violent gamblers.

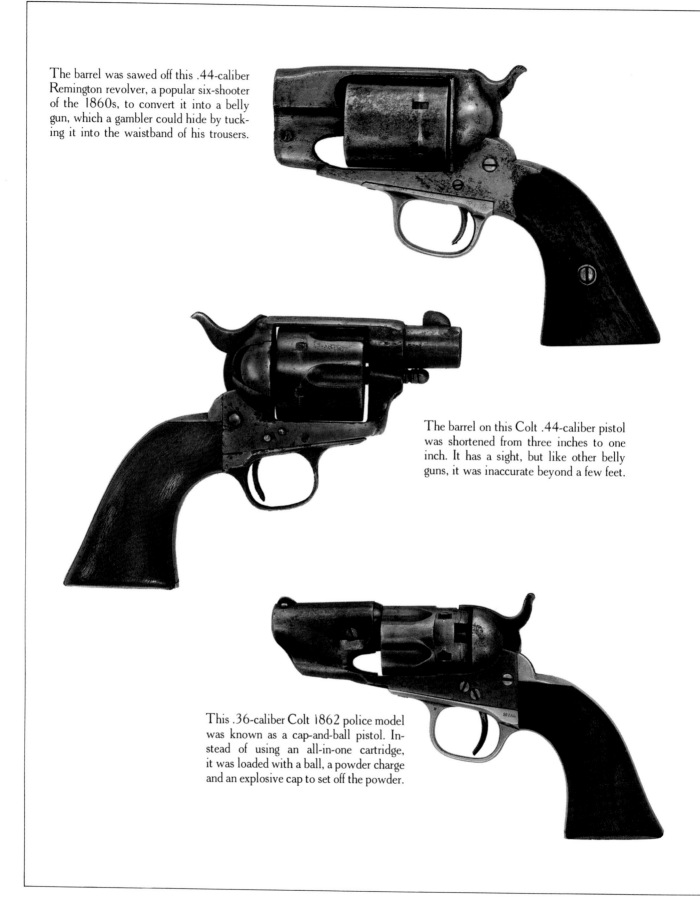

The barrel was sawed off this .44-caliber Remington revolver, a popular six-shooter of the 1860s, to convert it into a belly gun, which a gambler could hide by tucking it into the waistband of his trousers.

The barrel on this Colt .44-caliber pistol was shortened from three inches to one inch. It has a sight, but like other belly guns, it was inaccurate beyond a few feet.

This .36-caliber Colt 1862 police model was known as a cap-and-ball pistol. Instead of using an all-in-one cartridge, it was loaded with a ball, a powder charge and an explosive cap to set off the powder.

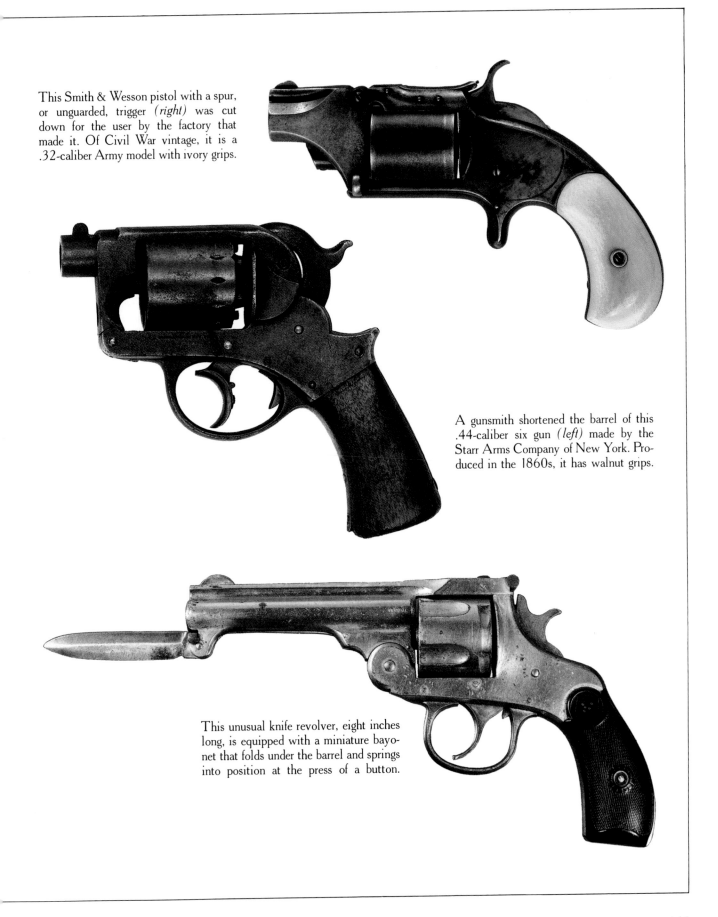

This Smith & Wesson pistol with a spur, or unguarded, trigger *(right)* was cut down for the user by the factory that made it. Of Civil War vintage, it is a .32-caliber Army model with ivory grips.

A gunsmith shortened the barrel of this .44-caliber six gun *(left)* made by the Starr Arms Company of New York. Produced in the 1860s, it has walnut grips.

This unusual knife revolver, eight inches long, is equipped with a miniature bayonet that folds under the barrel and springs into position at the press of a button.

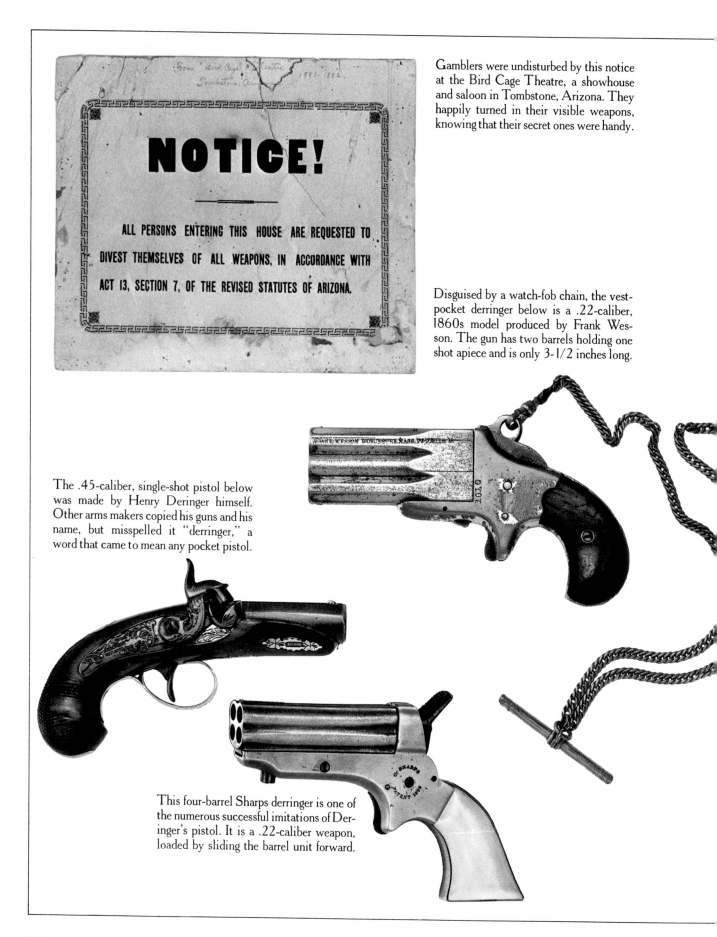

Gamblers were undisturbed by this notice at the Bird Cage Theatre, a showhouse and saloon in Tombstone, Arizona. They happily turned in their visible weapons, knowing that their secret ones were handy.

NOTICE!

ALL PERSONS ENTERING THIS HOUSE ARE REQUESTED TO DIVEST THEMSELVES OF ALL WEAPONS, IN ACCORDANCE WITH ACT 13, SECTION 7, OF THE REVISED STATUTES OF ARIZONA.

Disguised by a watch-fob chain, the vest-pocket derringer below is a .22-caliber, 1860s model produced by Frank Wesson. The gun has two barrels holding one shot apiece and is only 3-1/2 inches long.

The .45-caliber, single-shot pistol below was made by Henry Deringer himself. Other arms makers copied his guns and his name, but misspelled it "derringer," a word that came to mean any pocket pistol.

This four-barrel Sharps derringer is one of the numerous successful imitations of Deringer's pistol. It is a .22-caliber weapon, loaded by sliding the barrel unit forward.

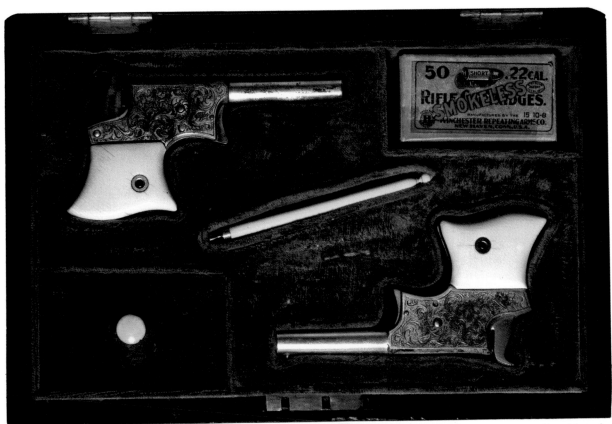

This set of Remington vest-pocket derringers, and a cleaning rod *(center),* is most unusual. The guns were usually sold singly.

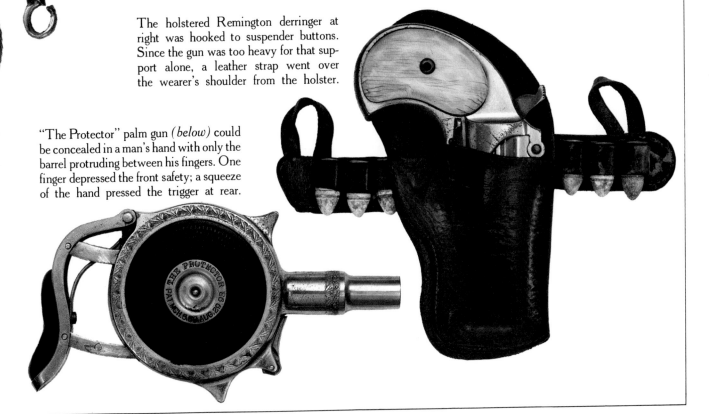

The holstered Remington derringer at right was hooked to suspender buttons. Since the gun was too heavy for that support alone, a leather strap went over the wearer's shoulder from the holster.

"The Protector" palm gun *(below)* could be concealed in a man's hand with only the barrel protruding between his fingers. One finger depressed the front safety; a squeeze of the hand pressed the trigger at rear.

5 | Booming business for boomtown gamblers

The Gem Lunch Counter *(center)* was the only structure on Block 16 in infant Las Vegas that was not a gambling establishment.

Have you ever, in the "Club Room,"
In a game run "on the square"
E'er wooed the "Fickle Goddess,"
And seen her bright smile there?

Although intended to immortalize the Arizona Club *(below)* in Las Vegas, the question posed by this 1908 doggerel could have been answered in the affirmative by miners, cattlemen and gamesters in any boomtown from Leadville to Tombstone.

Whether the stakes were a five-cent chuck-a-luck or a rich poker pot, the fickle goddess of the gambling tables was hearing appeals almost before the first bits of ore fell from the miners' picks or the odor of freshly seared cowhide faded from the cattlemen's irons.

From California and the Mississippi riverboats, gamblers beat a path to the Western big-money towns with the speed of vultures assembling over fresh-killed carrion. In Virginia City, Nevada, during the 1860s, the loyalties of the town's 15,000 inhabitants were apparent from the character of its structures: 100 gambling houses compared with a mere four churches.

Even the joys of marriage placed second to the alluring green baize. "What sensible man wants a wife," asked an 1877 *Butte Miner,* "if she refuses to support him, and even goes so far as to discourage his little recreations, such as faro, poker, etc.?"

Gamesters who rode the tides of Western prosperity

One morning in the 1870s, three tired-looking men perched on the steps outside a Denver bank that had not yet opened for the day's business. The man in the middle gripped a sealed envelope on which his companions kept a careful eye. Presently, the cashier arrived.

"Want to make a deposit, gentlemen?" he asked cheerfully. "Step inside."

"No, I want to negotiate a loan," replied the man with the envelope, "and there ain't a minute to lose. I want $5,000 quicker than hell can scorch a feather."

"What collaterals have you—Government?" inquired the bank official, hoping that the envelope might hold something as substantial as government bonds.

"Government, nothin'," the man snorted. "I've got something here beats four per cents all hollow. I've been sitting in a poker game across the street, and there's $4,000 in the pot. As I've every cent in the center the boys have given me thirty minutes to raise a stake on my hand. It's in this envelope. Just look at it, but don't give it away to these gentlemen. They're in the game, and came along to see I don't monkey with the cards."

The cashier ripped open the envelope. Inside were four kings and an ace, an unbeatable poker hand by the rules of the time. "This is certainly irregular," he said. "We don't lend money on cards."

"But you ain't going to see me raised out on a hand like that?" whispered the stunned poker player.

"Can't help it, sir," the cashier replied briskly. "Never heard of such a thing."

Out on the street, the disappointed gambler and his friends met the bank's president, who had just emerged from an all-night game of his own. When he saw the gambler's cards, the president ran into the bank, grabbed a bag of $20 bills, and followed the trio to their game. Ten minutes later he returned and tossed the bag and an extra handful of 20s on the counter.

"Here," he said to the startled cashier, "credit five hundred to interest account. Ever play poker?"

"No, sir."

"Ah, thought not—thought not. If you did you'd know what good collateral was. Remember that in the future four kings and an ace are always good in this institution for our entire assets, sir—our entire assets."

This tale of Western gambling was told in an 1896 book on the great American pastime of poker. Its author, John F. B. Lillard, all but swore that the events happened in Denver when he said they did. Other accounts placed the incident in other Western towns. But no matter where or when the loan was made, the story tells much about the heyday of boomtown gamblers from the mid-1860s until the turn of the century.

Gamblers appeared wherever there was a sudden eruption of easy money. Some came from the Mississippi riverboats; some moved from the maturing cities and towns of more settled California. Others, more venturesome still, forsook the urbanized East to try their gambling skills on the brawling frontier.

They did not much care where the money was. Like locusts, they moved from place to place, always ready to press on to greener fields. Gamblers could be found wherever construction gangs were pushing railroad tracks across the plains and through mountain passes. They set up games near logging camps and at trading posts where buffalo hunters came to sell shaggy hides.

The really serious money, wealth in quantities to tempt a gambler with great ambition, was found in the

---

Gaudy pictures of horses and lustrous abalone inlays decorate the rim of a seven-foot wheel of fortune. The agonizingly suspenseful slowing of such wheels attracted many a bet in boomtown gaming halls.

boomtowns. In Denver—and in Tombstone, Virginia City, Deadwood, Leadville, Creede and dozens of other mining towns—the lure was gold or silver clawed from the ground. In Kansas the cash that changed hands over the gaming tables came from the cattle trade, as cowboys drove enormous herds of longhorns north from Texas to Abilene, Hays City, Ellsworth, Wichita, Dodge City and sister settlements on the plains. But whatever the source of a boomtown's wealth, or the quality of its life, within the four walls of its gambling dens all was much the same. If a card player had passed out in Deadwood's No. 10 Saloon and awakened in Dodge City's Long Branch Saloon he would not have noticed much difference.

When a saloonkeeper first arrived at the site of a sudden gusher of money, he generally doled out his refreshments in a tent or dugout containing little more than a pair of barrels with a plank laid across them as a bar—not much in the way of gambling facilities. But if the camp prospered, the saloon improved. From a tent the saloonkeeper moved into permanent quarters, retailing his goods in a long, narrow, plank-walled room furnished with everything indispensable to a pleasant evening of fellowship: a simple bar, maybe a stove and a scattering of plain tables and chairs. Later, if the mines or the cow trade continued to thrive, the saloon was spruced up with mirrors, fancy glassware and paintings of buxom enchantresses, coyly posing in the nude.

Finally, in the best circumstances, the establishment blossomed like the Oriental Saloon in Tombstone in the early 1880s. An Eastern reporter said that the Oriental was "simply gorgeous. The mahogany bar is a marvel of beauty, the gaming room is carpeted with Brussels, brilliantly lighted and furnished with reading matter and writing materials for its patrons."

Professional gamblers were welcome citizens in the boomtowns. Together with the ever-present saloon-keepers, they generally arrived in a cattle town along with the first cattle drive, or showed up at the mining camps about the same time the miners did. Cattle driving was a tedious and low-paid occupation, and when cowboys reached the end of a trail they looked forward to the fellowship of a saloon and the chance to multiply their meager wages at the gambling table. Mining was probably the biggest business gamble the West had to offer, and games of chance were merely less strenuous extensions of gold panning or back-breaking pick-and-shovel work.

In many saloons the choice of ways to risk one's money was none too extensive, consisting only of a faro layout, a roulette wheel, a monte bank and a poker table. These facilities, meager as they might be, required at least a few good gamblers to run them. Ordinarily it took three to handle a faro game—a dealer, a lookout and a casekeeper who sat at the table with an abacus-like device to show which cards had been played. Other men were needed to manage the other games. Saloonkeepers hired their own professionals to man the card tables, or encouraged independent gamblers to set up business in their establishments. The more the merrier—and the brisker the trade.

Wages were relatively high but there were so few really top-notch professionals that proprietors were sometimes obliged to hire men of unseasoned ability. This could be a distinct liability when the host had to make good his resident gambler's losses. An Arizona businessman sank $1,000 in a new saloon and hired an unskilled gambler. Within four months, the place folded. In Tombstone, an unlucky saloon owner named George Hand lost as much as $700 some nights.

Such setbacks were the exception. Gamblers as a rule made fine profits, although not by playing for huge stakes, in the dramatic manner of frontier legend. Their considerable winnings usually came from a great volume of business rather than from the size of the bets. Most poker games had a one- or two-dollar limit; bets at faro usually ranged from 25 cents to a dollar; 10-cent chips at roulette were common and a gambler could play dice for as little as a nickel a throw.

The reason for such paltry stakes was purely economic. The ordinary miner in Leadville or Virginia City made a little less than $20 a week, pretty good wages for the period, but hardly enough to qualify him as a high roller. And the average cowboy, much as he enjoyed lavishing his earnings on liquor, prostitutes and gambling, seldom had large sums of money to spend. A young man often rode into a Kansas cattle town after a four months' trail drive from Texas with only about $120. But there were enough of these small-stake gamblers for the professionals to reap a rich harvest.

When gamblers first appeared during a boomtown's early period of joyful speculation, they were welcomed

$50 Reward

The above Reward will be
paid to the man who
cannot find the

KENO GAME

Which is now running in the

Alhambra Saloon.

FIRST ROLL FREE!

IKE.

REPUBLICAN PRINT, 306 FIFTH STREET.

WOODEN KENO CARDS

GOOSE AND BALLS

KENO: THE SOMETIME GOLDEN GOOSE

Of all the games offered in Western boomtowns, keno was one of the easiest to rig for cheating. The pivot-mounted device at far left—the goose—was spun to mix numbered balls within. When the conductor of the game, or "roller," pushed a lever, one ball dropped out. He shouted its number; if players had that number on the keno cards bought from the house, they covered it with a button. A player won when a row of five numbers was full. But when fitted inside with a device dropping prearranged numbers for a house shill, the goose turned golden only for the keno parlor.

While gamblers listen intently, a keno roller in the 1860s calls out the number of a ball prior to placing it in the master board before him.

John Wesley Hardin, a gunfighter known for "signing" cards with bullets to boost a casino of which he owned a share, was a poor loser at craps. He once recovered his losses at pistol point. Ironically, he was gunned down while rolling dice for drinks.

the card games that continued even as he mounted a makeshift pulpit, spoke the invocation. One member of his rowdy congregation, hit with a streak of ill fortune at faro, had just lost three times running. "Damn the luck!" he bellowed. Just then, the preacher, coming to the end of his prayer, intoned, "Amen."

At that, nearly everyone in the place whooped and roared with laughter. Someone set loose a couple of snarling canines who were being groomed for an upcoming dogfight. Yet the minister droned ahead with his service. Though few in the unruly crowd heard what he said, he persisted, delivered the benediction, took up a tidy collection, accepted the offer of a drink, and disappeared into the night.

Not until later did the patrons of the Gold Rooms learn that the dedicated man of the cloth was no clergyman at all, but a roving cardsharp, down on his luck and seeking to raise rent money and a small stake to finance his return to the gaming tables.

The early accommodations between gamblers and clergymen, or between gamblers and other respectable, responsible elements of Western towns, could not last. As stable businessmen, farmers and proper ladies moved in, gamblers came to be tolerated only as raffish inferiors. Finally, when respectability had fully triumphed, the gamblers often were ejected from the community under the concerted fulminations of the clergy, the chamber of commerce and perhaps the local chapter of the Woman's Christian Temperance Union. But until they were driven out or driven underground, the sporting men enjoyed their day in the sun.

Abilene, Kansas, the earliest of the great staging areas for the eastward rail shipment of Texas longhorns, began to blossom with the arrival of the first beef late in the summer of 1867. Up to this time, Abilene had been, according to an early inhabitant, "a very small, dead place, consisting of about one dozen log huts." Soon the village's dusty streets were swarming with free-spending cowboys and cattlemen, and with gamblers eager to relieve them of their hard-earned cash. Four short years later, Abilene had reached the peak of its prosperity, and notoriety. "I have seen many fast towns, but I think Abilene beats them all," recalled the gunman and frequent gambler John Wesley Hardin. "The town was filled with sporting men and women,

gamblers, cowboys, desperadoes and the like. It was well supplied with bar rooms, hotels, barber shops and gambling houses, and everything was open."

Hardin, surely no stranger to vice in any form, took an appreciative view of Abilene, but others regarded it with less relish. John Haynes, who drove 1,000 yearlings into town and sold them for $8,000, barely got out with the shirt on his back. As he remarked ruefully, his was a fate familiar to "any old trail driver who found himself rich in Abilene, Kansas, in 1871."

The rich and the would-be rich, searching for sport in Abilene, invariably found their way to the famous Alamo Saloon, whose luxurious trappings made it a seductive oasis for men weary of herding cattle across the dusty plains. A cowboy pushing his way through the Alamo's glass doors walked into a long room with a polished bar and gleaming brass fixtures. Nearly every foot of floor space was taken by gambling tables where a man could try his luck at cards or dice.

Another popular spot in Abilene was the Bull's Head Saloon, which was said to have the most expensive faro layout that money could buy. The Bull's Head opened its doors in the spring of 1871 under the proprietorship of Phil Coe, a dapper gambler from Texas, and Ben Thompson, a gunman with a considerable reputation as a professional gambler. For a time, the saloon turned a tidy profit for its two owners. Then, in a chain of events that helped to speed the end of Abilene's days as a gambler's town, Thompson and Coe ran afoul of the town marshal, Wild Bill Hickok.

The trouble seems to have started when Thompson refused Hickok's order to bowdlerize an allegedly obscene painting of a bull that graced the outside of his saloon. Hickok then hired a couple of painters to do the job. Coe escalated the feud by accusing the marshal of prejudice against Texans; Hickok claimed that Coe was running rigged games in the Bull's Head.

Smarting under this accusation, Coe went out on the town with a bunch of fellow Texans who were about to hit the trail for home. (Thompson happened to be away from Abilene recuperating from a broken leg suffered in a buggy accident.)

A townsman who saw Coe and his friends remembered them later as a "band of crazy men. They went up and down the street with a wild swish and rush and roar, totally oblivious to anything in their path." As the

A faro dealer in 1895 in Morenci, Arizona, removes a
losing stack of chips from the table as customers consider
their next bets. Players had to decide quickly; a fast game of
faro commonly let gamblers wager at least twice a minute.

revelers approached the Alamo Saloon, Coe, who was no marksman and seldom carried guns, whipped out a pistol and got off a wild shot. Marshal Hickok, drinking with his good friend Mike Williams at a bar down the street, heard the gunfire and hurried to investigate.

Entering the Alamo at the back, Hickok passed the gamblers at the tables and pushed his way through the front doors to the street, where he confronted the mob of Texans. "Who fired that shot?" he demanded.

Coe, still gripping his revolver, replied that he had shot at a dog. Hickok leveled his two guns at Coe, who also drew a bead on the marshal. It is unclear who fired first. But when the powder smoke drifted away into the night, Phil Coe, a gaping bullet wound in his abdomen, lay writhing in the street. Furthermore, Hickok's friend Williams was dead, shot accidentally by Wild Bill himself as he rushed to the marshal's aid. Coe lingered for three days before succumbing. "He was a gambler; but a man of natural good impulses in his better moments," remarked the Abilene *Chronicle*.

After the rampaging Texas cowboys were well on their way south to their ranches, the mayor and his council told Wild Bill that they were "no longer in need of his services." The local farmers had been constantly battling the cattlemen, whose herds trampled their land and subjected their livestock to foot-and-mouth and other diseases. Local real estate speculators wanted to clear the land of Texas cattle, as well. These interests joined the townspeople, who were genuinely fed up with the gambling and rowdyism of the cattlemen, in proclaiming that Abilene would no longer need a sheriff to keep the Texans in hand because "the inhabitants of Dickinson County will no longer submit to the evils of the trade."

Abilene was dead, at least as a gambling haven. Long live Newton, a Kansas town some 65 miles to the south that was willing to assume Abilene's role as a mecca for cowboys and gamblers, despite the evils.

Newton was a very short-lived cattle town. Its heyday lasted little more than a year before the railroad and the longhorns went elsewhere. But from late 1871 to early 1873 its candle burned brightly. And, of course, its citizens were possessed with "a mania for gambling," in the words of the Topeka *Daily Commonwealth*. Of a full-time population of about 800, Newton harbored at least 80 professional gamblers.

FARO: THE FRONTIER FAVORITE

Faro, sometimes spelled pharo, pharaoh or pharaon, was the West's most played casino card game. A faro table could be found in almost every saloon in almost every boomtown. Bettors could back a card of any rank by laying their chips on a reproduction of the card fixed atop the table. Suits were irrelevant. After the bets were placed, a dealer dealt two cards from a box. Those backing the card dealt first lost; bets placed on the second card won. Bets on other cards were either left for the next play or withdrawn by the players. If a pair was dealt, the bank took half of the money that had been staked on the paired card. Crooked dealers occasionally stacked the deck with many pairs.

On this 1868 Hart's pasteboard package, the makers advised faro dealers to avoid counterfeits by buying only cards "securely wrapped, signed with our name."

These six-sided tokens, called coppers because pennies were used originally, were put atop a bet to reverse the action—that is, to bet a card to lose instead of to win.

Players who ran short of chips could use their chips to place one bet and these oblong markers (left) to place additional ones. Since only one card could lose on any given play, the house could take the player's chips from his nonlosing bet to pay for a markered bet that was a loser.

This abacus-like device, known as a case-keeper, kept track of dealt cards and the gamblers could see instantly how many cards of any rank had been played. This 1860s model sports a rosewood frame, boxwood card faces and ivory counters.

This faro layout *(below)*, also called a spread, organized the wagers. Bets on one card were set on top of the card; bets on two cards at once were put between them.

HIGH CARD

This dealing box, used in Virginia City, Nevada, is made of sterling silver and accented with abalone-shell inlays. An honest box, it allows the dealer to slide out only a single card at a time. Some rigged boxes let dealers check the next card and pull out two at once to cheat the bettors.

The center of their activities was the Gold Rooms, run by Doc Thayer and Bill Pierce. Thayer supervised the gaming tables and was acknowledged as the local dandy, largely because he always kept his coat on and wore his pants outside his boots. Pierce handled the bar. It was said that nearly every man in Newton dropped by the Gold Rooms in the course of a day.

The Gold Rooms was, to say the least, inappropriately labeled. Even by boomtown standards, the place was sleazy. Despite its plural name, it was a one-room building about 60 feet long and 30 feet wide. Sunlight flickered through chinks in the walls of unseasoned lumber, and spider webs festooned its rough-hewn rafters. Its "mammoth" bar was 20 feet long and backed with barrels of the house rotgut whiskey and wine. (Rumor had it that several Newton saloons almost shut down because their liquor was so bad even rough-and-ready Texans could not stomach it.)

But patrons did not come to the Gold Rooms to find elegance and fine liquors. Customers came to gamble and they sat willingly at tables knocked together in much the same crude fashion as was the building itself. The unfinished boards of the square table tops were covered with heavy green cloth, and each table had a small semicircle sawed out of one side. Sitting in that cozy half-moon, the dealers were closer to their game layouts, and had better control of the action.

One of the Spanish monte dealers at the Gold Rooms was "Poney" Reid, whose white hat was a trademark that set him off in any crowd. Nearby sat another monte man, "Trick" Brown, a Texan who seemed to be indifferent to whether he won or lost.

At another table sat John Gallagher, a master at three-card monte, a variation of the shell game that never gave its victim a chance. Gallagher, known as "Three-Card Johnny" for his skill at this swindle, had worked his way to Newton along the Union Pacific's advancing right of way, leaving many a railroad construction worker with empty pockets. Though only 26, he was a veteran at the gambler's trade; it was said that he had started playing cards as soon as he was old enough to tell a club from a spade. Many of his colleagues believed in hitting a sucker hard right from the start, but Gallagher had a different strategy: he played a cat-and-mouse game, letting his victim win a little at first. "He is sure to come back at me again," Gallagher

was fond of saying, "and then I not only get his money, but his watch and revolver besides, if he has any."

As cowboys converged on other Kansas towns, the gamblers bypassed Newton and the Gold Rooms. Some set up their games in Wichita, others went on west to Hays City. Ben Thompson, late of the Bull's Head in Abilene, made his way with many of his fellow gamblers to Ellsworth, where for a time he ran the gaming tables in the back room of Joe Brennan's saloon on South Main Street.

But even Ellsworth, despite such imposing buildings as the stone, brick and stucco Grand Central Hotel, was fated to go the same boom-and-bust route as Newton and Abilene. Along with all the other erstwhile Kansas cattle centers, Ellsworth lost out to a town that was soon being called the "wickedest little city in America" and the "Babylon of the plains." Its name was Dodge City, and the gunslinging gamblers who flocked to its saloons and gambling halls were in no small measure responsible for its colorful reputation.

When Dodge City welcomed its first big wave of Texas cowboys and their thundering herds of longhorns in 1875, it was a town that had already earned a considerable reputation as a center of gambling and other frontier entertainments. It had been founded three years earlier to cater to the soldiers of nearby Fort Dodge and to the hunters who were decimating the buffalo herds that ranged the southern plains (200,000 hides were shipped East during the town's first winter). The tiny community was, in fact, first known as Buffalo City. A newspaper correspondent from Leavenworth, Kansas, visiting Buffalo City just a few months after it had begun to rise from the barren prairie on the north bank of the Arkansas River, counted about a dozen frame buildings and perhaps twice as many tents. Nearly every structure, he noted, "has out the sign, in large letters, 'Saloon.' "

Dodge City soon assumed its permanent name and got down to serious boomtown business. Along the main thoroughfare, Front Street, and in bystreets arose numerous gambling saloons; among them was a pool hall called variously the Billiard Saloon and the Main Street Saloon. Lest anyone fear that its equipment was inferior or rigged, the owner proudly advertised that he provided "round balls! and straight cues!"

Go west, young man—but don't gamble

When the renowned journalist Horace Greeley stopped at Denver in June of 1859, the city was scarcely more than a rude collection of log huts. But typical of many a nascent boomtown, casino gambling already flourished—a state of affairs so appalling to the abstemious editor that he felt forced to act.

In a bad humor from an accidental wound in the leg, and further irritated that his "room" at the Denver House was separated from the hotel's roisterous gaming hall only by a thin canvas curtain, Greeley mounted the soapbox right in the casino to deliver a strong antigambling address.

The speech had little effect. As Greeley telegraphed East, "The visitors of that drinking and gambling room had a careless way, when drunk, of firing revolvers—sometimes at each other, at other times quite miscellaneously—which struck me as inconvenient for a guest with only a leg and a half for dodging bullets. So I left."

Though Greeley departed in a huff, gold seekers by the thousands were pouring in and the owners of the Denver House moved fast to capitalize on the city's boom. They enclosed much of the block upon which the hotel stood and whimsically rechristened their enterprise the Elephant Corral, in deference to its ungainly dimensions.

Soon the Corral was the trade center of Denver, where miners bought supplies off the backs of wagons and purchased a pack mule or two before setting off. Ironically, organized card and dice gambling at the Corral ceased within two years. The owners of the business, whose hotel Greeley had sarcastically dubbed "the Astor House of the gold region," found more profit in running a livery stable than a casino.

Horace Greeley craved "deliverance at any price" from the Denver House.

Gold seekers pack up at the Elephant Corral, Denver's hotel, casino and trading post.

Virtually every Front Street saloon offered billiards as a relaxing accompaniment to drinking, and some of Dodge City's resident pool shooters became quite adept at the sport. One, Jacob Schaefer, graduated to world championship play after perfecting his skills hustling pool at the tables of Beatty and Kelley's saloon. But most of the cowboys, buffalo hunters and others who stormed into Dodge City were pining for indoor diversions more exciting than a gentlemanly game of billiards. Many of them, in addition to downing great quantities of good, bad or indifferent liquor, sought the services of the prostitutes who thronged Dodge City, as they did every other boomtown of consequence. But the most popular pastime in this last big, wide-open town on the high plains east of Denver was gambling.

Even in the popular Comique Theater, which specialized in tired vaudeville acts, the patrons' gambling proclivities were not forgotten. Actor-comedian Eddie Foy, who played at the Comique in the summer of 1878, attempted to evoke its atmosphere many years later: "The songs and patter from the stage at one end; the click and clatter of poker chips, balls, cards, dice, wheels and other devices at the other end, mingled with a medley of crisp phrases—'Thirty-five to one!' 'Get your money down, folks!' 'Eight to one on the colors.' 'Keno!' 'Are you all down, gentlemen?' "

So great was Dodge City's reputation that men for many miles around would save up their funds for one almighty fling. Wrote one local businessman: "There were numbers of people, to my certain knowledge, who would carefully save up from two hundred to five hundred dollars, and then come to Dodge City and turn it loose, never letting up until every dollar was gone. There were others whose ambition was higher. They would save up from five hundred to two thousand dollars, come to Dodge City and spend it all. There were still others who would reach out to five thousand dollars and upwards, and away it would all go, and, strange to say, these men went back to their different avocations perfectly satisfied. They had started out for a good time and had had it, and went back contented."

Perhaps this last statement smacks a bit of chamber-of-commerce boosterism. The frequency of violence in and around the saloons would indicate that at least some gamblers did not leave Dodge City perfectly content, especially if they suspected that they had been

Dance-hall girls and patrons pause for their portrait at a plush betting parlor in silver-rich Tonopah, Nevada. Besides live music, the casino boasted race results by wire and bookmaking on major sporting events.

Professional gambler Riley Grannan was such an openhanded friend to busted prospectors, as well as to other gamblers and prostitutes, that he was eulogized as a public benefactor when he died at age 37.

cheated. Buffalo hunters often turned up in the gambling saloons with large bankrolls. The typical hunter, described by an officer at Fort Dodge as "unsavory as a skunk," was ordinarily an easy mark for prostitutes and gamblers when he came in from the prairie.

One such man, known as "Dirty Face" Ed Jones because he never washed, fought an uphill battle to keep the hide money he earned one season. After selling his skins, he sauntered over to a saloon in clothes stiff with the dried blood of his quarry, his feet wrapped in buffalo skin held on with wire. Ed stood quietly warming himself in a corner, not drinking or gambling. But eventually he was persuaded by a saloon girl to try his luck once at roulette; when he won, Jones was hooked. He gambled all night and lost $2,000 in cash, his hide wagon and even his prized rifle.

Professional gamblers with bulging wallets also arrived to play against other professionals, mingling with amateurs on the customers' side of the faro tables. The *Globe,* a Dodge City newspaper, contrasted the professional gambler and the amateur in an 1879 article:

"The old professional takes off his coat, arranges it on the back of his chair, and sits down in front of the faro table with as much of an air of business and composure as a bookkeeper commencing his daily labor. He bets his 'system' without variation, and his countenance remains calm and immovable whether he wins or loses.

"The other class of gamblers are men who have other means of earning money, but who think they are just as liable to win as those more familiar with the game. They stand around the table until they think they see a card that is lucky, and immediately deposit their spare change on that card, and excitedly await developments. It is only a matter of time when their money is gone and they are left with their hands in their empty pockets, staring vacantly at the board."

Occasionally a highly skilled player, not a professional but one who nevertheless fancied himself a formidable sharp, would visit Dodge City in the hope of luring a few wealthy merchants into a poker game. In 1877 Thomas Carney, a rich businessman who had been governor of Kansas from 1863 to 1865, turned up with genteel larceny in mind. According to an obviously hostile item in the Dodge City *Times,* Carney announced that he had come to town to purchase buffalo hides, although actually he intended to "entice our unsophisticated denizens into the national game of draw poker. The Governor's reputation and dignified bearing soon enabled him to decoy three of our business men into a social game." The *Times* did not mention, and apparently no one bothered to tell Carney, that the three "business men"—Colonel Charles Norton, Robert Gilmore and Charles Ronan—were professional gamblers of renowned talents.

"The game proceeded merrily for a time," the report said, "until, under the bracing influence of exhilarating refreshments, the stakes were increased, and the players soon became excitedly interested."

In Carney's time the game of poker was still in a state of flux. It had been decided only recently that a flush—a hand of cards all of one suit—outranked a straight of five consecutive cards. But the straight flush, five cards of the same suit in sequence, had not yet been declared the premier hand in poker, beating even four of a kind. In those days there were two unbeatable hands: four aces, or four kings and an ace. Obviously, if a player held four kings and an ace, no one else in the

Wyatt Earp's name was a good drawing card for the Northern, a Tonopah, Nevada, saloon. Earp, famed as a lawman and gambler, backed the Northern but left its day-to-day management to a partner.

game could hold the superior hand of four aces. But sometimes poker was played with a 53-card deck that included a joker (also called a "cuter" or "imperial trump") that could be played as an ace. Carney somehow overlooked the fact that he was playing with such a deck. And in this deck, the cuter must have borne a dangerously close resemblance to the ace of spades, because Carney apparently mistook it for that card.

"At last the Governor held what he supposed to be an invincible hand," the *Times* said. "It consisted of four kings and the cuter or 'imperial trump,' which the Governor very reasonably supposed to be the ace of spades." The betting became brisk, with Norton and the Governor raising each other $100 at a crack.

"Governor Carney's eyes glistened with joy as he saw the pile of treasure which would soon be all his own, loom up before his vision, and he hastened to see the Colonel and add the remainder of his funds, his elegant gold watch and chain. Norton was still with the game, and the Governor finally stripped himself of all

remaining valuables, when it became necessary for him to 'show up' his hand.

"A breathless silence pervaded the room as Gov. Carney spread his four kings on the table with his left hand, and affectionately encircled the glittering heap of gold, silver, greenbacks and precious stones, with his right arm, preparatory to raking in the spoils. But at that moment a sight met the old Governor's gaze which caused his eyes to dilate with terror, a fearful tremor to seize his frame, and his vitals to almost freeze with horror. Right in front of Col. Norton were spread four genuine and perfectly formed aces, and the hideous reality that four aces laid over four kings and a 'cuter' gradually forced itself upon the mind of our illustrious hide and bone merchant.

"Slowly and reluctantly he uncoiled his arm from around the sparkling treasure; the bright, joyous look faded from his eyes, leaving them gloomy and cadaverous; with a weary, almost painful effort he arose from the table and, dragging his feet over the floor like balls

of lead, he left the room, sadly, tearfully and tremulously, muttering, 'I forgot about the cuter.'

"The next eastward bound freight train carried an old man, without shirt studs or other ornament, apparently bowed down by overwhelming grief, and the conductor hadn't the heart to throw him overboard. Gov. Carney is not buying bones and hides in this city any more."

It was a rare card game in Dodge City, or in any other of the Western boomtowns, that had such drama or such a spectacularly poignant conclusion. Most gambling proceeded in an uneventful and businesslike fashion, though on occasion Dodge City presented its gaming fraternity with comic vignettes that raised a chuckle for years afterward.

On one notable occasion, a gangly young man in well-worn work clothes strolled into the restaurant operated by James "Dog" Kelley, mayor of Dodge City, and shyly asked if anyone in town played poker. Kelley, whose nickname came from his large pack of hunting dogs, may have felt a certain responsibility as mayor for the welfare of out-of-town visitors. Admitting that poker was played on occasion, he advised the stranger not to get involved in any of the games. "You are no match for these card sharks," he warned. "And besides, in these games the sky is the limit."

The young man thanked Kelley profusely and strolled out to Front Street, where he gawked at the false-fronted frame buildings like a country boy who had never been to the city before. As the worldly Kelley watched him taking in the wondrous sights of Dodge City, he marked him as a wide-eyed bumpkin trying to play at being a Westerner.

That night, the youngster wandered into the Lady Gay Saloon and sat alone at a corner table. He turned down several free drinks, explaining that he never touched liquor, and he seemed content enough just watching the progress of a high-stakes poker game.

The bait was too inviting for one cardsharp. Sauntering over to the innocent, the gambler asked him if he would care to try his hand at a little poker. The young man agreed, but said he probably could not play for long. "I ain't got much money," he admitted.

The Lady Gay's bartender felt sorry for the kid, but not sorry enough to be a spoilsport and discourage him from playing. He felt even sorrier when he saw the

young man ask how to shuffle and deal, and then proceed to handle the cards as if he had 10 thumbs.

But when the playing began, the youth seemed to be blessed with a streak of beginner's luck a mile wide. As he took pot after pot, the gamblers began to wonder if he learned awfully fast or knew more than he had let on. By dawn, only one of his five original opponents was still in the game, and that one did not last much longer. After raking up the chips, the young man cashed them in and walked out the door without a word.

The amazed bartender, who had stayed through the night to watch the game, followed the younger man to the sidewalk. There he saw the youth join a well-dressed stranger, and together the two mounted their horses and spurred them toward the city limits.

Later in the morning, the discomfitted gamblers gathered at Dog Kelley's restaurant for breakfast.

When Kelley learned of the game's outcome, and remembered the young "greenhorn" whom he had warned to stay away from the tables, he observed, "Mark Twain was right; you can't tell how far a frog can jump by looking at him."

Professional gamblers, ex-governors, cowboys and buffalo hunters were not the only lambs fleeced in Dodge City. Soldiers from Fort Dodge were cheated regularly out of their meager pay—in the 1870s a private made $13 a month—and were subjected to verbal and physical abuse in the seamier gambling saloons. In 1878 a group of soldiers returned to the fort and complained to their company commander, who marched them back into town, fully armed, and ordered them to fire several volleys through the side of a particularly offensive establishment. On his command they fired, too high to kill anyone but low enough to terrify the sharps inside. Gunfire on that scale must have been disquieting to the honest citizens of Dodge City as well, and surely did nothing to tone down its reputation as one of the West's most dangerous places.

Some travelers, indeed, feared even to pass through Dodge City on their way to points farther west. In 1877, one timid young man, 15 miles from the city limits, wrote to his father that he had "laid over here to wait for a larger crowd so as to be perfectly safe going through Dodge." On another occasion, the surgeon at Fort Dodge visited a westering wagon train that had halted for the night near the post. He found the settlers gathered in prayer. On the journey they had survived hailstones, floods, thirst and parching heat, raids by horse thieves and attacks by Indians.

"But now, oh, Lord, we face our gravest danger," prayed the minister—or so the surgeon said anyway.

The count and his ill-fated "fairyland"

The Broadmoor Casino was built by Count James Pourtales (*inset*); a genial snob, he attempted to exclude "the lower classes."

Western gambling took on a glamorous, European look with the 1891 opening of the Broadmoor Casino near Pikes Peak in central Colorado. The guiding spirit behind this grandiose establishment was Count James Pourtales, a German nobleman who had been scouring the New World in search of good investments to bail out his impoverished ancestral estate, Glumbowitz, in Prussian Silesia.

Pourtales bought into a huge dairy farm near Colorado Springs, then decided he could do better by founding a resort town on part of the property. To lure buyers of lots, he built a pleasure palace the likes of which had never been seen in the West—"3000 acres turned into Fairyland," as a Denver newspaper called it.

The Broadmoor Casino stretched for 244 feet along a 15-acre artificial lake. Its exterior was graced by 32 Corinthian columns and its rooftop terrace commanded spectacular views of the mountains. Inside, the entrance hall was paneled in dark oak and its double staircase led to a grand ballroom and concert hall, three dining rooms and a salon for the ladies.

The gaming rooms were on the first floor; patrons played against one another, not against the house. Although the count made nothing on the gambling, he hoped to realize a handsome profit on the sale of liquor—which was a major attraction, since nearby Colorado Springs was a dry town.

Pourtales installed a resident orchestra of European musicians, imported a French chef and an experienced resort manager, planted 10,000 trees and stocked his man-

made lake with trout so that his guests could play at being fishermen. To promote his enterprise he even hired a lady parachutist (who promptly landed in the lake) and organized a pony race between wealthy "cowboys" and neighboring Ute Indians.

The opening of the casino on July 1, 1891, was a glittering private affair. A few days later, on the Fourth, a crowd of more than 15,000 swarmed over the resort.

But success was short-lived: expenses were gargantuan, few of the wealthy bought lots in Broadmoor City, and with the Panic of '93 Colorado's main industry, silver mining, came to a virtual standstill. Pourtales declared bankruptcy, and four years later his Monte Carlo in the Rockies burned to the ground.

"Dodge City lies just ahead, and we must pass through it. Help us and save us, we beseech Thee. Amen."

The wagon master's request for a military escort through the sinful precincts of Dodge City was turned down, but the surgeon volunteered to take the wagons through the next morning. He knew, of course, that Dodge City's rowdies were creatures of the night who seldom roused themselves before noon. He knew, too, that the town was not nearly so dangerous as it was sometimes claimed, though there was a grain of truth to the advice that a seasoned cowhand once gave to some younger men: "Dodge," he said, "is one town where the average bad man of the West not only finds his equal, but finds himself badly handicapped."

Much of the gunplay that gave Dodge City its rough-and-ready reputation stemmed from cheating at cards or other games of chance, though at least one slick operator managed a novel way out of a possibly fatal exposure as a cheat. Realizing that his poker opponents suspected him, quite accurately, of secreting an ace up his sleeve, he nonchalantly ordered a sandwich from the bar. When his snack arrived at the table, the sharper flicked the extra card from its hiding place and slipped it into his sandwich, which he proceeded to munch until he had swallowed the incriminating evidence. Someone must have seen his maneuver, however, for he was promptly nicknamed "Eat 'Em Up Jake."

The cattle trade brought on the boom in Kansas, but in much of the inland West, precious metal — and the arts of finding it, mining it and spending it — reigned supreme. The gambling mania that gripped the mining camps was, if anything, even more feverish than the Dodge City craze. Professional gamblers, lured by visions of riches, quickly descended on the mining camps.

When the discovery of silver turned Virginia City, Nevada, into a boomtown during the winter of 1859-1860, the first rushers lived in tattered tents and holes burrowed into the hills. Yet even in those conditions many betting men were on hand to minister to the miners' gaming instincts. In November 1859, a Sacramento *Union* correspondent observed that only about one sixth of the 300 or so inhabitants were bona fide miners. As for the rest, they were "the prospecting gentry, speculators, loafers, and gamblers. The town is full of gamblers and their booths are full every evening."

The largest and most comfortable structure in town was a combination saloon and gambling hall, housed in a 25-by-40-foot tent stretched over a frame of boards.

Gamblers in this place and Virginia City's other entertainment spots worked themselves ragged the first season. The bitter winter cold often kept the miners from their claims, and they took to gambling day and night. Cash was in short supply, and games were sometimes played for interests in mines instead of money.

Denver, which had a brief career as a rough-and-ready boomtown before becoming a supply and financial center for the Rocky Mountain West, was equally well supplied with gambling saloons from its early days.

Gambling by men in high public position was commonplace in Denver, and few of them made any effort to cover it up. At the popular Denver House, a local judge once gambled away 30 city lots in less than 10 minutes, and the county sheriff had to pawn his sidearm for $20 to keep afloat in a faro game. In the 1888 Senatorial election, Republican candidate Edward O. Wolcott was accused by his opponents of losing $22,000 in a night of poker playing at Ed West's gaming rooms. "It's nobody's business but my own," bellowed Wolcott, "and besides, I had won the money at the races the day previous." He went on to win at the polls, too: Colorado voters sent him to Washington for two consecutive terms. (The high-rolling Senator Wolcott later died while on a visit to the gambling capital of Europe, Monte Carlo.)

As Denver became more civilized, its gambling fever abated and sporting men turned to newer, less refined boomtowns. One of the wildest of these was Leadville, tucked away in the Rocky Mountains 75 miles southwest of Denver. Leadville had only 100 inhabitants when it was incorporated in February of 1878. A year and a half later, choking on a population of nearly 15,000, the silver town boasted four banks, 10 dry-good's stores, 31 restaurants and a whopping 120 saloons and 118 gambling houses and private club rooms. Any town where a man could invest $17 in a silver mine and sell his share a year later for a cool one million dollars — as the famous silver magnate Horace Tabor actually did — was ripe for all sorts of hazards of fortune, including games of chance.

For its more righteous citizens, Leadville also sprouted four churches. Pap Wyman's, one of the most

BUCKING BAD ODDS AT ROULETTE

The faint click, click of the roulette ball was a familiar noise in most Western gaming halls, but gamblers who bet on it seldom won. Gambling houses often rigged roulette games with magnets or by tilting the wheels. Even when the games were honest, players bucked great odds. Early American wheels had 28 numbered slots and three unnumbered ones, marked with an eagle, 0 and 00. Though the wheels had 31 slots, the house paid only 26 to 1 on single-number bets and enjoyed a 13 per cent advantage. In the 1890s gamblers got better odds when casinos imported European wheels with 36 instead of 28 numbers: only 0 and 00 cut into the payoff ratios.

This decorated wooden bowl was used in the Southwest to play canute, a Mexican cousin of roulette. A ball, spun down the sloped sides, could stop against one of the 16 slotted wedges or fall into the center.

Two betting layouts and some $20,000 in gold coins and chips flank a roulette wheel in a mining-town casino. The heavy legs of tables like this one were occasionally hollowed out to hide cheating devices.

"You win at will," hawked H. C. Evans & Co. when it advertised this covered roulette game in 1909. The lid, which had to be lifted to see the result, could direct the ball anywhere a cheating croupier wanted.

popular gambling emporiums, had at its entrance a Bible said to be well thumbed—although it is unclear whether it was consulted for spiritual guidance or for some mystic hint of a lucky number to play. Inside this pleasure palace, a newspaperman who visited in 1879 found "every game of chance known to the fraternity in full blast" and behind the bar a huge clock bearing on its face the pious admonition "Please Do Not Swear."

Such displays of piety had little impact on Leadville residents. Their excesses caused heads to shake even in Dodge City, where astonished readers of the Dodge City *Times* were told that their own brawling community had been surpassed in wickedness by the upstart mining town. "This is a fast age," a correspondent wrote, "and Leadville is up with the times. We formerly had the opinion that Dodge City was the banner City for pure cussedness, but Leadville is 40 degrees nearer hell than any City in the Union. You Dodge City folks are Sunday-school children in comparison."

Not least of the reasons for Leadville's fearsome reputation was the occasional presence in its gambling saloons of cool, deadly professionals like Luke Short. Raised in Texas, Short had hit a number of the Kansas cattle towns as a cowboy. There he had been fascinated by the easy life of the gamblers, and he determined to make his way in the world by shuffling cards rather than herding cattle. After a couple of years in Nebraska—where he sold forbidden whiskey to the Sioux Indians—Short moved on to Denver, outfitted himself with fancy clothes, and struck out for Leadville. In a specially made, leather-lined pocket of his trousers he toted a Colt revolver with a sawed-off barrel.

Short arrived in Leadville in late 1878 or early 1879, and he soon had occasion to draw his weapon. The first time, he merely used the heavy Colt to club a barfly who had snickered at his dandified suit and flicked the brim of his tall silk hat. After one or two more such defenses of his sartorial tastes, Short gained considerable respect in Leadville's saloons and gambling dens. Then a local roughneck called Brown decided one night to test the dapper Short's mettle again.

Short was immersed in faro at the time, watching intently as the dealer pulled the cards from their box and matched them against bets made on replicas of cards on a table layout. As Short placed a bet on the layout, Brown leaned over his shoulder. "That ain't the play," he sneered, and he moved the chip to a different spot. Short returned the chip to the place he had chosen and waited for the turn of the card. When he lost, Brown whooped with laughter.

Brown deliberately meddled with Short's bets twice again, determined to provoke the gambler. After the third incident Short turned to him and said evenly, "Stranger, I make the bets with my money. You make 'em with yours."

The words were mild enough but they served Brown's purpose. He responded with a few choice oaths, moved back from the table, and went for his gun. But he was not fast enough. Short whipped out his snub-nosed Colt and squeezed off a quick shot that tore through Brown's face from cheek to cheek.

Brown's wound was not fatal, and Short was not charged with any wrongdoing. It was hardly a crime, said a law officer, for a man to protect his right to bet without interference. Laws were formed on the spot, as they were needed, in a town as rough as Leadville.

Though exonerated, Short did not stay in Leadville long. Instead, he drifted to other Western boomtowns, among them Cheyenne, Wyoming, and Deadwood, in the Black Hills of Dakota Territory. Short's wanderings eventually took him to Arizona Territory, where he dealt faro beside Bat Masterson and Doc Holliday at the Oriental Saloon in Tombstone. Wyatt Earp was there, too, as part owner of the Oriental.

Tombstone's legend began in 1877, when a prospector named Ed Schieffelin found silver on the spot where a friend had told him, "Instead of a mine, you'll find a tombstone." Then came the deluge of miners, claim jumpers, con artists, painted women, gunmen and gamblers. Law and order, of sorts, followed in the persons of the Earp clan and Doc Holliday. But these "lawmen" were a wild bunch; when their sulfurous careers blew up at the famous battle at the O.K. Corral, they were chased out of town by a sheriff's posse. No wonder the entire country, from the White House down, saw Tombstone as a hellhole where at least one murder was committed every day. On May 3, 1882, President Chester Arthur issued a proclamation stating that "it has become impracticable to enforce by the ordinary course of judicial proceedings the laws of the United States" in Tombstone and other Arizona trouble spots, and calling on "insurgents" to "disperse

A Tombstone gallery of high rollers and low dealers

In its heyday, Tombstone, Arizona, was packed with sporting men of every description, from the obscure to the renowned, tinhorn to high roller, blackguard to philanthropist.

Charley Recanzone, head bartender at Billy King's Saloon, dealt for the house as adroitly as he mixed a whis-key sour. Pete Spence was a low-life varmint who held up stagecoaches and spent the proceeds on royal gambling and drinking sprees. After serving a stretch in jail, he switched to a new profession: jumping silver-mine claims. Homer Dubois operated a crooked faro game by using a device he worked with his knee. As a kid, Bones Brannon played faro for jack-knives, using homemade equipment; eventually he set up at the Alhambra, a gambling emporium whose owner, Dick Clark, could fleece a million-aire senator or restore a poor man's lost stake with equal *sang-froid*.

CHARLEY RECANZONE

DICK CLARK

BONES BRANNON

PETE SPENCE

HOMER DUBOIS

CASTING THE LOT

Most hazard operators dropped the dice through a dice horn *(right)*, which was much like two funnels joined tip to tip. Others used a rotating wheel *(below)*, marked with dice symbols, to simulate a throw. Some used a tin hazard horn, originating the term "tinhorn gambler."

THE BAFFLING BOARD

On the hazard board below, players could make short-odds bets on the roll being a high or low number, and long-odds wagers on the chance that all three dice would show the same number, called a "raffle."

and retire peacefully to their respective abodes."

As with all Western boomtowns, there was a reputable side to Tombstone. In this case it was literally one side of Allen Street, the main thoroughfare. Decent folk confined their activities to the shops and restaurants on the south side of the street. But the heart of the town was the north side of Allen Street, where the saloons, dance halls and gambling dens reigned supreme. A tax on the saloons and the equally flourishing red-light district provided the sole support for Tombstone's school system.

The Alhambra, one of the better gambling establishments in Tombstone, belonged to a man who came to be admired and respected as few boomtown gamblers ever were. Richard Brinsley Sheridan Clark was born in Cayuga, New York, in 1838. No one knew why his parents had given him the name of the great 18th Century Irish dramatist, but his later propensity for elegance in behavior and dress accorded well with the playwright's acidulous comedies of manner. In fact, Dick Clark had little education and never wasted his time reading books. Soon after his parents migrated to Saginaw, Michigan, Dick, though still a child, decided that what he wanted most in life was to be a real high roller. Throughout his youth, with single-minded determination, he set about perfecting his technique, learning to cut, shuffle and deal with precision, training his eyes to take in every detail of a game including the strengths and weaknesses of his opponents, cultivating the gambler's controlled detachment.

He played cards with Michigan farmers and lumberjacks, but this small-fry gambling hardly fed his ambitions. Before he was 21, he left his family and turned to the West, the gambler's land of opportunity. By the time the Civil War began, Clark was a veteran player who needed new fields to conquer. He knew soldiers had money and little to spend it on, so he joined the Union Army—not to fight, but to gamble. According to Dick's thinking, a soldier did not earn his pay anyway, so there was nothing wrong with taking it away from him. In this endeavor he was so successful that he re-enlisted for another year after the War ended; the vineyards had not been picked clean. When he was mustered out at last he was a quartermaster sergeant.

By then the Western cattle towns were beginning to boom and Clark got in on the ground floor. He was in

Players and kibitzers gather around a poker table in an Anaconda, Montana, saloon around 1895. A photographer set up the scene — and the club flush held by the player at right — to capture the flavor of a boomtown card game.

Abilene when it all started, in 1867, then moved on to Dodge City, where his winnings were so heavy that he wore out his welcome and had to leave town.

A chance glimpse of the young Dick Clark during his wanderlust years is afforded by "pen portraits of the professional gamblers" sent from robust Newton, Kansas, to the Topeka *Daily Commonwealth* in September 1871. "Dick Clark and Jim Moon deal monte," runs the pertinent passage. "The former's travels have thrown him principally in the southern country. He, too, is widely known, and has the reputation of being one of the best-hearted men and cleverest poker players in the country. His face, while engaged in play, is one of the most impassive and stony I ever saw."

When Clark ran out of cattle towns he began to cultivate buffalo hunters, as he had earlier cultivated soldiers and lumberjacks. Following the men who followed the bison, he migrated as far south as Fort Mobeetie, Texas. He was fond of reminiscing in later years about how he once shot up the place and had to leave in a hurry. Actually, Clark was not fond of violence, but he knew how to handle a pistol when necessary and faced dangerous situations with cool courage.

Once he was held up in his own gambling saloon by a desperate character named Fred Kolan. It was 4 a.m., the customers had all left, and Dick was sitting sleepily counting the take at the faro table with Billy King, a younger sidekick. Kolan, coming up from behind and leveling his .45 at them, told the gamblers to get their hands up and to hand over the money. Dick grinned and said he could not hand over the money with his hands in the air; Kolan let him lower his arms to scrape up the cash. When Dick reached into the drawer and pulled out a fistful of bills of chicken-feed denomination, Kolan ordered him to dig deeper — and then made the error of reaching past Billy King's ear to scoop up some money lying on the table. With lightning speed, King grabbed Kolan's gun arm with his raised right hand; the gun went off, and a bullet whistled harmlessly between Clark's knees. A second later Clark knocked Kolan senseless with the barrel of his six-shooter.

To avoid bad publicity, Dick never pressed charges, merely seeing to it that Kolan left town. But the demonstration was enough to remind the temptable not to be fooled by Dick Clark's quiet, gentleman's manners or his fancy diamond studs and Prince Albert coat.

The Silver Cup paid off when both wheels stopped with a player's color lined up between arrows that were cast into the case.

The drop of a nickel and a tug on the Wasp's crank set spinning a color wheel embellished with five Victorian beauties.

Symbols on the Horseshoe correspond to predictions on the framed card, hence qualifying the machine as a fortuneteller.

Winner's Dice Game, ostensibly a gum machine with cigar bonuses for the lucky, probably was played more often for cash.

Beetles decorate the cast nickel front of Little Scarab, a bar-top roulette machine. The winning wagers were paid in tokens.

The Victor, which could be played for either nickels or pennies, riffled real playing cards to create random poker hands.

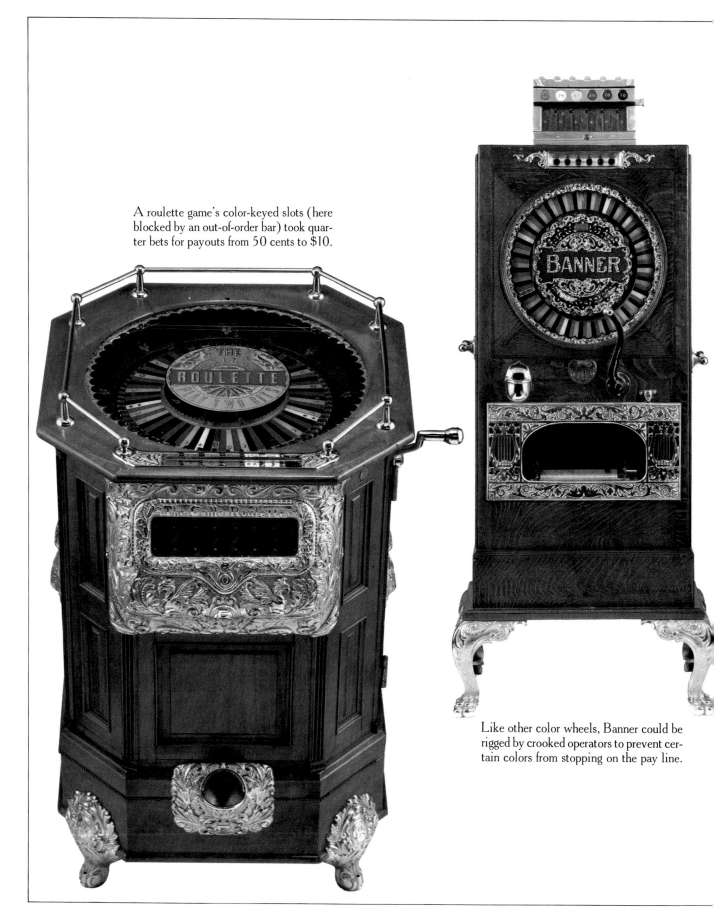

A roulette game's color-keyed slots (here blocked by an out-of-order bar) took quarter bets for payouts from 50 cents to $10.

Like other color wheels, Banner could be rigged by crooked operators to prevent certain colors from stopping on the pay line.

Quintette sometimes chided a player for losing by showing a winning poker hand in one of the five windows he had not chosen.

Cricket challenged a gambler to bounce a nickel through rows of springy pins into the one-dollar slot in the left side.

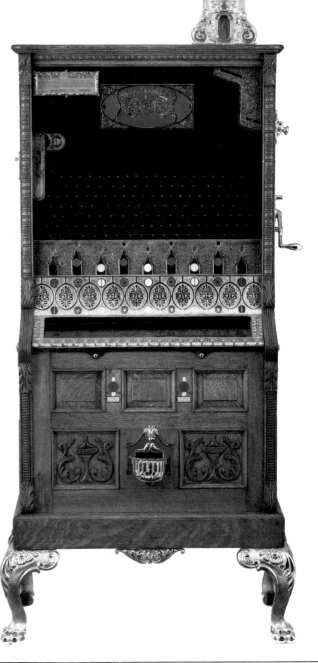

6 | Thundering hoofs and hammering fists

Galloping flat out, four quarter horses churn up a billow of dust as they race along a crowd-lined Socorro, New Mexico, street in 1884.

A barrel of brandy against two horses and five dollars: those were the wagers on a Los Angeles horse race run in 1839. After the race, one rider accused the other not only of blocking his way but of striking his horse and sought a ruling from the local judge. But the magistrate chose instead to fine each rider $10, because their race course was improperly fenced.

That contest exuded the essence of Western horse racing. Westerners would bet almost anything on a favorite steed. And when the law got involved in racing, it usually was not to forbid the sport but to regulate it. Dakota Territory, among others, even ruled that the debts of horseplayers were the only legally binding gambling obligation.

Of course, disputatious gamblers sometimes tried to settle arguments out of court, as many a bloody lip and bruised knuckle testified. And as likely as not, some bystander would wager on the outcome of the altercation as soon as the first punch was thrown, because fisticuffs, like horse races, were among the West's favorite gambling opportunities. And like horse racing, which moved from Main Street to elegant race tracks, boxing moved from sand lots into arenas to provide Western sporting men and visiting Easterners with some of the best fight action ever seen anywhere.

Fast horses, tough boxers and big-time betting

In the spring of 1861, several members of Denver's gambling fraternity organized what promised to be one of the year's most colorful local events—a race between two swift horses named Rocky Mountain Chief and Border Ruffian. Chief, known as "the Greer horse" for the brothers who owned him, was something of a local champion. Border Ruffian was comparatively unknown. He was a newcomer owned by A. B. Miller, a local plunger who along with the brothers Greer arranged the tantalizing test of horseflesh.

The race was to take place in three heats, each a single lap around an oval dirt track variously reported to be either a mile or a half mile in circumference. The winner of two out of three heats would take the purse.

Word of the race spread throughout Denver and the surrounding mining camps. On the big day a huge crowd—including not only high-rolling sports and professional gamblers with their shady ladies but family men with their wives and children—assembled to enjoy the festivities. Few of them seemed bothered by a spell of blustery wind that, according to the *Rocky Mountain News,* "increased to a perfect gale, filling the air with dust and gravel." The sandstorm delayed post time but the racegoers, spirits undimmed, filled in the time with brisk betting and visits to the beer barrels set up around the track.

When the wind died down, the starters walked the well-groomed horses into position. Leading Rocky Mountain Chief by the bridle was a man named Tom Hunt, whom Denver race fans knew as a one-time Border Ruffian supporter. His appearance as starter for the other side must have raised some eyebrows, even

Elias J. Baldwin, audacious speculator in horseflesh, mining stocks and California real estate, takes the pot in a scene he staged to show his amazing skill at cards.

though Hunt had foreshadowed this change of allegiance two weeks earlier when he announced a bitter falling out with A. B. Miller, Border Ruffian's owner. At that time the Greer brothers had accepted his offer of his services. What they did not know was that Hunt had put his money on Border Ruffian.

When the starting gun cracked, Border Ruffian surged forward but Chief did not; Hunt was still clinging to his bridle. Gene Teats, Chief's 14-year-old jockey, frantically yelled at Hunt to let go, and Hunt did so, but only after pulling the horse into a shallow ravine alongside the track. Scrabbling his way out of the loose dirt, the late-starting Chief made a valiant effort to catch up. But Border Ruffian galloped home with several yards to spare and was declared the winner of the first heat.

Outraged cries of "Foul!" filled the air, and losing bettors spilled onto the track with pistols drawn. The treacherous Hunt was permitted to escape with his skin only after he promised to leave town by sundown. The losers paid off their bets on the first heat with much grumbling, and new wagers were placed for the second heat.

The horses jumped off to a clean start, and by the time they turned into the home stretch Border Ruffian had taken the lead again, this time by about 10 yards. At that point a Chief supporter, a Denver gambler and saloonkeeper named Charley Harrison, suddenly appeared riding on a horse alongside the track and urged his favorite on; there were those who claimed that he threatened to shoot the Greer horse's jockey out of the saddle if he did not whip his steed to victory. Whatever the reason, Rocky Mountain Chief did indeed spring ahead, and he crossed the finish line nearly three lengths ahead of his rival.

Despite the contention of Border Ruffian's backers that outside parties had interfered with the race, the judges declared Chief the winner. Several fights immediately broke out at trackside. Border Ruffian's owners, now certain they could not win, withdrew from the contest. Rocky Mountain Chief then ran the last heat alone and was declared the winner of two out of three.

According to some accounts, the Greers enjoyed their horse's winnings hardly long enough to count them. The brothers spent the night after the race gambling with Charley Harrison at his Criterion Saloon. By sunup they had been relieved of their winnings. So the big winner of the occasion was the hard-riding Harrison, who not only won his bet on Chief, but got Chief's prize money as well.

Although the Chief-Ruffian contest had been distinguished from start to finish by boisterous excess, it was not an unusual event. Similar challenges, though not necessarily accompanied by cheating and pistol-point intimidation, were settled almost daily in one or another mining camp or emerging town or at some ranch or farm throughout the West. It is easy to see why. Horse races were exciting events, with an ebb and flow evident to even the most unschooled spectator. Moreover, they were open to the wildest speculations about their probable outcomes—just the thing to bring out the bettor in the bystander.

Gradually, as wealthy men made a hobby or a sideline of breeding horses, Western races became more carefully orchestrated, the crowds grew and betting flourished. Indeed, gambling and a day at the races became virtually synonymous. And when Westerners got around to staging formal stakes races the prizes were sometimes much richer than those back East. In 1873 what was billed as "The richest race in the world" was run at Ocean View Park in San Francisco. The winner's purse was $20,000 in gold. In the same year New York's famous Belmont was worth only $5,200 and Maryland's Preakness a mere $1,800.

Boxing matches underwent a similar development in the West, which became the scene of some of the greatest fights in ring history. Fisticuffs were common among roistering frontiersmen, and it was a short step from gambling on impromptu saloon bouts to betting on organized endurance contests in which the number of rounds was determined by the stamina of the fighters. Noting the popularity of such spectacles, entrepreneurs with a keen eye for profit presented prize fights for the diversion of entertainment-starved miners, lumberjacks and railroad workers. Civic-minded townsmen promoted big-money bouts as publicity devices to attract high rollers to their communities. In doing so they catered to the red-blooded Western male for whom there was nothing more exhilarating than the pitting of man against man or horse against horse—nothing, that is, except gambling and winning on either kind of contest.

Horses had been raced in the West ever since the conquistador Hernán Cortés brought them to Mexico in 1519, and by the time of the California gold rush, wealthy descendants of Spanish noblemen were betting on a grand scale. In 1852 in Los Angeles, Don Pío Pico, who had been the last Mexican governor of California before it was annexed by the United States after the Mexican War, matched a stallion named Sarco against Black Swan, a mare owned by José Andrés Sepúlveda, one of the great landowners of southern California.

According to an eyewitness, "the length of the course was nine miles, or more properly speaking, three Spanish leagues. Everybody in the country was present and the whole country as far north as San Luís Obispo and south to San Diego was depopulated. They all came to see the great race." Black Swan won by 75 yards and Sepúlveda collected what was probably the biggest horse bet that had been made in North America to that time: 5,000 pesos and 1,000 head of cattle.

It was inevitable that betting on horse races should become just as popular among Americans out West as among Spaniards. Almost anyone owning a swift mount was ready to take on all comers, accepting a challenge with anything from a pinch of gold dust to a town lot bet on the outcome.

The horse was not always the principal contestant in equine races. In 1868, a Californian named Edward Whipple declared categorically that no horseman alive had the endurance to cover 300 miles in 15 consecutive hours. Others disagreed and two men bet $2,000 against Whipple's $2,250 that one Neel H. Mowry, an experienced horseman, could accomplish the feat. Side bets against Mowry blossomed as the day of his highly publicized ride drew near, and his chances seemed to be so slim that anybody who was betting for him did so at favorable odds.

TOUTING FOR A GROWING SPORT

During the 19th Century, Western horse racing advertisements like these reflected the development of the sport itself. In the 1835 event in Texas advertised by the broadside at right, the turf was open countryside. As real tracks were laid out at state and county fairgrounds, races drew bettors with eye-catching handbills such as the fold-open cardboard jockey's cap below. By the late 1800s, the West could boast elaborately appointed racing facilities like the Oakland Track in California, which appeared in a newspaper promotion picture *(below, right)* in 1897.

COLUMBIA JOCKEY CLUB

The Races over the Columbia Turf will take place on the 4th Monday in May ensuing, in the town of Columbia. Weights according to the rules of the Turf:

The 1st day.—A sweep stake for one mile, free for any horse, mare or gelding in the Province,—Entrance $100.00

The 2nd day.—One mile and repeat $100.00

The 3rd day.—Two miles and repeat $100.00

The 4th day.—Three mile heats $125.00

The 5th day.—One mile heats, 3 best in 5 $150.00

The liberality of the public spirited proprietors has rendered this one of the pleasantest, and most eligible situations in Texas for the sports of the Turf. It is anticipated by the Club, that the races contemplated will be among the most interesting ever holden in Texas. —Their fine horses are already entered.

Gentlemen at a distance wising to enter horses, and procure stables, will do well to address the proprietor J. H Bell, Esg. or the Secretary of the Club:

By order of the C. J. Club:

A. C. AINSWORTH, Sec'y

Columbia, April 11, 1835.

NEBRASKA STATE FAIR RACES

September 8th to 12th, 1890.

$6,500 in Purses. Entries close Sept. 1st. All purses four monies: 50, 25, 15 and 10 per cent Entrance fee 10 per cent of purse.

Best Half-mile Track: Best Speed Barns: Best Accommodations in all Respects, in the West: Pure water: Hydrants at barn door: Cash paid at the Close of Race. For further particulars address the Secretary,

ROBT. W. FURNAS, BROWNVILLE, NEB.

CALIFORNIA JOCKEY CLUB

At 4:40 a.m. on August 2, Mowry spurred his horse to a gallop. Thirty additional horses stood by to relay him on his 300 laps around the mile-long track at Bay View Park in San Francisco. He rode his own familiar mount for the first four miles, but thereafter changed horses after no more than three circuits of the track, planning to remount the horses as often as necessary to complete the distance. When he had covered 200 miles Mowry was far enough ahead of schedule to take a 20-minute break, and those who had bet against him were dismayed that he still had nearly seven hours to complete the remaining third of his race against time.

Back on the track once more, Mowry pressed ahead, but the effects of his arduous ride were beginning to show; as he came closer to the 300-mile goal he had to be helped to the ground each time he dismounted, and then boosted back into the saddle. Still he kept at it, and at 6:49 p.m. he passed the judges' stand for the 300th time. The ride had taken him just 14 hours and nine minutes. But Mowry was not finished yet. As the few happy winners counted their spoils, Mowry galloped a victory lap around the track—"for luck," he explained. Then he hobbled off to doctor his thighs, chafed raw by loose longjohns.

The unusual nature of Mowry's marathon ride attracted an uncommonly large number of gamblers and curious onlookers, but even the most conventional Western horse-racing event drew big crowds. On July 6, 1872, when a Wichita mare took on a Texas racer at a track just north of Wichita, so many townsfolk turned out that a local newspaper reported that Main Street, for an hour or so, seemed almost deserted." In addition to the thousand or so men who attended, there were five carriages crammed with soiled doves from the lusty cattle town's bordellos and dance halls. Betting was brisk, though the wagers were not large: the reporter who covered the race noted only that "more than a thousand dollars changed hands" on the race, which was won handily by the hometown favorite.

Most of the contestants in the Western races were quarter horses. A compactly built, powerfully muscled runner capable of dazzling spurts of speed for distances up to a quarter of a mile, the quarter horse was the preferred mount of Western ranchers and cowhands. As a work horse, it was ideal for cattle drives and roundups, where sudden, swift moves were often nec-

essary to control the milling herds. As a racer, it was the best thing on four legs for a short, swift dash, and spur-of-the-moment contests became so common that some towns passed laws banning racing in the streets. Many communities boasted of hometown champions that could outrun any challenger.

In 1856 there lived in Lancaster, Texas, just such an equine paragon, a durable quarter horse called Steel Dust. Although nearly 12 years old, not much to look at and lethargic in temperament, he was still capable of bursts of speed astonishing enough to infect the whole town with champion-horse fever. It happened that the citizens of nearby McKinney, Texas, were in the throes of the same disease. They regarded a big bay stallion named Monmouth as well-nigh unbeatable. Inevitably, Steel Dust and Monmouth were scheduled for a contest. Both horses were famous along the frontier; each had won many races. And when they finally came head-to-head, some 2,000 people—an enormous crowd for Texas at that time—gathered at McKinney from as far as 100 miles away to see the action. The Foote House, the town's only hotel, reportedly put up 32 guests in its four rooms; everyone else camped out. In Whiteley's Saloon seven bartenders poured whiskey until the supply was exhausted.

Residents of both towns plunked down all their available cash on their favorites and then put up livestock, wagons, tracts of land, saddles and bridles. By the time the final bet was made it seemed conceivable that either Lancaster or McKinney might be economically demolished by the outcome.

The race was run at half a mile, down the main street of town, apparently a compromise between Steel Dust's quarter mile and the full mile that Monmouth usually raced. The jockeys were Tom MacKnight, a young black boy, aboard Steel Dust, and Bob Rudolph, a white horseman who handled Monmouth.

The race did not last long. A spectator posted near the finish reported what he saw as the horses approached him: "Big Monmouth was taking gigantic strides but the little mousey horse was making two jumps to old Monmouth's one. They were not long strides but he was making them faster. Steel Dust was on the left with the little Negro boy lying squat down on his back. Bob Rudolph was thrashing Monmouth but I could not see that the Negro boy was doing

anything to Steel Dust. Before we could think, they were at the finish line, Steel Dust three lengths in front. Steel Dust turned sharp off the track and plowed to a stop. Old Monmouth kept right on and ran into a thicket, sweeping Bob off his back (both jockeys rode bareback) and disappearing from view, crashing off down into the woods."

For the next two days, according to reports, a great caravan of wagons, buckboards, traps and surreys wound its way south from McKinney to Lancaster, carrying the plunder that Steel Dust had won. Not much was heard of Monmouth in later years but Steel Dust founded a line of outstanding quarter horses that would remain prominent for decades.

A certain virulent strain of champion-horse fever attacked individuals rather than whole communities, and one of its victims was a wealthy New Mexico rancher, Lucien B. Maxwell, who would learn that horse racing could be an expensive hobby for both himself and his loyal neighbors.

In the summer of 1866, Maxwell decided to promote a race on a crude track on a ranch near the sleepy village of Las Vegas, New Mexico. His prize horse was a fast mare named Fly, a breeze at short distances and the winner of several contests against respectable opponents. Flushed with confidence, Maxwell let it be known across the Southwest that he would back Fly against any challenger for a wager of either $1,000, $5,000 or $10,000—challenger's choice. So certain was Maxwell that his horse would win that he brazenly offered to cover any challenger's expenses for bringing a horse to the race and taking the defeated animal home afterward. Maxwell, of course, would add to his own winnings with healthy side bets in livestock and cash.

Two sporting gentlemen, remembered only as Foster and Rogers, snapped at Maxwell's bait and brought up from El Paso a little-known but promising bay named Bald Hornet. They were ready, they announced, to go for the highest stake.

By race day a crowd said to number some 5,000 fans had shown up in the vicinity of the track to make camp and place a wonderful miscellany of bets. The renowned Kit Carson himself was there, a celebrity among the mass of assembled ranchers and cowhands, miners and army officers, women and children, Indians and Mexicans, traveling men and professional gam-

James Ben Ali Haggin's enthusiasm for fine horses was demonstrated by the grandiose scale on which the lawyer-rancher-capitalist pursued his passion. His California stable of 2,000 thoroughbreds was the largest that was ever assembled.

The rags-to-riches climb of Irish-born Marcus Daly led from a Brooklyn leather factory to part ownership of the Anaconda Copper Mine. The Montana stud farm he established with his fortune was second in size only to that of James Ben Ali Haggin.

The bristly mustachioed Theodore Winters' turf achievements were the pride of two states. He was California's first serious breeder of thoroughbreds, but later moved to Nevada, where he raised his finest horses, including the famed Norfolk.

In a painting called *The Last Race*, the gaily decorated "Opposition" flies past a rival rig between Oakland and San Jose. Stagecoach races and the betting they engendered were a brief sidelight of the rivalry between coaching lines in the 1860s.

blers. All together they laid out a reported $300,000 on the race in the form of currency, gold dust, gold mines, cattle herds, a piano and a variety of clothing ranging from serapes to baby slippers.

Hopes and bets ran high on Fly. Kit Carson, for one, had so much riding on Maxwell's perky mare that he jokingly threatened to shoot the jockey, a little fellow named Betts, if he failed to win the race. Betts's wife, a domineering Mexican woman of formidable proportions, was loyal to the core; she put every cent of her $800 savings on the fleet-footed Fly.

Excitement was at fever pitch as Fly and Bald Hornet, the latter ridden by one Johnny Frey, tore off from the starting line and headed down the mile-long track. Fly was looking good, eating up the course with her usual sizzling speed, and visions of easy money danced in many a head. But there was one thing the mare's backers had failed to consider: Fly, a superb short-distance sprinter who had started her career as a cattle pony, had never been extended beyond a half mile, while Bald Hornet was a durable full miler. With a sinking heart the overconfident Maxwell saw his pride and joy fall back after the first couple of quarters, and Bald Hornet surged ahead to win the race by a good three lengths.

Kit Carson, seeming almost serious this time, whipped up his shotgun and trained it on the unfortunate Betts, but was restrained by three local stalwarts. The real threat to Betts turned out to be his wife, her $800 wiped out in the debacle. When a downcast and apprehensive Betts crept home after his bad day at the track, Mrs. Betts—so the story goes, and there is none to deny it—bundled him into a sack and vindictively slung him into the Purgatoire River. Fortunately, four of Betts's neighbors rallied around as he bubbled his way toward extinction, and fished him out just in time.

Maxwell himself was spared violence but very little else. By the time all the bets were paid off he had lost $15,000 in cash and a considerable number of horses, sheep and cattle. In addition to that, he found that he was having to provide food for an enormous gathering of indignant and indigent losers until they set out for home.

Maxwell's mistake was to underestimate the competition, but then that is what makes a horse race, as John Markesbury of Mesa, Arizona, found out when the entire countryside steadfastly refused to underestimate his horse Crowder. Markesbury had acquired Crowder, a well-bred quarter horse, on an 1882 jaunt east to Missouri. For the next two years, he trained the horse diligently until it was ready to race.

Crowder was so ready that in meet after meet he left the field trailing far behind him and carried away the purse for his proud owner. Whether the competition was one horse or eight, it made no difference—Crowder was always the winner, even when Markesbury offered the competing horses head starts of 20 to 35 feet. After a while most Arizonans simply refused to race against Crowder, and almost everywhere that Markesbury went in search of a race for his wonder horse he ran afoul of uncooperative horsemen and self-contradicting racetrack posters with such slogans as "Free for all—Crowder barred."

Crowder's racing career came to a premature end when some sportsman injected the horse with a debilitating drug before a race, leaving him too sluggish to compete against even an untrained saddle nag. It was the last straw for Markesbury; he retired the much-abused Crowder and quietly made plans for a new racing and wagering technique that would leave many betting men scratching their heads and wondering how Markesbury was able to outsmart them.

Crowder had sired two colts, and Markesbury trained these mounts not only as racers but as work horses, training them to pull a wagon with a heavy load. The older colt, in particular, showed impressive sprinting speed, and it was with this animal that Markesbury intended to make up what he had failed to win with Crowder.

Too well known at home in Arizona to pull off his scheme there, Markesbury traveled to Texas with a mule team, the two Crowder colts, the aging Crowder himself and a freckle-faced kid.

When Markesbury learned about a race in the making, he would send the youngster ahead to mingle with the race-track crowds. After a discreet interval, Markesbury himself would arrive on the scene in a wagon drawn by the two colts. Looking over the race horses at the track, he would say something like this: "These are pretty fair ponies, I guess, but back in Arizona where I come from they use this kind to run cattle on. Why, I've got a workhorse here. . . ." Or else he would tout his pair as a powerful pulling team and offer to match them against any of the other heavy haulers around. Then he would subtly change his tune and wind up betting that one of his work horses could whip one of the fancy race horses.

The trick worked every time. Horse-proud Texans were only too happy to wager their money on a seasoned Texas race horse—a leadpipe cinch to beat a lumbering work horse. Delighted chortles at the prospect of putting the Arizona rube in his place grew even merrier when Markesbury called for a volunteer jockey and a silly-looking freckle-faced boy stepped out of the crowd, allowing as how he had ridden a burro so he sure could ride a horse.

He could indeed. As the little caravan moved on through Texas, Markesbury's sensational colt and expert jockey wiped smug smiles off a good many faces while picking up thousands in purse money and side bets. Finally, in Fort Worth, Markesbury called it a day, after winning $2,500 plus side money in a quarter-mile race against the fastest quarter horse in that part of Texas. Having proved that the work-horse stunt was a sure money-maker, and realizing that a wise man quits while he is ahead, he sold his traveling stable—the two colts and Crowder himself—for more than $7,000, and went home a rich man.

Betting-mad Westerners did not restrict their race wagering to contests of horseflesh. A more unusual event than anything ever cooked up by the ingenious Markesbury took place in New Mexico in 1888, following a convivial conversation on the relative capabilities of horses and men. Dr. W. S. Bolton of El Paso, Texas, argued that a bicyclist could outpace a horseman over a long-distance course. J. W. Clayton, a New Mexico cattleman, disputed it, and the two men arranged to test their hypotheses with a race for a purse said to be worth $5,400. It was agreed that the race would be run from the Timmer House in Silver City, New Mexico, to the railroad hotel in Deming, about 50 miles to the south. Bolton was permitted to name the cyclist of his choice, and Clayton was allowed to choose the horse and rider.

After examining a number of mounts, Clayton purchased Rattler, a long-legged horse known for his speed and endurance as well as for his meanness. Casting around for a rider who would be able to manage this spirited steed, Clayton found the man he was looking for in a seasoned horseman named J. E. Wilson. At Bolton's request, an experienced racing cyclist named H. J. Kennedy came down from Denver, surveyed the route, and announced that he would attempt the rugged course if a new two-wheeler was positioned every 10 miles along the way.

There was considerable public interest in the race as the riders buckled down to strenuous training on the road between Silver City and Deming. Each man faced different problems. Wilson would be riding an unpredictable horse that reacted violently to spur and whip and sharp sounds. Kennedy would be pedaling over an obstacle course of a road that was far from ideal for even the most accomplished cyclist: 10 or 12 miles through a recently washed-out canyon, a long stretch of rocky outcroppings and loose pebbles, and six miles of heavy sand. Bettors were as divided on the outcome as its sponsors, Bolton and Clayton.

At 6:30 a.m. sharp on race day, Mayor Jack Fleming of Silver City fired his six-gun to signal the start. Rattler bucked wildly at the report, lunging about in every direction except toward Deming. An excited Wilson nudged him with a spur, which riled the horse even more and wasted precious seconds while Kennedy pumped his bicycle into the distance.

According to one version of the race, the cyclist was almost seven miles out of Silver City before the horse began to gain on him. He continued in the lead for several miles, sailing on serenely as if oblivious to the thundering hooves coming up behind him. Then, when the rocky stretch loomed up, Wilson made his move with Rattler. He delivered a couple of stinging whacks with his quirt—a chancy tactic, considering his mount's aversion to such persuasion—and the irate beast thundered past the bicycle, kicking a shower of dirt and pebbles into the cyclist's face. Kennedy spluttered, lowered his head into the storm and pedaled his two-wheeler furiously to regain the lead.

He never did. For mile after mile Wilson kept Rattler, kicking up pebbles like buckshot, squarely ahead of the bicycle. Kennedy, helpless and tiring, had to drop back. Horse lovers cheered as Rattler galloped across the finish line at the railroad hotel in Deming. He had run the 50-mile course in three hours and 40 minutes, claiming a national long-distance record.

One hour and seven minutes later a winded and disgusted Kennedy straggled up to the hotel. The cyclist's supporters swarmed around him, denouncing Wilson in unprintable terms and claiming that the cowboy had deliberately fouled their man by forcing him to ride amid a fusillade of rocks. But the voices of winning horse players drowned out the complaints of losing bicycle backers, and the race stood as run.

Wild-eyed Western gamblers loved to bet on novelty events like horse-and-bicycle races. But there existed a saner class of bettors, men with an empirical turn of mind who preferred serious races and who studied the race horses' parents and past performances for promise of future victories. And for that, horse race aficionados required an organized system of professional races, legitimate race tracks and, above all, a network of dedicated breeders to supply the pedigreed horseflesh necessary to make betting on the nags a true challenge of divination.

The West's first major thoroughbred breeding venture germinated in a spirited rivalry between two dedicated turfmen, Theodore Winters and Judge Charles H. Bryan. The hot competition between the two led Winters to bring in from the East the horse that was to become the granddaddy stud of California winners.

The men were neighbors when the struggle began. Theodore Winters, a rich Sacramento speculator nicknamed "Black T." for his luxuriant black moustache, raised thoroughbred race horses on the Rancho del Sierra near Virginia City, Nevada. In the same town, Charles Bryan, a former California judge, had a law practice that earned him more than enough to support a fair stable and feed an appetite for betting on horses.

On many a weekend at local race tracks in Nevada or in California, Charlie Bryan matched his horses against those of Black T. And on as many a weekend he went home a losing bettor with a losing horse. Exasperated by repeated failure, Bryan nipped off to Kentucky in 1864 and, for the handsome price of $12,000, purchased a sleek four-year-old stallion named Lodi. Put through his paces at the San Jose race track in California, Lodi ran effortlessly ahead of all contenders. At last Bryan had a winner to beat Winters who, in the meantime, had purchased an impressive Kentucky-bred horse for himself: a three-year-old champion named Norfolk.

When Charlie Bryan confidently challenged Winters to race a horse against Lodi, Winters was ready with Norfolk. Three two-mile heats were scheduled to take place on May 23, 1865, at Ocean View Park in San Francisco, to be followed by a rematch on another track at a later date.

Race fans everywhere, particularly in California and Nevada, went into a frenzy of excitement as newspapers spread the word of the contest. Betting pools materialized all over the country. For a mere five dollars, anyone could enter. "Wives neglected their puddings to dabble in pools," one reporter declared, "and men gathered in saloons and street corners to talk about the races." As far away as New York City, side bets were placed to the tune of $150,000.

Some 8,000 fun-lovers were reported present at the San Francisco track on race day, but not every spectator was a singleminded racing fan. One trackside reporter had a haughty sniff for some of those in attendance. "Harlotry was there in profusion," he wrote, "girls with painted faces and sepulchral smiles, and loud blasphemous talk. It was their outdoor saturnalia." For most of the sports fans present, however, the meet was a significant event in the history of Western racing—a two-out-of-three-heat duel between two im-

peccably pedigreed bluebloods, for a purse of $2,500.

There was considerable excitement and curiosity among the spectators as the two horses were led to the starting line. Most racegoers were familiar with Lodi, but Norfolk, making his first appearance at a California track, was something of an unknown quantity. In contrast to the well-behaved Lodi, he seemed a bit skittish, and many bettors, particularly the women, took this as a point in Lodi's favor. But persistent trackside rumor had it that some knowledgeable plungers were offering odds of 5 to 4 on Norfolk.

At the start of the first heat, such optimism seemed misplaced. Charlie Bryan's Lodi took the inside track and a quick one-length lead, which he held to the half-mile mark. Then Norfolk closed the gap, and at the end of the first mile he had left Lodi trailing by nearly a length. But Lodi regained the lost ground and caught Norfolk at the finish line. The judges called a dead heat, and all bets were off. But most of Lodi's supporters, impressed with his showing at the finish, bet him in the second heat, convinced that the Bryan horse still had the winning spirit. Perhaps the jockey would make his move a hundred yards earlier this time, and Lodi would overtake Norfolk at the wire.

It was not to be. Lodi took an early lead in the second heat, but Norfolk swept by to win by nearly four lengths. Jubilant bettors rushed to collect their winnings on Norfolk, then offered odds of 5 to 2 against Lodi for the final heat, which Norfolk won handily by five lengths. Lodi fared no better in two rematch races run the following September. After the third defeat, Bryan had had enough of horses and racing in general and Lodi, Norfolk and Winters in particular. The judge retired from active racing and sold the disappointing Lodi.

But Winters' Norfolk proved to be the pride of his stable, as indefatigable and successful a stud as California had ever seen, siring a galaxy of stakes winners and making Winters the acknowledged father of California breeding and racing.

A generation later, there were dozens of California breeders, chief among whom was San Francisco's James Ben Ali Haggin, a former Kentucky lawyer whose middle name came from his Turkish grandfather. Settling in San Francisco in 1850, Haggin made a fortune during the gold rush through land purchases and mining investments. Around 1880 he acquired the 44,000-acre Rancho del Paso on the northeastern outskirts of Sacramento, where he took up thoroughbred breeding on an extensive scale.

Between 1881 and 1891 his horses captured a good many prized racing purses in the West—as well as in the East, where the greater prestige of the racing events made up for the risks to horses on the long and hazardous journey from California—and offered a rich harvest to legions of bettors. But in one of Haggin's major victories, he was unable to wager on his winner.

In 1886 Haggin took his horse Ben Ali, a spectacular success on California tracks, to Churchill Downs for the Kentucky Derby. Reckoning that a Western horse shipped two thousand miles across country shortly before a big race would go to the post a long shot, Haggin was hell-bent on cleaning up a packet by betting heavily on Ben Ali. Much to his consternation, however, the Churchill Downs's bookmakers called a strike for the day of the Derby, the track owner having

Convinced that racing horses had, at one point in their stride, all four feet off the ground, Stanford got photographer Eadweard Muybridge to take this sequence that showed a trotter in mid-air.

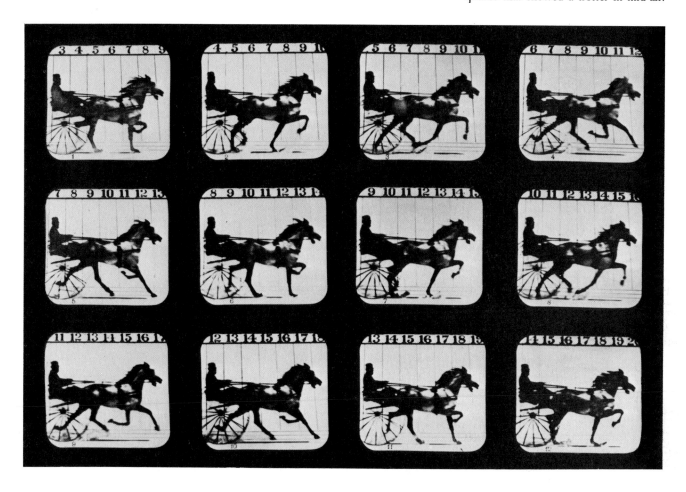

demanded three times the usual fee for permitting the bookies to operate.

Haggin raged, pleaded, even offered to pay the difference between the standard and inflated bookie fee; but all his ploys failed and the bookies remained on strike. Ben Ali won the Derby but Haggin lost his chance to make a killing.

Some wealthy horsebreeders, such as Leland Stanford, were not interested in betting on their horses. A native New Yorker, Stanford made his name in the West as governor of California and founder of Stanford University, and he made his fortune as a czar of the Central Pacific Railroad Company. Stanford's interest in horses began, as he once explained, "through ill health. My doctor had ordered a vacation for me and had told me I must go away on a tour." Although advised to leave as quickly as possible, the overworked railroad tycoon was not able to get away.

Instead, he recalled, "I bought a little horse, that turned out to be remarkably fast, and it was in the using of it that I became interested in the study of the horse and its actions."

It was a costly hobby. In 1876, Stanford purchased some land close to San Francisco and expanded it over the years into an 11,000-acre ranch. There he bred trotters and trained them in something similar to a progressive school for humans—pioneering methods that altered the course of harness racing. The nursery pampered young horses with every conceivable comfort to ensure their physical and emotional well-being. Neither oaths nor an angry tone of voice were allowed in the presence of the foals. Future champions were trained from the beginning for speed rather than endurance—this was the opposite of conventional training wisdom—and schooled at a rate that matched their individual abilities.

Bodine, although foaled in New York, raced in California and was dubbed "The Trotting Whirlwind of the West." In 1877 he defeated Leland Stanford's aging star Occident (*opposite*) four times.

BODINE. The Trotting Whirlwind of the West.

Stanford's methods produced spectacular results. Horse after horse trotted into the winner's circle, forcing other trainers and breeders to adopt Stanford's methods if they hoped to remain competitive. Harness racing profited immensely from these developments, as did the betting public, which generally preferred to wager on horses that trotted quickly than on horses that trotted slowly.

Stanford placed himself rather above all this. Ever the doting headmaster, he would settle into a swivel chair in the infield of the kindergarten track and intently study his pupils, caring far more about their progress than about the money they might win at the races.

Hundreds of miles to the south, near Los Angeles, Elias J. "Lucky" Baldwin was breeding fine thoroughbred horses, working as hard to improve Western thoroughbred racing as Stanford was to improve harness racing. But there the similarity between the two men stopped. Stanford had an analytical mind; Baldwin often acted impulsively. Stanford's demeanor was sober almost to the point of priggishness; Baldwin, although not a drinking man, was a high liver. Stanford earned his fortune step by logical step; Baldwin lucked into most of his millions—as his nickname indicates.

In the 1860s, Baldwin bought numerous shares in the rich silver mines of Nevada's Comstock Lode. He had accumulated the money for this venture through years of labor at miscellaneous enterprises that ranged from itinerant peddling and horse trading to running a livery stable in San Francisco.

Baldwin hung onto his silver stocks through ups and downs until 1867, when he sold shares in three mines as the value of the stock peaked. Then he locked the depressed stocks of other mines in a safe, left instructions with his broker to sell them if they reached his original purchase price, and took off on a lengthy tour of the Orient.

Back in San Francisco the next year, Baldwin learned that the stocks he had ordered sold at a break-even price had soared to unbelievable heights. The old horse trader shrugged philosophically and called upon his broker to buy up a few more low-priced shares—only to find that the stocks had not been sold after all.

The California-bred Occident rose from bakery-cart nag to 1873 world record holder. His rags-to-riches success as much as his speed made him popular with California bettors throughout his long career.

The California Wonder OCCIDENT, owned by Gov. L. Stanford.

In his haste, Baldwin had forgotten to give the broker a key to the safe. "By gad!" Baldwin blurted in a rare burst of emotion; when he had recovered his poise he sold the neglected shares and became an instant multimillionaire.

Thereafter he was known as "Lucky" Baldwin, though he steadfastly denied that luck had anything to do with his success.

Baldwin had always had an eye for fine horses, but he did not begin his career as a serious turfman until the 1870s, when he bought two prize stallions, eight mares and the 8,000-acre Rancho Santa Anita in the San Gabriel Valley not far from Los Angeles. All this formed the nucleus of a racing stable and breeding farm that was, for a period of about 25 years, one of the most successful in America.

Baldwin lived in great style, as befitted a bonanza king, entertaining the cream of the nouveaux riches and a string of beauteous actresses. One of his frequent visitors and fellow racegoers was ex-lawman Wyatt Earp, well known in sporting circles during the '80s and '90s. Earp raced trotters and thoroughbreds,

which he often worked out on Santa Anita's half-mile training track.

Earp's wife, Josephine, became well acquainted with Baldwin, and recalled later that he was an exemplary character who did not drink, smoke or swear. She also made the startling claim that he never bet on his own horses. Baldwin may not have bet in her company but he certainly did on other occasions, once losing a $20,000 side bet on one of his star mares, Molly McCarthy.

On his way to success and riches, Lucky Baldwin earned a reputation as a womanizer and sharp operator. In the eyes of many of his contemporaries, Mrs. Earp notwithstanding, his only redeeming features were his intense interest in horses and his scrupulous honesty in all matters concerning breeding and racing. As Edward Morphy, editor of *The California Turf* in the 1890s, wrote of Baldwin years later: "His name is known throughout the sporting world, but I never knew but one good thing about him; he never threw a race."

Such faint praise was not Baldwin's idea of crowning glory. What he wanted above all, in his declining years, was to open the biggest and best public race track in America on his own property. And in December 1907, he presided over the inauguration of the elegant and commodious Santa Anita track, considered by many enthusiasts to be the best in the West, if not in the nation. *The San Francisco Call* was almost reverent in its coverage of the event. "Lucky Baldwin has realized the greatest ambition of his life," it observed. "Nearly eighty years of age, he has suffered many reverses and achieved many successes, but the climax of his career, his fondest hope, was the establishment of a modern racing plant on his famous ranch, Santa Anita.

" 'I desire no other monument,' said Baldwin when the first day's races at his new track had been run. 'This is the greatest thing I have ever done, and I am satisfied.' " The *Los Angeles Express* was considerably less enthusiastic, and made snide remarks about the booze that flowed freely both inside and outside the grounds, and the touts, bookies and gamblers who arrived for the opening festivities.

Bookmakers, named for the ubiquitous notebooks in which pioneering practitioners of the art had recorded and computed odds, were in full flower at Santa Anita that day. As at most tracks, they occupied a circle of elevated stalls near the finish line. Stalls were equipped with blackboards, used to post the odds on each horse in each race. According to one account of Santa Anita's first round of races, the betting ring was "so jammed with excited men that you had to squirm and wriggle through like a weevil boring through cheese."

Bookmakers were almost indispensable to the operation of a race track, replacing an earlier and wildly impromptu betting system in which spectators dashed frantically about seeking to line up wagers with other fans. Bookmakers established an orderly betting process that made it convenient for anyone to participate.

Some bookmakers operated on a grand scale. One, George Rose, based in San Francisco, had five assistants running bookie stalls at Western tracks, and employed 33 clerks to tally bets and compute odds. At one series of races lasting 24 days, he won $50,000.

A bookie generally posted opening odds that were based on his personal assessment of each horse's prospects. As the race approached and betting intensified, a bookie adjusted his odds to assure that he could pay off the winning bettors after a race with money wagered by the losers and leave himself a comfortable margin of profit. One means to this end was to lower the odds on favorites and to raise the odds on unpopular horses. This maneuver attracted bets away from favorites and in favor of longshots, thereby assuring a pool of losers' money to pay off the winners. Generally, bookies at a track offered roughly the same odds. For one thing, betting trends were similar throughout the circle of oddsmakers; for another, bookies kept an eagle eye on their neighbors' blackboards to remain competitive.

At its best, oddsmaking was more art than science, so it was possible for bookies to make financially disastrous mistakes. To narrow the margin for error, successful bookies cozied up to jockeys, trainers and stablehands in search of inside information on the condition of each horse. Then, armed with a fair notion of who the winner was likely to be, they dispatched touts to circulate among gullible bettors and spread the word that a nag with no chance of winning was a sure thing. Eager to make a killing, suckers would rush to the bookie's stall, lay their money on a sure loser and make the bookie a sure winner.

Among the touts on hand for opening day at Lucky Baldwin's Santa Anita track was one who seemed to stand several cuts above most members of his profession. "He is fashionably and rather sportily dressed," recalled one racegoer, "with the inevitable field glasses hanging from his shoulder. When the horses are led in the paddock to be saddled for the race, he stands in front of one of them, leaning on his light cane watching the grooms with a most critical and severe air as they unwrap the binding from the horses' legs. You are not sure, looking at him, whether he owns all the horses or just this one, or whether it's the track. He says nothing—just stands there with a magnificent air of self-satisfaction and sufficiency."

For all his lordly airs, this classy tout's job was simply to deceive the betting public, though it was said that he worked with such persuasive style that he could "lose your money ten times running and meet you on the eleventh day at the paddock gate with the same magnificent air of condescension—and probably get your money again to bet and divide."

Track owners generally tolerated such hanky-panky on the part of bookies. The public wanted to gamble,

Scenes of "Lucky" Baldwin's Rancho Santa Anita decorate playing cards made, with the owner's usual flamboyance, for his adjoining

and horse-race entrepreneurs feared that gate receipts would plummet if the bookies were barred; moreover, bookmakers paid dearly for the privilege of setting up their stalls and blackboards. It was not uncommon for track owners to demand that each bookie pay $100 every day he opened his stall.

Most bookies accommodated all comers, no matter how small their bets. But some, like a man known by the curious name of Virginia Carroll, had little use for penny-ante gamblers. Once, when the ill-tempered Carroll was having a streak of bad luck in calculating his odds, a farmer paused in front of Carroll's stall and perused the blackboard. Waving his umbrella to attract the bookmaker's attention, the farmer called out, "Give me one dollar on April Shower."

This incident was too much for the long-suffering Carroll. Snatching the umbrella from the farmer's grasp, he hurled it into the stands and then bawled out to his bemused clerk: "Five umbrellas to one umbrella against April Shower!"

Bookies were forced to deal with such pikers as the umbrella-toting farmer, and they also had to contend from time to time with big operators who were clever enough to beat them at their own game. One such plunger was George E. Smith, who got his gambling start in Pittsburgh and was given the nickname "Pitts-burgh Phil" to distinguish him from another betting man who was also named George Smith.

While playing the horses at the Bay District track in San Francisco in the 1890s, Phil started to suspect that conniving owners and trainers were rigging races that had left him a loser to the tune of about $50,000. One day while he was sitting in the grandstand contemplating his losses, a jockey named James Forman "Todhunter" Sloan sat down next to him and struck up a conversation. Sloan, whose grandiloquent nickname had evolved from his being called "Toad" because of his short legs, proved to be a talkative sort. Through his discussion with Sloan, Phil confirmed his suspicions that many of the jockeys—including Sloan himself—were being bribed to hold back their mounts and fix the races.

Phil decided to turn the tables and win back his losses from the bookies. He figured that one good jockey—and Sloan was one of the best American jockeys ever—riding to win would regularly finish first in races where other jockeys were riding to lose, even if his horse was not the fastest. So Phil offered to guarantee Sloan a flat $400 for every race that he won, more money with less risk than the jockey earned by cheating. "I'll do it," said Sloan. "I'll put all I know into every race that I ride. You can bet on me every time."

216

Oakwood Hotel. His passion for breeding fast thoroughbreds made Baldwin one of the most successful American turfmen of the 1890s.

Phil replied that, in order to conceal their complicity for as long as possible, he would bet on Sloan only if he rode the best horse, but that he would pay him the $400 whether or not he had bet on him.

Sloan began to win race after race, just as predicted. Phil, to avoid rousing the suspicions of bookmakers who might wonder why one man was putting so much money on a single jockey, employed agents to place his wagers in the betting ring.

Unfortunately for the bookies, the scheme worked superbly. By the end of a month, Phil was almost $80,000 ahead. But other bettors had noticed that Sloan seemed to be winning an uncommonly large number of races, and began betting heavily on the jockey, thus ruining the odds on his mounts.

Phil knew that his game was up for good when he chanced to get into a conversation with a bookmaker who mentioned that he suspected there was something fishy about Sloan's constant victories. In the future, said the bookie, he would not be offering favorable odds on any horse ridden by Sloan, and most of his brethren in the betting ring were taking the same precaution. Within days, Pittsburgh Phil had packed his bags and headed back for the Eastern tracks. Only later, when Phil began telling the tale himself, did his bookmaker-victims realize what had happened to them.

Next to horse racing, probably no sporting event was closer to a Westerner's heart or more likely to induce him to bet his bottom dollar than a fight to the finish between a pair of hammer-fisted boxers, professional or otherwise. Western boxing had a long and lusty history. The sport was particularly relished in the mining towns, whose citizens—possibly because of the speculative and sometimes dangerous nature of their occupations—were enthralled by the excitement of man battling against man.

Railroad construction crews enjoyed bare-knuckle blood-letting as much as miners did, frequently staging hotly contested bouts on Sunday mornings. Rival camps would choose their champions, put up a purse of $50 or so, and then gather outside a saloon to watch the stalwarts slug it out. They fought under London Prize Ring rules: a round ended only when one fighter went down; there was no limit to the number of rounds, and a match lasted for as long as both fighters could throw a punch.

Betting was brisk at such affairs, and conflict was not always limited to the boxing ring. In 1863, when a referee at a prize fight in Virginia City, Nevada, ruled after the 14th round that one of the contestants had lost the match because he had delivered a foul blow, gunfire and fist fights erupted at ringside as the

Bookmakers like George Rose, sporting the derby in this 1898 program of the Pacific Coast Jockey Club, were celebrated figures. A

GEO. ROSE, THE POPULAR BOOKMAKER.

bookie's assistants included spies who reported on competitors' odds and paddock men who assessed the condition of the horses.

AND HIS STAFF OF ABLE ASSISTANTS.

disgruntled bettors refused to honor their losing wagers.

One of the best-known boxers of the early West was a Denver blacksmith named John C. "Con" Orem, who gained considerable fame—and won a good deal of money for his partisans—with his 102-round victory over the Briton Enoch Davies in 1861. About 2,000 spectators gathered on the outskirts of Denver to observe this match. Possibly because of all the gold dust carried by eager bettors, the bleachers collapsed under the weight of the crowd. No one was hurt outside the ring that day, but inside the ropes Con Orem thrashed his opponent so severely that Davies took two weeks to recover.

Not long after the Davies fight, Orem retired from the ring and reopened his blacksmith shop in Denver. There he learned that a famous Western boxer, like a gunfighter with a reputation, was sometimes hounded back into the arena by his past. Challenged disparagingly by one Hugh O'Neil to fight for a $5,000 purse, Orem felt compelled to step back into the ring. There he did battle for 185 rounds; the referee finally declared the fight a draw and all wagers were canceled. But Orem made it up to his fans in a rematch some months later, when he beat O'Neil on a foul.

By 1895, a Texas saloonkeeper and sportsman named Dan A. Stuart had decided to offer Western boxing fans a considerably more edifying spectacle. What Stuart had in mind was a prize fight between James J. "Gentleman Jim" Corbett, the heavyweight champion of the world, and Robert Fitzsimmons, holder of the world's middleweight championship.

Boxing had undergone substantial changes in form and reputation from the rough-and-tumble days of the Orems and O'Neils. The brutal London Prize Ring rules had generally given way to the slightly more refined Marquis of Queensberry regulations. Padded gloves were mandated for the boxers. Though fights could still continue for any number of rounds, under the new rules rounds were to last three minutes each and the match was over when one fighter failed to rise by the count of 10.

At the time, scarcely a state in the union allowed public prize fighting within its borders, either because of the mayhem that occurred within the ring or because of the gangs of unsavory gamblers, bookies and assorted cheats that seemed always to congregate at ringside.

The ambitious Stuart pressed on anyway with his plans for the Corbett-Fitzsimmons match, a gambling opportunity that the betting public would be a long time forgetting. But it would be nearly two years before fans could lay money on the fight.

Texas had no law against boxing, so Stuart selected Dallas as the battleground. Stuart had promised a purse of $15,000. To add to the action and excitement—and perhaps to convince the public that it would be a fair fight—Corbett and Fitzsimmons bet an additional $10,000 against each other. Sparing neither effort nor money, Dan Stuart confidently began building an arena. Construction was well under way when the promoter and eager bettors were dealt their first blow.

Texas Governor Charles Culberson refused to permit the match. There would be no prize fighting in his state, he declared; it brought in too many undesirable elements. There was no law on the books to back him up, but Culberson was undeterred: he convened a special session of the legislature and pushed through a bill prohibiting boxing contests in the Lone Star State. End of round one.

Stuart was down but not out. He turned his attention to Hot Springs, Arkansas, whose citizens were readily persuaded that a prize fight offered great profit-making possibilities for their town. Then Dan Stuart was floored for the second time. From Governor James P. Clarke in Little Rock came a notice that there was to be no fight.

What followed is not completely clear. Corbett's manager, William A. Brady, claimed many years afterward that he and Stuart, along with Corbett and Fitzsimmons, were summoned to the state capital. There, he said, the fighters were put in the custody of two tough-looking sheriffs, each of whom seemed itching to add another notch to his gun. Governor Clarke then announced that he did not intend to go to the expense of convening the legislature to pass a law that would stop the proposed fight. "I have a simpler way," he said. That way was to permit his lawmen to carve their notches if Fitzsimmons and Corbett so much as batted an eye at each other while in his state, after which the fighters would be shipped home in pine boxes.

Bowing to the inevitable, Dan Stuart continued the search for a site for his prize fight. He finally located it in Carson City, Nevada.

For several years, Nevada had been suffering an economic decline, and desperately wanted some spectacular attraction to bring in spending money and publicize the state. The Corbett-Fitzsimmons contest seemed made to order, and on January 29, 1897, Governor Reinhold Sadler signed an act of the legislature that made Nevada the only Western state to specifically authorize public prize fights.

Fitzsimmons, meanwhile, had not been idle. Just a few months earlier, in San Francisco, he had been in a match that demonstrated why boxing had fallen into such disrepute. Fitzsimmons was heavily favored to be the winner during the weeks preceding the fight, however, on the day of the event the betting shifted to his opponent, Tom Sharkey; the word was out that the referee intended to hand the match to Sharkey. What added spice to such rumors was the identity of the official: he was Wyatt Earp, the well-known frontier marshal and gambler.

When Earp stepped into the ring and peeled off his coat, it was apparent that the two boxers were not the only ones prepared for action. Buckled around the old lawman's waist was a large revolver, which was promptly removed by a police captain. Later, Earp remarked to his wife that he had carried a gun for so long that "I forgot I had the damn thing on." Even so, he was fined $50 for carrying a concealed weapon.

As far as Fitzsimmons' partisans were concerned, the hidden pistol represented the least of Earp's malfeasances that night. They contended that, round after round, the usually eagle-eyed Earp was blind to obvious fouls committed against Fitzsimmons by Sharkey. But in the eighth, Fitzsimmons seemed to settle the issue when he floored Sharkey with a hard slam to the body followed by a vicious blow to the head. As Sharkey lay on the canvas, Earp stood over him and counted to 10. Then the referee reached down and waved the fallen Sharkey's arm in the air. Fitz-

A miner competing in a 1904 Tonopah, Nevada, drilling contest pounds a steel bit into a granite block. Spectators at these mining town competitions bet on who could bore the deepest hole in 15 minutes.

simmons, he ruled, had thrown a foul punch, and Sharkey was the victor.

The bettors who lost their shirts on Fitzsimmons claimed that Earp had been involved in a fix, and called his decision the "greatest scandal of the modern ring." Earp, it is said, dismissed such charges as "rubbish," and his wife later claimed that he, like his friend Bat Masterson, had bet on Fitzsimmons and lost heavily on Sharkey's win. Whatever the truth might have been—and boxing fixes are difficult to prove—the controversy surrounding the disputed decision gave boxing a bad name in California for years.

The pall over boxing in California stopped at the Nevada state line, however, and preparations continued apace in Carson City for the Saint Patrick's Day bout between Fitzsimmons and Corbett. Stuart supervised the construction of an arena on the outskirts of town. Sales of tickets, ranging in price from five dollars to $40, got off to a brisk start and reporters flocked into Carson City to cover what was billed as "The Battle of the Century."

The hopeful citizens of Carson City predicted that 30,000 big spenders and high rollers would crowd into town for the fight, and anticipated that the bout would attract a high class of sporty capitalists and even some nice ladies.

As it turned out, all of the rosy predictions were sadly off-target. After the initial flurry of local ticket-buying, sales dropped off sharply since the out-of-town fans were understandably doubtful that the twice-postponed fight would ever take place. Only six or seven thousand people turned out for the event—and these, as Nevada journalist Alf Doten noted in his diary on March 15, included a large proportion of "pugs, gamblers, newspaper reporters, scrubs, whores and sons of bitches in plenty."

Doubts that kept fans away from the fight had little effect on their betting. Wagering was brisk as March 17 dawned and the fighters weighed in, Fitzsimmons at 167 pounds, Corbett at 183. Nevadans tended to favor the graceless but hard-hitting Fitzsimmons in spite of his weight handicap. Cornish miners also put their money on the Cornwall-born Fitzsimmons, and the boxer's loyal Chinese cook urged Orientals from San Francisco to take a flier on his boss as well. Miners of Irish extraction supported the Irish-American Cor-

bett, as did Eastern connoisseurs, who considered him a more scientific boxer than Fitzsimmons. At fight time, Corbett was the national favorite at 5 to 3.

With veteran Chicago referee George Siler officiating, the fighters bounced out of their corners shortly after noon and slugged away more or less evenly for the first five rounds. Then, in the sixth round, Corbett went all out and punished Bob Fitzsimmons with a flurry of well-placed jabs. According to one report, blood was "flowing freely from Bob's mouth and nose" and dribbling almost down to his soft leather shoes. In the frantic ringside betting, in which the odds were changing from round to round, Corbett had become the 5 to 1 favorite.

Then Corbett battered Fitzsimmons to his knees. Siler began the count. Mrs. Rose Fitzsimmons leaned over the ropes and screamed at her husband to get up. Fitz rested until the count of nine, and then rose. Bet-

ting at ringside was that he would not last 10 rounds.

In the seventh round he rallied astonishingly, while Corbett became increasingly wild, his punches frequently missing the mark. Fitz, his wife yelling advice and encouragement through the ropes, pummeled away at a tiring Corbett. In the 14th round, Fitzsimmons feinted a right to the jaw and landed a pile driver of a left in the pit of Corbett's stomach at a point just under the heart—a blow that would become famous as the "solar plexus punch." Corbett dropped to the mat, clutched feebly at the ropes, and distantly heard referee Siler counting him out.

For lucky bettors who went along with the doughty Fitzsimmons despite the odds against him, the fight was a bonanza. But for Stuart and Nevada it was less than the moneymaker of the century. It appeared at first that Stuart had lost his shirt because of the expense of his false starts in Texas and Arkansas and poor atten-

dance in Nevada. But when the movie of the fight was distributed, it grossed three quarters of a million dollars and saved Stuart from ruin. The fight brought little money into Nevada, but the enormous publicity it engendered was not forgotten by the state's boosters and businessmen, who figured there must be a way to turn such intense public attention into cash. The citizens of Goldfield were the first to discover it.

Goldfield, born of a rich gold strike in 1902, had rapidly developed into an exuberant boomtown. By 1906, with a stock exchange of its own, several prosperous banks and an abundance of gambling dens and saloons, Goldfield was afire with plans to publicize its attractions and sell stock in its mines. In July, civic leaders met to discuss a number of proposals, including one to dig a huge pool in Main Street and fill it with fresh beer twice a day. Then Tex Rickard, a Goldfield saloonkeeper, came up with the more practical public relations scheme of securing for Goldfield a title bout between two well-known lightweights, Battling Nelson and Joe Gans.

George Lewis Rickard had been, in the course of an adventurous career, a Texas cowboy, rancher and town marshal, a successful fortune hunter in the Klondike and a lifelong gambler. At the time he turned his multifarious talents to the fight-promotion game he owned a controlling interest in The Northern, a gambling and drinking establishment in Goldfield that was generously described by rival saloonkeeper Douglas Gillespie, proprietor of The Owl, as "the biggest sporting house in America."

Rickard knew how to promote a fight. Dipping into his own and other bulging Goldfield pockets, he raised a $30,000 purse for the event. The prize astounded the boxing world and made newspaper headlines, for it was the largest ever to be put up for a boxing match. When the fighters accepted the bid, Rickard displayed the $30,000 in the window of a Goldfield bank, neatly stacked in piles of freshly minted $20 gold pieces. This stunt caused another sensation and led to yet more front-page stories. Mine operators, stock promoters, gamblers and other worthy Goldfielders cooperated enthusiastically in further publicizing the fight by financing the circulation of 37,000 promotional postcards and 30,000 letters. On the tide of this unprecedented publicity campaign, a horde of newspapermen

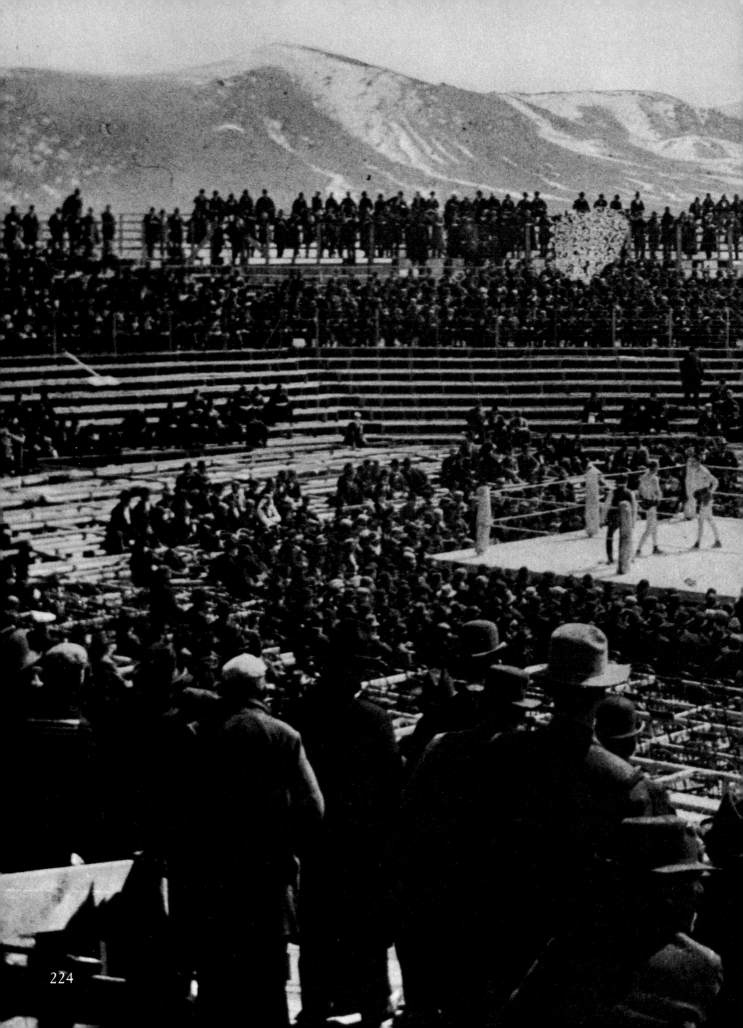

In front of a Carson City crowd of less than 7,000, Jim Corbett and Robert Fitzsimmons meet in their twice-postponed 1897 battle. The fight, recorded by movie cameras concealed in a ringside booth, ended when underdog Fitzsimmons knocked Corbett out in the 14th round.

JEFFRIES
VS. JOHNSON

RETURNS FROM THE BIG FIGHT
BY SPECIAL WIRE
DIRECT FROM THE RINGSIDE TO

Las Vegas Hotel

JULY 4   JULY 4
First Class   Accommodations

BEALE & HORDEN
LAS VEGAS - NEVADA

His face bloodied and swollen, Jim Jeffries grapples ineffectively with heavyweight champion Jack Johnson in their 1910 Reno bout. One of many "white hopes" to face Johnson during the black boxer's seven-year reign, Jeffries was favored 10 to 6. Bettors elsewhere—including fans lured to the Las Vegas Hotel by the broadside opposite—got a round-by-round telegraph account of Jeffries' defeat.

surged into Goldfield to report prefight activities and cover the match, which was scheduled for Labor Day.

Giving an additional fillip to the forthcoming event —and arousing a great deal of interest among bettors— were the vastly different techniques and reputations of the two fighters. Oscar Matthew Battling Nelson, who had been born 24 years before in Copenhagen, Denmark, was credited with having a granite jaw and the thickest skull bones since Neanderthal man. His strategy in the ring was to allow his opponents to wear themselves out by slugging away at his invulnerable hulk while he worked on them with low blows and other foul tactics. On one occasion, asked by a sportswriter why he had so viciously and repeatedly butted a willing but aging fighter in an exhibition bout, Nelson had replied: "Butt him? I didn't butt him. I was only rubbin' my hair in his eyes."

Nelson came to Goldfield accompanied by his manager, Billy Nolan, who was a cynical and hard-nosed character. Nolan had insisted that his fighter be guaranteed $22,500 of the purse—which had since grown by $3,500—win or lose.

Nelson's opponent, Joe Gans of Baltimore, was an elegantly scientific black boxer nearing 30. He had besmirched his record by throwing several fights at the behest of his erstwhile manager. This double-crosser had cleaned up by betting against Gans and then had dropped him because, he explained, he did not wish to be associated with a dishonest fighter. Thus Gans came to Goldfield with neither a manager nor the funds to put up the $5,000 weight-and-appearance forfeit demanded by Billy Nolan. Enter L. M. "Shanghai Larry" Sullivan, a freewheeling stock manipulator.

Sullivan had earned his nickname as operator of a sailors' rooming house years earlier in Seattle, where his sideline was procuring reluctant seamen for crew duty on the China run. Now he proceeded to tie up Gans, taking charge of his affairs and putting up money for the forfeit as well as for the fighter's training expenses. Gans's side of the bargain was simple: he had to defeat Nelson, or else.

George Rice, Sullivan's business partner, later recalled Sullivan's admonition to the fighter: "Gans, if you lose this fight they'll kill you here in Goldfield;

227

they'll think you laid down. I and my friends are going to bet a ton of money on you, and you must win." Gans promised to do his best, and as proof of his good intentions he bet his share of the purse on himself.

Tex Rickard, who was betting on Nelson, had chosen George Siler, the same man who had officiated at the Corbett-Fitzsimmons match, to referee the fight. Siler was noted for his impartial honesty, but Sullivan was taking no chances. When the referee arrived in Goldfield, Shanghai Larry took him aside and accused him of prejudice against blacks, and reminded him that Nelson was a notoriously dirty fighter. Siler promised that he would show his fairness to Gans by giving him the benefit of every doubt, and the conversation, according to Rice, ended with a warning from Sullivan: "Remember, if you don't keep your word you'll have just as much chance of getting out of this town alive as Gans will have if he lays down! You understand?" The referee understood.

As the day of the fight drew near, Gans was the 5 to 3 favorite, despite his reputation for taking dives. Betting ran high on both boxers. "It looked like the California days of '49," wrote a reporter from the New York *Evening World*. "Miners came in with their buckskin bags of dust and nuggets. Here and there a miner would offer to bet his gold mining claim against another." The local miner's union, after insisting that Gans prove his fitness in a rigorous physical examination by the union's own doctor—Gans passed with flying colors—bet its whole surplus fund on the black fighter.

For the first 10 rounds of the bout, such hopeful wagers seemed well placed. The agile Gans fell to his task with a will, outboxing and outslugging his lumbering opponent. Then in the 11th round Nelson's manager, Billy Nolan, grew impatient and instructed his man to start playing rough. Nelson obliged with wrestling holds and a rich assortment of butts, gouges and low blows, all illegal under the Queensberry rules. In the 15th he tripped and fell. Gans reached out a helping hand and pulled him to his feet; Nelson, hanging on with one hand, hammered at Gans with the other, and followed up with a kick to the shins. The odds at ringside lengthened to 3 to 1 on Gans, but at that price drew no takers.

Siler, perhaps mindful of his fate if Shanghai Larry Sullivan disapproved of his refereeing, repeatedly warned Nelson about his continued fouls against Gans. But Battling Nelson kept right on gouging and butting, urged on by Billy Nolan's cries of "Foul him! Foul him!"

Despite the punishing pace, both men diligently slugged away until the 42nd round, when Nelson struck Gans in the groin with a vicious blow that sent him rolling to the canvas. Gans might have faked the injury, but screams of "Foul! Foul!" nevertheless ricocheted across the arena, Shanghai Larry yelling loudest of all. Pale and shaken, Siler did the only thing possible. He disqualified the foul-punching Nelson and declared Joe Gans the winner.

Gans, the hero of the hour, hobbled back to his dressing room, where he disclosed that he had been fighting since the 32nd round with a broken bone in his left hand.

Tex Rickard, the promoter, and Goldfield, the host city for the fight, were in better shape than Gans. The gate receipts went well beyond $60,000, an unprecedented haul for a bout in a small mining town. After paying off the fighters and settling miscellaneous bills, Tex netted $13,215 in personal profits—pin money, perhaps, but enough to start him thinking about a new career. Goldfield's mine shareholders and speculators reaped an incalculable bonanza in low-cost publicity that helped inflate the prices of their stock, and within a few months the little town climbed to dizzying heights of prosperity. The good times lasted until 1910—and then the bubble began to deflate. Flood, fire, drastically dwindling gold production and the collapse of overpriced stocks transformed Goldfield into a ghost town within a few years after its heyday.

By then Tex Rickard had moved on to the greener pastures of Ely, Nevada, where he opened another Northern—this one a hotel—and awaited an opportunity to exploit his new-found talents as a ballyhoo artist and put on another big show for the gambling public. The chance came to him in 1909 with a fight between Jim Jeffries and Jack Johnson.

James J. Jeffries had retired from fighting in 1905, an undefeated heavyweight champion. The title passed to Tommy Burns of Canada, who lost it in 1908 to John Arthur Johnson, the Texas-born son of a black preacher. Reaction in the sporting world was a racist outcry for a "white hope" to recoup the crown. The best prospect was Jeffries, and after months of pressure, he announced his comeback and started training at his alfalfa farm on the outskirts of Los Angeles. He and Johnson agreed to meet in the ring sometime during July 1910.

Boxing promoters fell over one another to submit their competitive bids for handling the match. Among the bidders was Tex Rickard, whose offer was embellished with characteristic—and effective—showmanship. Sealed proposals from the would-be promoters were ceremoniously opened in Hoboken, New Jersey, on December 1, 1909, in the presence of Johnson—Jeffries was inexplicably absent—the bidders and a gaggle of newspapermen. All the envelopes contained a written bid and a certified check for $5,000. But Rickard's envelope showered fifteen $1,000 bills onto the table along with the check.

After that display of cash, the bid itself—a package that guaranteed the fighters at least $101,000—was an anticlimax. All eyes were riveted on the money. Jack Johnson, a perennially broke free spender, was deeply impressed. "Those checks may be all right," he reportedly said, "but they don't look so good to this baby as those bills with big numbers on them." Rickard's offer was accepted over others that appeared at least as attractive.

Jeffries was the favorite from the start. He was, after all, the great white hope; he had never lost a fight; he had spent more than a year getting back in shape and was reported by eminent physicians to be in perfect condition. But contributing to Jeffries' popularity with the bettors was the word that the fix was in. The rumor was, plausibly enough, that Johnson had agreed to throw the title bout on the understanding that Jeffries would retire permanently after the fight. As former champion, Johnson would then reclaim the crown.

Persuaded to stage the bout in San Francisco, despite California's legal prohibition of prize fighting, Rickard rented an empty lot in the Bay City, made arrangements to build a 30,200-seat arena, and started taking ticket orders. Rickard, having a wonderful time providing colorful copy for the newspapers, steadfastly denied the persistent stories that Johnson would take a dive. In fact Johnson, determined not to degrade himself, his race or the championship, had not agreed to throw the fight to Jeffries.

Odds were running about 10 to 6 for Jeffries, and wagers were astronomical. One Clarence Berry of Los Angeles bet $50,000 on Jeffries against $35,000 laid on Johnson by a Fred Meyerstein of San Francisco. With money like that riding on the outcome of the match, it was crucial that the fighters settle on a referee who would be scrupulously fair and observant. As Thomas A. Dorgan, a sportswriter and cartoonist noted later: "Every day the talk was of a fake, frameup, double-cross. No matter where you went you were bound to hear some of that crooked chatter. There was too much money bet. The man selected had to be purer than the driven snow. Picking the right man seemed impossible."

But Jack Johnson had a brilliant idea. He suggested Tex Rickard for the referee, and Jeffries readily agreed. The betting public warmly seconded the choice: Rickard was not betting on the fight; and his only interest in the whole affair was to make money by presenting a successful boxing spectacle.

Rickard philosophically assumed the added burden. Then, with $133,000 worth of ticket orders in and well over $30,000 spent on the stadium and other expenses, he received a staggering setback. The anti-boxing element of California used cries of fix and fake to persuade Governor James N. Gillett to enforce legislation already on the books and prohibit the fight. "We've had enough of prize fights and prize fight promoters," the governor announced little more than two weeks before the July 4 fight date.

Rickard's howls of protest were in vain. The governor's decision was final. Badly out of pocket and running short of time, Rickard sped by train to Nevada, that state of last resort, and made hasty arrangements to transfer the fight to Reno, whose indulgent city fathers offered to build a 20,000-seat arena for him in record time. It was completed the day before the fight.

At noon on July 4 the fight fans began to troop into the arena—cowboys, farmers, gamblers, ex-boxers, pickpockets and sportsmen from all over. It was an amiable crowd, and everyone seemed happy—everyone except Jim Jeffries who, having come to the realization that he had no chance whatever against Johnson, had become moody and withdrawn.

Although some fans continued to think the fight was fixed, odds on the outcome went to even money almost

as soon as the boxers stepped into the ring, and it was evident by the third round that the onetime champion had little chance of regaining the title. His splendid physique was a façade. "The great Jeffries was like a log," the Associated Press reported. "The reviled Johnson was like a black panther, beautiful in his alertness and defensive tactics. Jeffries could not reach the black man effectively. The blows landed with nearly all the speed taken out of them. It was like hitting a punching bag."

In the 15th round Johnson slammed Jeffries halfway through the ropes, and stood over him as he staggered up at the count of nine. Johnson battered him down for a second time, and then for a third. Cries of "Stop it! Stop it!" came from all sides, and Jeffries' own seconds called on him to quit. At that, Tex Rickard placed his hand on Johnson's shoulder and declared him the winner.

For those who had believed in Jeffries or doubted that the fight would be honest, the outcome was a stunning blow. For a moment the crowd was silent, and then the arena exploded with cheers for the man most of the spectators had bet against. "Hundreds," reported a correspondent, "swallowed the bitter pill of financial loss." Johnson and Jeffries were not among these losers. Johnson won $70,600 and Jeffries $50,400 in purse and Rickard's bonus money; later they took in more from movie rights. As for Rickard, the move from California to Nevada had been a costly but not disastrous one. His gate receipts amounted to $270,775 —which was almost $100,000 more than the take for that year's five-game World Series—and after paying all of the expenses he was left with a tidy profit of $60,000 or more.

Tidiness of that kind was a Tex Rickard trademark. For nearly three decades, it identified an array of successful endeavors that ranged from his Northern Hotel in Ely to cattle ranching in Paraguay after the Johnson and Jeffries fight. Then Rickard stormed New York, where he staged pugilistic spectacles that lay beyond the capabilities of Eastern promoters and gave Americans some of the best fights they had ever seen or bet on. It was fitting somehow that the boxing capital of the East became the last arena for Tex Rickard, a classic example of the rough-and-ready Westerner coming to show those know-it-all Easterners how it was done.

231

The night they shut Nevada down

By the end of the 19th Century, nearly every Western state and territory had laws regulating or prohibiting gambling. Antigambling legislation was widely regarded as a badge of respectability by lawmakers who wanted to clean up the wide-open frontier image of their domains.

Nevada was the last state to crack down. In 1909 it passed an antigambling law making it illegal to so much as flip a coin for the price of a drink.

The law went into effect on October 1, 1910. The night before, patrons mobbed the few gaming houses that had not already closed in anticipation of the deadline. In Reno, respectable townswomen who had never darkened a casino door showed up in hordes to inspect the houses and make a few daring wagers. Longtime customers had to fight their way to the tables to place their last bets. Promptly at midnight, all play ceased. "Stilled forever is the click of the roulette wheel, the rattle of the dice and the swish of the cards," reported the *Nevada State Journal* the next day.

The eulogy was premature. Within three weeks, the same paper informed its readers: "If you are properly armed with the high sign and the counter sign, and the address, it is said that there is a place in town where the roulette wheel spins nightly and where the faro bank is dealt as of old." Throughout the state, gamblers had matter-of-factly set up operations underground. There the games continued to flourish until Nevada legislators, deciding that the state needed the tax revenues and tourist business generated by gambling, legalized it again some two decades later.

On Nevada's last night of legal gambling in 1910, customers jam the bar of the Louvre, one of Reno's three gambling halls. Curious women who had crowded the casino were asked to leave at 7 p.m.

234

from the David R. Phillips Collection. 172: Courtesy Pioneer's Museum, Colorado Springs, Colorado—Courtesy Denver Public Library, Western History Department. 174, 175: Benschneider, courtesy Museum of New Mexico; courtesy California Historical Society/L.A. Title Insurance and Trust Collection—John Zimmerman, Collection of Robert C. Pollock. 177: From *Billy King's Tombstone*, by C. L. Sonnichsen, Tucson: University of Arizona Press, 1972 (5). 178, 179: John Zimmerman, Collection of William R. Williamson (2). 180, 181: Courtesy Library of Congress. 183: John Zimmerman, Collection of Frank Roza Jr. 184: Benschneider, courtesy James Andrews, Leadville, Colorado (22). 186, 187: Courtesy Denver Public Library, Western History Department. 188: Courtesy Marshall and Frank Fey Collection. 189: John Zimmerman, Marshall and Frank Fey Collection. 190: John Zimmerman, Collection of Frank Roza Jr.—Bill Malone, Collection of Jack Williams; Henry Groskinsky, Collection of Jack Williams. 191: Henry Groskinsky, Collection of Jack Williams—John Zimmerman, Collection of Marshall and Frank Fey; John Zimmerman, Collection of Frank Roza Jr. 192, 193: John Zimmerman, Harrah's Automobile Collection, Reno, Nevada (2); Henry Groskinsky, Collection of Jack Williams; John Zimmerman, Collection

of Frank Roza Jr. 194, 195: John Zimmerman, MGM Grand Hotel, Antiques, Las Vegas, Nevada. 196, 197: Joseph Smith photographer, David R. Phillips Collection. 198: Courtesy California Historical Society. 201: Courtesy Beinecke Rare Book and Manuscript Library, Yale University—Courtesy Nebraska State Historical Society (2); courtesy California Historical Society. 202, 203: Courtesy Wells Fargo Bank History Room. 205: Collection of The National Museum of Racing, Inc., Saratoga Springs, New York—Courtesy Montana Historical Society—Courtesy Nevada Historical Society. 206, 207: Courtesy The Bancroft Library. 210, 211: Stanford University Museum of Art, gift of Jane Lathrop Stanford; Stanford University Museum of Art, Muybridge Collection. 212, 213: Courtesy Library of Congress (2). 215: John Zimmerman, Harrah's Automobile Collection, Reno, Nevada. 216, 217: Courtesy The Huntington Library, San Marino, California (6). 218, 219: Courtesy California Historical Society. 221: Courtesy The Nevada State Museum. 222, 223: Courtesy Nevada Historical Society. 224, 225: Courtesy The Bancroft Library. 226: Courtesy Rockwell Collection, University of Nevada, Las Vegas Library. 227: Nevada Historical Society. 230, 231: Courtesy Nevada State Museum. 232, 233: Courtesy Library of Congress.

ACKNOWLEDGMENTS

The index for this book was prepared by Gale Partoyan. The editors give special thanks to Richard Dillon, Mill Valley, California; Dr. Bernard Fontana, University of Arizona, Tucson; Leonard V. Huber, New Orleans, Louisiana; Nat Loubet, *Ring Magazine*, New York; John Luckman, Gamblers Book Club, Las Vegas, Nevada; Dr. Noel Neifert, Tell City, Indiana; Duane Smith, Durango, Colorado; and Walt Wiggins, Roswell, New Mexico, who read and commented on the text. The editors also thank: Lillian Alves, Benecia Public Library, Benecia, California; Susan Anderl, Ann Dean Kepper, Special Collections Dept., University of Nevada, Las Vegas; Jim Andrews, Leadville, Colorado; B. K. Beckwith, Pasadena, California; Raymond Blake, Independence, Missouri; Donald Britt, Mark Curtis, Clyde Wade, Harrah's Hotels and Casinos, Reno, Nevada; Ronald Brooks, Virginia City, Nevada; Ernie Bryan, Portland, Oregon; Amelia Buckley, Cathy Cooper, Keeneland Association Library, Lexington, Kentucky; Peter J. Buxton, San Francisco, California; Eslie Cann, Phillip I. Earl, Lee Mortenson, Guy Louis Rocha, Nevada Historical Society, Reno; Emory Cantey Jr., Fort Worth, Texas; Tamra S. Carboni, Robert R. Macdonald, Louisiana State Museum, New Orleans; Donald Clowser, Deadwood, South Dakota; Kent Cochran, San Mateo, California; Pamela Crowell, The Nevada State Museum, Carson City; Arthur H. Davis, Lead, South Dakota; Carl S. Dentzel, The Southwest Museum, Los Angeles, California; Laverne Dicker, Catherine Hoover, Garry Kurutz, The California Historical Society, San Francisco; Mildred B. Dillenbeck, Remington Art Museum, Ogdensburg, New York; Don Dilley, Eleanor M. Gehres, A. D. Mastrogiuseppe, Kendallyn Schober, Denver Public Library, Colorado; Lawrence Dinnean, The Bancroft Library, University of California, Berkeley; Gary Dubnoff, Vallejo, California; Catherine Engel, Judith Golden, The State Historical Society of Colorado, Denver; Valerie Enholm, Robert C. Pettit, Nebraska State Historical Society, Lincoln; John C. Ewers, Paula Fleming, Barbara Stuckenrath, National Museum of Natural History, Washington, D.C.; Bert R. Fenn, Tell City, Indiana; Ruth Ferris,

Brentwood, Missouri; Marshall Fey, Liberty Belle Saloon and Restaurant, Reno, Nevada; Mary Fleming, Janet Sporleder, California Thoroughbred Breeders Association, Arcadia; Joe Foster, The Lovelace Foundation for Medical Education and Research, Albuquerque, New Mexico; L. Thomas Frye, Brian Suen, Oakland Museum, California; Elaine Gilleran, Joan Salz, Wells Fargo Bank History Room, San Francisco, California; Deborah L. Ginberg, The Society of California Pioneers, San Francisco; Craddock Goins, Ann Serio, National Museum of History and Technology, Washington, D.C.; Joe F. Goodson, Dallas, Texas; Gail Guidry, Bonnie Wright, The Missouri Historical Society, Columbia; Ann S. Gwyn, Howard Tilton Memorial Library, New Orleans, Louisiana; Dr. Jack Haley, University of Oklahoma Library, Norman; Gladys Hansen, San Francisco Public Library, California; Hugh Hayes, Stockton, California; Rosemary Hetzler, Pioneers' Museum, Colorado Springs, Colorado; Sandra Hinson, Orlando, Florida; James R. Hunt, The Public Library of Cincinnati and Hamilton County, Ohio; Larry Jochims, Marlaine Lamar, Joseph Snell, Kansas Historical Society, Topeka; Irene R. Johnson, Fountain Hills, Arizona; Bernique Langley, Santa Fe, New Mexico; Walter Latzko, Hall of Fame of the Trotter, Goshen, New York; John H. Lawrence, Rosanne McCaffrey, Historic New Orleans Collection, Louisiana; Henry Leifermann, Washington, D.C.; Del McBride, Washington State Capitol Museum, Olympia; Bill McDonald, Dallas Historical Society, Texas; Alexander Mackay-Smith, The National Sporting Library, Middleburg, Virginia; Dr. Malcolm McLean, The University of Texas at Arlington, Texas; Robert McNellis, El Paso, Texas; Margaret Marshall, Wing Luke Memorial Museum, Seattle, Washington; Greg Martin, San Francisco, California; Thomas Martin, Capistrano Beach, California; John Marvin, Tombstone Courthouse State Historic Park, Arizona; Glenn Mason, Lane County Pioneer Museum, Eugene, Oregon; Jeff Millett, Newport Beach, California; Robert D. Monroe, University of Washington Libraries, Seattle; Anita Mozley, Stanford University Museum of Art, California; Roxanne-Louise Nilan, The

Stanford University Libraries, California; Mrs. L. M. Pettis, Bonham, Texas; Robert C. Pollock, Carson City, Nevada; Frederic Renner, Paradise Valley, Arizona; Frank Roza Jr., Consolidated Coin Co., Carson City, Nevada; June Sampson, University of South Dakota, Vermillion; John Skold, Nebraska State Fair Office, Lincoln; Sandra Snider, Dept. of Arboreta and Botanic Gardens, Arcadia, California; C. L. Sonnichsen, The Journal of Arizona History, Tucson; Gary Steven-son, Virginia City, Nevada; Mr. J. W. Todd, Seattle, Washington; David W. Toll, Gold Hill News, Virginia City, Nevada; Paul Treece, Granville, Ohio; William F. Tuttle, The United States Playing Card Co., Cincinnati, Ohio; Frederick Way, Sewickley, Pennsylvania; Virginia Wayland, Pasadena, California; Jack Williams, Dallas, Texas; Susan Williams, Oakland, California; Janice Worden, Oregon Historical Society, Portland; Oren H. Yeager, Lakewood, Colorado.

BIBLIOGRAPHY

The Abilene Chronicle, "Gambling," June 1, 1871, Kansas.

Alta California, "Local Intelligence," August 3, 1868, San Francisco.

Amaral, Anthony, "The Great Horse Race Feud," *Nevada Highways and Parks,* Vol. 30, No. 1, Spring 1970.

Asbury, Herbert:
   The Barbary Coast. Capricorn Books, 1968.
   Sucker's Progress. Dodd, Mead & Co., 1938.

Beckwith, B. K., *Step and Go Together.* Arco Publishing Co., Inc., 1967.

"Betsy Taliaferro Diary," Western Kentucky Library, (unpublished manuscript).

Borthwick, J. D., *The Gold Hunters.* Gryphon Books, 1971.

Brodhead, Michael J., "The Great Prize Fight," *Nevada Highways and Parks,* Vol. 38, No. 3, Fall 1973.

Catlin, George, *North American Indians,* Vols. I, II. Ross & Haines, Inc., 1965.

Chafetz, Henry, *Play the Devil.* Clarkson N. Potter, Inc., 1960.

The Commonwealth, "Newton, A Description of the Gold Room," Sept. 17, 1871, Topeka, Kansas.

Cooper, Courtney R., "Easy Come, Easy Go," *The Saturday Evening Post,* Dec. 3, 1927.

Culin, Stewart:
   The Gambling Games of the Chinese in America. Gambler's Book Club, 1972.
   Games of the North American Indians. Dover Publications Inc., 1975.

Daniel, Daniel M., "Golden Anniversary of Fitz-Corbett," *The Ring,* May 1947.

The Denver Post, "Denver Pioneer Tells of Thrilling Ride in Race for $80,000 Block of Gold," Oct. 7, 1923, Colorado.

Devol, George H., *Forty Years A Gambler on the Mississippi.* Johnson Reprint, 1892.

Dodge, Richard Irving, *The Hunting Grounds of the Great West.* Chatto & Windus, 1877.

Dorsey, George A.:
   The Mythology of the Wichita. Carnegie Institution, 1904.
   Traditions of the Skidi Pawnee. Houghton, Mifflin and Co., 1904.

Earp, Josephine S. M., *I Married Wyatt Earp,* edited by Glenn G. Boyer. Univ. of Arizona Press, 1976.

Elliott, Russell R., *Nevada's Twentieth-Century Mining Boom.* Univ. of Nevada Press, 1966.

El Paso Times, "Horse Vs. Cycle," Aug. 15, 1888, Texas.

Emerson, Elliott, *Bet and Win at Harness Racing.* Gambler's Book Club, 1966.

Faulk, Odie:
   Dodge City. Oxford Univ. Press, 1977.
   Tombstone. Oxford Univ. Press, 1972.

Finger, John R., "Henry Yesler's 'Grand Lottery of Washington Territory,'" *Pacific Northwest Quarterly,* Vol. 60 (July 1969).

Fleischer, Nat and Sam Andre, *A Pictorial History of Boxing.* Citadel Press, 1975.

Fleming, Mary, "Leland Stanford," *The Thoroughbred of California,* Vol. LXVII, No. 2, August 1978.

Frank, Wallace, "History of Thoroughbred Racing in California," (unpublished doctoral dissertation, University of Southern Calif., June 1964).

Fuller, Alfred, "The Story of Crowder," *Arizona Cattlelog,* April, 1953.

Gard, Wayne, "Racing on the Frontier," *The Quarter Horse Journal,* Vol. 7, No. 7, April 1955.

Gilbert, Kenneth, *Alaskan Poker Stories.* Western Printing Co., 1974.

Glasscock, C. B., *Lucky Baldwin.* The Bobbs-Merrill Co., 1933.

Greeley, Horace, *An Overland Journey.* Alfred A. Knopf, 1964.

Green, Jonathan H., *Gambling Exposed.* Patterson Smith, 1973.

Hereford, Robert A., *Old Man River.* Caxton Printers, Ltd., 1942.

Hunter, Louis C., *Steamboats on the Western Rivers.* Octagon Books, 1969.

Jackson, Clarence S., *Picture Maker of the Old West, William H. Jackson.* Charles Scribner's Sons, 1947.

Jones, Thomas R., *You Bet, How the California Pioneers Did It.* Copyright by Mrs. Lesley Mate, 1936.

Kansas City Journal, "America's Most Wicked City," Dec. 13, 1908, Missouri.

King, Jack, *Confessions of a Poker Player.* Gambler's Book Club, 1970.

Koschitz, Joseph, *Koschitz's Manual of Useful Information.* McClintock & Koschitz Publishers, 1894.

Lardner, Rex, *The Legendary Champions.* American Heritage Press, 1972.

Lewis, Marvin, ed., *The Mining Frontier.* Univ. of Oklahoma Press, 1967.

Lewis, Oscar, *Sagebrush Casinos.* Doubleday, 1953.

Longrigg, Robert, *The History of Horse Racing.* Stein and Day, 1972.

Longstreet, Stephen, *Win or Lose.* The Bobbs-Merrill Co., Inc., 1977.

Los Angeles Express, "Santa Anita Race Track Now Open," Dec. 7, 1907, Calif.

Los Angeles Sunday Times, "Fortunes Are Lost or Won at Arcadia," Dec. 8, 1907, Calif.

McCallum, John D., *The World Heavyweight Boxing Championship.* Chilton Book Co., 1974.

McLean, Malcolm D., *Fine Texas Horses.* Texas Christian Univ. Press, 1966.

Maskelyne, John N., *'Sharps and Flats.'* Gambler's Book Club, 1971.

Matson, Daniel S. and Bernard L. Fontana, eds., *Friar Bringas Reports to the King.* Univ. of Arizona Press, 1977.

Meyer, Joseph E., *'Protection,' The Sealed Book.* Joseph E. Meyer Publisher, 1911.

Miller, Nyle H. and Joseph W. Snell, *Great Gunfighters of the Kansas Cowtowns, 1867-1886.* Univ. of Nebraska Press, 1967.

National Institute of Law Enforcement and Criminal Justice, *The Development of the Law of Gambling: 1776-1976.* U.S. Gov't. Printing Office, Nov. 1977.

Neisler, Will, "Frontier Sports," *The Mustang,* Vol. 1, No. 2, May/June 1939.

Nordell, Philip G., "Pattee the Lottery King," *Annals of Wyoming,* Vol. 34, No. 2, October 1962.

Parmer, Charles B., *For Gold and Glory.* Carrick and Evans, Inc., 1939.

Pourtales, James, *Lessons Learned from Experience,* translated from the German by Margaret W. Jackson. The Colorado College, 1955.

Quinn, John P., *Fools of Fortune.* G. L. Howe & Co., 1890.

Rice, George G., *My Adventures with Your Money.* Bookfinger, 1974.

Richardson, Albert D., *Beyond the Mississippi.* Johnson Reprint Corp., 1968.

Roberts, Gary, "The Night Wyatt Earp Almost KO'ed Boxing," *The West,* Vol. 4, No. 5, April 1966.

Robertson, William H. P., *The History of Thoroughbred Racing in America.* Bonanza Books, 1964.

Rocky Mountain News, "Yesterday's Race," June 5, 1861, Denver, Colo.

Rosa, Joseph G., *They Called Him Wild Bill.* Univ. of Oklahoma, 1974.

Rust, John A. and Huey Shelton, *The Howards: Master Steamboat Builders.* Amon Carter Museum of Western Art, 1978.

Samuels, Charles, *The Magnificent Rube.* McGraw-Hill Book Co., Inc., 1957.

Scarne, John:
  Scarne on Cards. Crown Publishers, Inc., 1974.
  Scarne on Dice. Stackpole Books, 1974.
  Scarne's Complete Guide to Gambling. Simon and Schuster, 1961.

Smith, Bradley, *The Horse in the West.* World Publishing Co., 1969.

Smith, Duane A., *Rocky Mountain Mining Camps.* Univ. of Nebraska Press, 1974.

Smith, George E., *Racing Maxims and Methods of "Pittsburg Phil."* Edward W. Cole, 1908.

Sonnichsen, C. L., *Billy King's Tombstone.* Univ. of Arizona Press, 1972.

Soulé, Frank, John H. Gihon and James Nisbet, *The Annals of San Francisco.* New York, 1855.

Sprague, Marshall, *Newport in the Rockies: The Life and Good Times of Colorado Springs.* Sage Books, 1961.

Streeter, Floyd B., *Ben Thompson, Man with a Gun.* Frederick Fell, Inc., 1957.

Treece, Paul Robert, "Mr. Montana: The Life of Granville Stuart, 1834-1918," (unpublished doctoral dissertation, Ohio State University, 1974).

Underhill, Ruth M., *Papago Indian Religion.* AMS Press, 1969.

Vestal, Stanley, *Queen of Cowtowns, Dodge City.* Univ. of Nebraska Press, 1972.

Wayman, Norbury L., *Life on the River.* Crown Publishers, Inc., 1971.

TEXT CREDITS

Chapter I: Particularly useful sources for information and quotes in this chapter: George Catlin, *North American Indians,* Vols. I, II, Ross & Haines, Inc., 1965; Stewart Culin, *Games of North American Indians,* Dover Publications Inc., 1975; Richard Irving Dodge, *The Hunting Grounds of the Great West,* Chatto & Windus, 1877; Oscar Lewis, *Sagebrush Casinos,* Doubleday, 1953; Albert D. Richardson, *Beyond the Mississippi,* Johnson Reprint Corp., 1968; Paul Robert Treece, "Mr. Montana: The Life of Granville Stuart, 1834-1918," (unpublished doctoral dissertation, Ohio State University, 1974); Ruth M. Underhill, *Papago Indian Religion,* AMS Press, 1969. Chapter II: Herbert Asbury, *Sucker's Progress,* Dodd, Mead & Co., 1938; George H. Devol, *Forty Years A Gambler on the Mississippi,* Johnson Reprint, 1892. Chapter III: Herbert Asbury: *The Barbary Coast,* Capricorn Books, 1968; Herbert Asbury, *Sucker's Progress,* Dodd, Mead & Co., 1938; J. D. Borthwick, *The Gold Hunters,* Gryphon Books, 1971; Robert A. Hereford, *Old Man River,* Caxton Printers, Ltd., 1942; Thomas R. Jones, *You Bet, How the California Pioneers Did It,* Copyright by Mrs. Lesley Mate, 1936; Marvin Lewis, ed., *The Mining Frontier,* University of Oklahoma Press, 1967; John P. Quinn, *Fools of Fortune,* G. L. Howe & Co., 1890. Chapter IV: *The Abilene Chronicle,* "Gambling," June 1, 1871, Kansas; Herbert Asbury, *Sucker's Progress,* Dodd, Mead & Co., 1938; Hubert Howe Bancroft, *California Inter .Pocula,* Vol. 35, Arno Press in cooperation with McGraw-Hill, 1967; Courtney R. Cooper, "Easy Come, Easy Go," *The Saturday Evening Post,* Dec. 3, 1927; H. C. Evans, *Catalogue,* H. C. Evans & Co., 1909-1910; *Kansas City Journal,* "America's Most Wicked City," Dec. 13, 1908, Missouri; John N. Maskelyne, *'Sharps and Flats',* Gambler's Book Club, 1971; Philip G. Nordell, "Pattee the Lottery King," *Annals of Wyoming,* Vol. 34, No. 2, Oct. 1962. Chapter V: Herbert Asbury, *Sucker's Progress,* Dodd, Mead & Co., 1938; *The Commonwealth,* "Newton, A Description of the Gold Room," Sept. 17, 1871, Topeka, Kansas; Odie Faulk, *Dodge City,* Oxford University Press, 1977; Kenneth Gilbert, *Alaskan Poker Stories,* Western Printing Co., 1974; Nyle H. Miller and Joseph W. Snell, *Great Gunfighters of the Kansas Cowtowns, 1867-1886,* University of Nebraska Press, 1967; C. L. Sonnichsen, *Billy King's Tombstone,* University of Arizona Press, 1972; Stanley Vestal, *Queen of Cowtowns, Dodge City,* University of Nebraska Press, 1972. Chapter VI: C. B. Glasscock, *Lucky Baldwin,* The Bobbs-Merrill Co., 1933; *Los Angeles Sunday Times,* "Fortunes Are Lost or Won at Arcadia," Dec. 8, 1907, California; Charles Samuels, *The Magnificent Rube,* McGraw-Hill Book Co., Inc., 1957; Bradley Smith, *The Horse in the West,* World Publishing Co., 1969.